THE WAR WITHIN

THE MEANING OF LIFE & MY JOURNEY TO FIND IT

DR. MICHAEL COCCHINI

For inquiry or wholesale, please contact TheWarWithin.me

ISBN Paperback: 979-8-9894166-1-5

ISBN Hardback: 979-8-9894166-2-2

ISBN Ebook: 979-8-9894166-3-9

Table of
CONTENTS

An Arrogant Introduction   i

01.   Einstein's Error   1

02.   The Language of Love   11

03.   The Silence of Slaves   25

04.   Deathbed Diaries   39

05.   A Tale of Two Toddlers   49

06.   The Accidental Ape Theory   63

07.   Mutant Memes   77

08   Mario's Matrix   91

09.	The Will of the Wielder	105
10.	The Conservation of Content	117
11.	The Prophets of Nun	133
12.	Apples & Addicts	153
13.	The One You Feed	171
14.	The Wages of Sin	183
15.	Identity Dissonance	193
16.	Men Worth Marrying	203
17.	Emotional Support Jesus	219
18.	The 7th Sola	235
19.	Citizens Under Siege	253
20.	All Things to All Men	269
21.	Closing Prayer	279
	End Note	281

An Arrogant
INTRODUCTION

I have no problem humbly admitting that I struggle with narcissism.

I tried to pry the pride from these cold dead pages. But sin is so hardwired into my flesh, that I'm afraid it was to no avail. The best way I've heard it described is that most people wait until they have flushed sin out of their lives before undertaking a ministry calling of this magnitude. Instead, I jumped off the cliff hoping a parachute would magically materialize on the way down.

It was important to me that this book be real, and as a consequence of that, it's going to be messy. In order to truly change, all masks must burn. You have to smash all the pseudo personalities of your soul into one very real, very raw, very messed up person. And then allow God to change that single, consistent person day by day. I am still half-baked and ironing out the kinks somewhere along the way.

I'm that guy who swears in front of the pastor at church, then preaches the Gospel to the drunkard at the bar. If you would say it in private with your friends, then say it in public to the Pope. Otherwise, you're just pretending. If you're a different person everywhere you go, which version of you is God actually transforming? I am the last person who deserves the wisdom God has bestowed upon me and I'm still trying to figure out how to best steward the honor of sharing it with the world. Please be patient with me during this process.

At the time of writing this, I struggle daily with pornography, lust, pride and vulgarity, predominantly. And then secondary sins like anger, driving people to wrath and a lack of mercy... and probably a list of tertiary sins I am not even aware of. I'm sure looking back, in the years to come, I will cringe at my own youthful writings. I can only hope that God allows this work to be a blessing in my generation for the people it was intended to help.

These writings are going to sound initially arrogant until you find them for yourself inevitably accurate. I ask that you forgive me ahead of time for any unintentional air of arrogance in the pages to come. I pray that it will not deflate the meaning or purpose. After all, it is not that I am brilliant, it is that the Bible is accurate.

This book is not authoritative, nor is it informative. I am no subject matter expert. I'm just a sinner like you trying to compare notes from my own broken journey.

It seems clear that God has created some sort of theological Tower of Babel. Only this time, it's not meant to drive us apart, but unite us as a whole. If we each have only a piece of the puzzle, we have to join forces in love and truth to patch it altogether. Until the puzzle is complete, we see through a glass darkly. And so we find that love is the answer, as well as the goal and process.

The War Within is my piece of the puzzle. And sharing it with you is my show-and-tell contribution to the whole. I pray it is a blessing to you, and guides even just one to the foot of the cross. Above and beyond simply poking holes in each other's worldview, let us genuinely seek truth together, wherever it goes. The topics discussed in this book are literally the most hotly disputed issues of all mankind. I expect some backlash. Please love me enough to correct me before you condemn me. I will thank you for it.

The only thing I am sure of at this point, is of my own ignorance. The more I learn, the less I know and since science is most aptly defined as "the belief in the ignorance of experts", I suppose I'm finally qualified to write this book.

You will find parts of this book insightful, at least until the point that the analogies become too esoteric for your current life experiences. At which point I fear you may disregard the entire thing. Sometimes when we learn new things, it's like being handed a series of bowling balls. If you try to hold too many at once, you'll drop them all.

As you read, these ideas will stay with you like rocks rumbling around in your shoe. You will start to see the parts of this book you found most offensive play out in your daily life. Eventually your real life experience will catch up to what you have read and you will hopefully realize that maybe there's something to it after all.

This process of initial rebellion, followed by inevitable acceptance will continue as you wrestle your way through the very difficult topics discussed in this book. It is all just a lot to take in at first because you have to accept that your life is basically a lie and everything you've ever been told is an insidious crock of shit.

This book is dangerous. The War Within is for the truth seeker willing to take the Red Pill of reality and eat the truth tacos of life, without feeling the need to ask who's sacred cow we slaughtered to make them.

This book will offend you. It is highly controversial, quite vulgar and extremely politically incorrect. Possibly the most vulgar "Christian" book ever written. That's because it's not written from the perspective of religious piety but rather from the blood soaked trenches of the battlefield of life. It's more of a soul survival guide than it ever was a line item on my ministry résumé.

This is very much an "all things to all men" type book, written by a saved sinner who wants to share his cup with a lost and dying world. After all, if you are a Christian, and you don't try to tell others that they are about to die... you're either a coward or a monster. And it's hard to tell which one is worse.

During the 7 years it took me to write this book, I shared these ideas, in person, one by one, with well over 4,000 people. Towards the end of the project, I intentionally became homeless myself for 6 months. Many of the hardest teachings in this book were written out of the back of my van, while living at parks, gyms and homeless rescue missions.

I figured I couldn't write something raw and real unless I was living in a gutter of pain myself, suffering along side the same spiritual patients I was going to prescribe this book to as medicine, once it was finished.

You could think of it as a doctor giving himself cancer, in order to motivate himself to cure it, so that he could share that cure with his cancer patients, who otherwise might not be cured. It's amazing what you can accomplish when you put yourself in a situation, in which you have no choice.

As a Medical Doctor, studying Orthopedic Surgery, who was supposed to be making $320,000 a year, I can tell you that pissing in a milk jug, in the back of a van, in the middle of a parking lot, in the dead of winter, is not just humbling, it's humiliating. But come to find out, some stars can only be seen from the bottom of a well.

During my trial of dedicated homelessness, I would go to the nicest gym in town in the mornings, and share these ideas with multimillionaires in the sauna. After that I would go to hipster coffee shops to write, and would start up conversations about the meaning of life with hypersensitive college students, studying for their liberal arts degrees.

Then, in the evenings, I would go deliver food in my van, so that I could chit chat with average middle class working families. I would also talk to fast food employees and "salt of the earth" type folks, struggling to pay their bills. Finally, I would go to sleep at Centennial Park in Nashville, and share these ideas with my fellow homeless compatriots, who would lovingly call me "high class homeless", since I had a van to sleep in, while they were sleeping on the grass, benches and sidewalks.

It was very interesting to see an absolute unity of response across such a diverse audience. Despite having different struggles, education levels, socioeconomic classes, life experiences, political opinions, religious backgrounds, sexual orientations, media preferences and spiritual beliefs, everyone said the same thing... "If there is a meaning to life, it sounds like you've cracked the code."

During this difficult, yet fruitful, season, I would intentionally talk to the hardest cases about the most offensive topics. I would go up to the business man in the Ferrari and talk to him about how the love of money is the root of all evil. I would start a conversation with the 20 year old, vegan, transvestite college student, with pink hair, a gay pride shirt and a gluten sensitivity, and talk to them about gender confusion, the meaning of sexuality, the importance of identity and the roles of traditional marriage.

In every case it challenged their beliefs, but for about 99% of them, they thanked me for loving them enough to help them work through a struggle everyone else was too afraid to address. And I would say in every single case, they walked away at least one step closer to finding peace, just on the other side of the discomfort I had left them to wrestle with.

While the individual people openly accepted my teachings, I found that institutions did not. My church reprimanded my methods, my family stopped talking to me, my girlfriend broke up with me, other medical professionals distanced themselves from me, my first publisher tried to drop me as the content of the book took form and my employer fired me for being "too assertive" in my spreading of these beliefs, and this was at a supposedly Christian workplace.

Anyone with a preconceived expectation of what I was, and was not allowed to say, based on how my words affected their brand or lifestyle by proxy, ran for the hills. Conversely, anyone who met me with no expectations other than to consider the meaning of life itself, wanted to buy me a beer and hear more of what I had to say. The institutions called me arrogant, hateful and mean, while the people called me humble, loving and kind.

In actuality, my teachings were undermining the social matrices that these institutions relied upon to survive. I was tugging at the threads of the fabric that they had worked very hard to weave into the minds of their captives. I was encouraging the individual to break free, think for themselves and question everything. That's not too far off from how Jesus lived His life as well.

But this is only beneficial to the individual, while it is detrimental to the collective. It serves no purpose for a mental plantation to lose a slave. And as such, you brand yourself as one who is at enmity with the system. Who do you think engineered those social mores in the first place? Apparently, people in the matrix take themselves very seriously, and then there are those of us who are just trying to wake each other up before the clock strikes midnight.

Sociological groups of people were screaming at me to stop, but psychological individuals were begging me for more. The institutions were telling me that I was hurting people, hardening hearts and overcomplicating things. But the people themselves were telling me that they had never felt so loved, comforted and free in all their lives.

And that's when I knew I was onto something. That's when I knew that what I was saying needed to be shared with the world. If it cost me my life and livelihood, so be it.

If we are going to talk about the most difficult things in life, we better just go ahead and accept up front that it's going to be an emotional, offensive and uncomfortable process. The content in this book has already been banned in literally every single test group in which it was posted. It has been banned by theists, philosophers and atheists alike. This book was published by the skin of its teeth, for the purpose of saving you by the skin of yours. It has cost me everything.

I don't know how many books get banned before they even get published, but I sort of wear that as a badge of honor. If there's one thing I've learned from video games, it's if you're encountering enemies, you're going the right way.

It's a fallacy to believe that things are true simply because they are offensive. But I think we can all agree that whatever the truth winds up being in the end, it's probably going to be controversial, offensive and inconvenient. And so if you claim to be seeking truth, but you're not actively pissing anyone off, you're probably not seeking truth.

For this, I cannot apologize. The risk of being offended is a necessary prerequisite in order to discuss important ideas. The War Within will break down every inch of your perceived existence and call you to live a higher standard of life than you have ever previously been held to. I'm not trying to make any friends here. This is not because I think I am right. It is because it has become evident that everyone is wrong about something (myself included).

This book will likely destroy my ability to get hired or work as an MBA or Medical Doctor for the rest of my life. "Greater love hath no man than this, that he would lay down his life for his friends". And so for all of you, I die on this hill hoping to purchase your attention for a time... that you too might be saved. I suppose the greatest physician of all never worked in a hospital either. And so I delight to share in the sufferings of Christ.

As you read through the hurtful truths in the pages ahead, please know that each word is wrapped in the love with which I wrote it. The love hidden behind the pain rests in the price it cost me to share it with you. It would have been easy to go about my business, take the paycheck and not rock the boat. Please know that I did this because I love you and let that love carry you through the discomfort of the soul surgery you're about to endure.

It is through tears, with a scalpel and by the ink of blood that I write this love letter to you, my estranged spiritual family. I'm writing to tell you about our Father whom you may have never met. I'm writing to tell you about His will and your name written in it, that we may share in an unearned mutual inheritance some glorious day.

In my research to write this book, I read the entire Protestant Bible, Catholic Apocrypha, Ethiopian Canon, Quran (of Islam), Book of Mormon, Egyptian Book of the Dead, Bhagavad Gita (of Hinduism) and every other holy book on earth I could get my hands on. I'm still working on the Jewish Talmud, as it alone is a 7 year read, but I already know what it says, because they all say the same thing.

I also read The Selfish Gene by Richard Dawkins, The Theory of Everything by Stephen Hawking, 12 Rules for Life by Dr. Jordan Peterson and many... many other religious, spiritual and influential books I was once searching fruitlessly for meaning in. 72 titles and counting.

As my initial reading list died down, I realized how much more there was to read: Plato, Aristotle, Socrates, Freud, Kant, Darwin, Dante, Jung and more.

And so, confused about the point at which I would know enough to start writing, I asked my professor at Georgetown University for guidance. His advice was this:

"You have to pick a point, run to it, and let the chips lie. It's impossible to "know everything" and ultimately that's not the point. The way I describe a book like you're doing is like a museum exhibit. You are the curator and you bring together the paintings that you think tell the story. It's not every painting, and it's likely going to miss many. But, you're the curator so as you guide people through, be intentional about it. Don't apologize for not having every painting. Decide what you want, have those, and then let people experience it."

And so, I took this advice, suspended my studies for the time being and completed the first draft of what is sure to become a lifelong project.

The War Within is for the Christian, the Atheist, the Scientist, the Philosopher and the Agnostic. It answers the 3 biggest questions of life:

- Is there a God?
- If so, which one?
- What does He want?

This is not a self help book. Nor is it about religion or apologetics. All sources of information are considered, and from all angles. I am a scientist of sorts and so my worldview lens tends to be the scientific method. If this book had a genre, it would be: "Belligerent Truth Seeking".

The War Within is written to answer each community's questions and get us all on the same page of truth. This is going to require us all to take a step back in humility and accept that our perception of reality itself, which we have used to build our current worldview, is arbitrary on every level. The reason you cannot trust your current worldview is because the way you built it was heavily subjective in the first place. You form your worldview:

- By storing inaccurate "facts",

- When you hear them repeated enough times,
- From sources you shouldn't trust,
- Via communication mediums you don't understand,
- Through an environment that skews the information,
- To subsidize an identity crisis you won't admit you have (caused by traumas you don't know exist),
- And all for motives you're not being honest with yourself about.

Any resulting worldview from such an inaccurate set of sensory perceptions, presuppositions and external influences... can only be false. Your life is a lie, and deep down you know it. If you want to fix that, read on.

But know this here and now that you cannot unread this book. If you start it, please finish it. As I break down the worldview you once believed was reality, there may not be enough pillars of perception left to support the weight of your sanity. Unless you are guided safely to the other side, you may experience an existential crisis by stopping in the middle. If you are going to read it, read all of it.

This book is about the Meaning of Life. And unlike many books before it, it actually answers the question. But don't say I didn't warn you: no matter who you are, the answer is not pretty. It is not going to be something you want to hear. Be sure you really want to escape from the Matrix before you go down this rabbit hole. You have been warned.

Please bear with me as we crawl through these truths together. If you will have the humility to bite your tongue through the things you think you already know, you will see that they eventually turn into things you have never truly considered. And once the dust settles, they inevitably open the door to a deeper understanding of things you've heard before but never fully understood.

The whole point is to start with something simple and familiar, and then trail off into the abyss of the unknown, hand in hand. You will feel at some points that I am over explaining the concepts. While this may be annoying in the beginning, you will appreciate this simple and thorough approach by the end, as we dive deeper into abiogenesis, quantum mechanics, metaphysical anatomy, hermeneutics, attachment theory, spiritual warfare, entropic thermodynamics, constraint theory and much more.

If you're not familiar with these references, concepts or correlations... no worries. It doesn't matter whether or not you know the difference between Schrödinger's Cat and Pavlov's Dog. We will cover them all later in this book, as simply as possible. It's also ok if there are still some undigested kernels of truth in the factual feces of what you get out of this.

The goal is to explain difficult topics, as simply as possible. If your biggest complaint at the end is that I made it too simple, that's a win. Your patience is appreciated. At the end of the day, I wrote this book as if I was explaining these things to my younger self. This is the book I wish existed back then. And so if it feels patronizing at times, it's not that I think you're stupid, it's just a reflection of how hopelessly dense I was, and arguably still am.

Also know that there are always deeper explanations than what you see on the surface. You have to know at least twice as much as what is in the book, to write one properly. And 4 times more than what is in the book to explain it simply. For as much as is crammed into this book, there has been much more removed. Please be cautious in your assumptions about what you think I mean.

For example, when I talk about your "immortal soul", some people are quick to point out that the Bible says the soul can die. But I never said it couldn't. That's a false assumption. Being immortal is not the same thing as being indestructible. Jelly fish are immortal... right up until their eternity is interrupted by a speed boat propeller. The Devil is truly in the details. Please give me the benefit of the doubt and hear me out. I am not saying this book is perfect in the first place.

I will do my best to be brief, lighthearted, hilarious, vulnerable and insightful. No one likes an author who hides their one relevant point in a mountain of pretentious fluff to sell a book. No one needs another lecture from someone who thinks they are somehow exempt from the problems being discussed. Truly I tell you I am the worst of you, the least of these and the assistant chief of sinners.

In the Bible, God sent a eunuch to teach you about lust, a dead man to teach you about life, a celibate to teach you about marriage, a poor man to teach you about wealth, a sinner to teach you about righteousness and a murderer to teach you about forgiveness.

Now, in His cosmic sense of humor, He has sent a narcissist to teach you about humility.

CHAPTER 1

Einstein's Error

You... will... die. And on your deathbed you will not just look back on the good times in life. You will stare forward into the endless abyss and whisper into the darkness, "Was it good enough?"

This book helps you answer that question.

The meaning of life is not the Pursuit of Happiness, but the Seeking of Righteousness. It's going to take the rest of this book to unpack exactly what that means.

You don't have a soul. You are a soul. Your soul has a body and your soul has a spirit. Your body is your soul's interface with the physical world and your spirit is your soul's interface with the spiritual world. The death of your physical body triggers a series of events that will determine where your immortal soul will spend eternity.

This life is a war for your soul, between your flesh and your spirit. The one that wins is the one you feed.

When attacked, it's important that we orient ourselves to the battle field, enemy and weapon formed against us and then inventory our own weapons and armor to respond, rather than react.

The most insidious attacks facing us today are complacency, overconfidence, distraction and systematic desensitization. It doesn't matter that you're being eaten alive if you have already lost the will to live. Learned hopelessness means that you can be killed by an inferior or defeated enemy simply because you don't care enough anymore to fight back. The battle is already won or lost in the heart and mind before the first blow is ever dealt.

We have formed entire industries around entertainment to distract ourselves from the fact that we are all racing towards death. We have created celebrities of those among us who are best at the craft of distraction. That's probably why you picked up this book in the first place. To be amused. I'll play the fool if I must to hold your attention. But truly I tell you, this is no laughing matter.

Imagine if the victims of the World Trade Center on 9/11 created a currency of paperclips and gave a few to Bob for showing them a magic trick and a few more to Jeff for telling a funny joke. Because just for a moment, the magic trick and the joke distracted them from the looming smoke and flames about to engulf their bodies. For just a moment it increased their confidence that it was all going to be alright. And then they died, never having lived at all.

Their time would have been better spent looking for a makeshift parachute. The joke and the magic trick ate up the time that could have been used to escape death. The same is true of your soul. The reason you're so susceptible is precisely because you're so entertained. An idol mind is the Devil's workshop. King David was supposed to be at war when he saw Bathsheba bathing on the roof. He went to the roof looking to be entertained because he was bored. And he found his entertainment at the cost of his kingdom.

We can hustle for cash and elevate our entertainers. But in the end, it's all just paperclips and parachutes. Entertainment and increased confidence evoke a false sense of calm before the storm. They do not change the fact that the storm is still coming.

This life is a test. But luckily the test is open book. For those who study, there is nothing to fear from death. If you know it's coming, why stick your head in the sand? Why not talk about it? Why not prepare for it? Why not conquer the fear of death so you can live your life in peace?

The Bible is obviously the official text book for this final exam. But you can think of The War Within as the cliff notes or cheat sheet of the text book. It's not a replacement for it. But rather an introduction to it.

If you expect to know the password to the eternal treehouse when this is all over, you better make sure it's not in a language you never learned to speak.

The deathbed question of "was my life good enough to carry me across the chasm to whatever's next" really breaks down to 7 simpler questions. And these are the only 7 questions worth asking in this life:

- Who
- What
- Where
- When
- Why
- By whom, and
- How

And the greatest of these is "Why".

These questions represent the proverbial return to the first principles of existence. "First principles" is an engineering term that means rebuilding a machine or system from the ground up. I would add the nuance here that returning to first principles should not simply be the arrogant revisiting of what we know to be true, but rather an acknowledgement of our own ignorance. Returning to first principles is the deconstruction of what we think we know, not just a building back up from it. It is humility. It is accepting our own mental fallibility.

These questions are so hardwired into our society that entire fields of study have popped up around each:

- Who am I? (Psychology & Sociology)
- What am I supposed to be doing? (Ethics)
- Where did we come from? (Quantum Mechanics)
- When did creation begin? (Cosmology & History)
- Why are we here? (Philosophy)
- By whom were we created? (Metaphysics)
- How did we get here? (Evolution)

It's worth noting that these are not flawless correlations and that there are many other such fields, as well as subdivisions of each field, including: astrophysics, ontology, epistemology, etc.

The reason that "why" is the greatest of these questions is because if life was an equation, then "why" would be the answer. Another way to think of "why" is that all the rest can be derived from it.

Such an equation might look like this:

Who + What + Where + When + How + By Whom = Why

This concept of an equation for life is nothing new and I am certainly not the first to try to solve it. It was originally conceptualized by the Greeks and later mathematically formulated by Issac Newton. Albert Einstein then attempted for 30 years to "read the mind of God" by figuring out the unified "Theory of Everything" that is now referred to as "The God Equation."

The God Equation was Einstein's attempt to find the meaning of life, using mathematics. It would be a single equation that combines what we think we know and might look something like this:

Gravity + Electromagnetism + Weak Force + Strong Force = The God Equation (also known as the "Meaning of Life")

But Einstein, like Newton before him, failed, swallowed up in death before victory.

This may have not been Einstein's fault at all. The larger problem may have been the limited language in which he pondered these things in the first place. The 7 Presuppositions of Science are assumptions accepted by anyone who designates mathematics, science and human level logic as their worldview language.

These are the 7 Presuppositions of Science:

1. The mind is the primary organ of understanding, not the spirit.
2. Mathematics is the correct language in which to solve the equation of life (and Base 10 is the correct dialect).
3. A Creator God must also be limited to our rules of logic, 3 dimensions, and inability to harness the wonders of the quantum level (which is a paradoxical space that by its very nature defies logic).
4. The creation singularity (Big Bang) and the energy which powered it (from the quantum level) had no intent from a Creator on the other side of the quantum curtain.
5. The purpose of why we were put here (which is the static, philosophical, divergent understanding of wisdom) can be derived from the mechanism of how we got here (which is the dynamic, scientific, convergent conceptualization of knowledge).
6. If it cannot be measured, quantified, qualified, or otherwise observed... it doesn't exist.
7. And of course, the most egregious of all, the grand presupposition

of science that "Anything is possible... unless it's God." The idea that any evidence that leads back to God must automatically have a "more reasonable" (which often means more complicated) explanation, despite the scientific consensus of Occam's Razor (which states that the simplest explanation is usually correct).

The scientific community takes a self admitted 1% knowledge of everything and uses it to create rules, absolutes, derivations, assumptions and limits of the 99% of creation they openly admit they don't understand. This wouldn't be so bad if they just admitted they were a faith based religion like everyone else. But they arrogantly claim to be "the lack of all beliefs", and then they proceed to make grand assertions that there is no God in the other 99% of everything they are yet to discover, or reverse engineer.

As a medical doctor and a former atheist myself, I realized that I had two very different definitions of the word "nothing". If you asked me what happened when we die, I would say "nothing". And if you asked me to define "nothing" I would laugh and say "What do you mean? Nothing is the absence of everything. There is literally nothing to define".

But if you asked me to describe the "nothingness" from which the universe came, I would define it as having gravity, laws of thermodynamics, quantum level energy, a multiverse generator, light, space, time, matter and star dust. That's not exactly "nothing".

This cognitive dissonance weighed on me, and so to alleviate the guilt of feeling like a hypocrite I collapsed the two definitions into each other. Come to find out, "nothing" + "nothing" can equal "something". I realized that if the universe actually created itself on accident, from nothing, then it was also scientifically possible that some form of heavenly afterlife could just spring up from the next "nothingness" that happens after we die.

I realized that my beliefs were largely a product of what I had been told and the limits of the language in which I had formed my worldview. I also recognized that I was outsourcing a lot of my faith to celebrity scientists I didn't know, movies I hadn't watched, studies I didn't read, organizations I didn't belong to and mathematicians I didn't understand. They discovered these supposed truths, but I didn't have the time or specialization to double check their work. I had to just assume they were right and bake their "facts" into the foundation of my worldview. I didn't know what else to call that other than "faith".

The criteria with which I determined my trusted sources was problematic as well. I realized that there were certain "facts" I would believe the first time I heard them, while others I had to hear a few times before I would inculcate them. Once I had accepted something as fact, I would start evangelizing the concept to other people as if I had created it myself. I realized that there was a dopamine reward in this transactional type of behavior and I was receiving some sort of social currency as a dividend from being perceived as intelligent.

If someone disagreed with one of these "facts", I would begin to defend the idea as if I was somehow offended they had the nerve to challenge it in the first place. Didn't they know I had done my due diligence in research?! Didn't they know I was intelligent?! After all, I was the one with all the degrees and everyone already agreed that I was brilliant... after hearing all of my facts.

Debate was a declaration of war. A warfare I would become quite proficient at over the years. An attack on my facts was an attack on my person. I began to fight to the death as I accepted my growing collection of facts as my right, honor and obligation to protect and defend. I began to notice these behavioral patterns forming, but I didn't know why.

Even if it was all true and I could verify it, none of these "great" men actually invented any of the things they were studying. Instead, they were reverse engineering an already created clock and using their data to explain to the rest of us that there therefore must be no clockmaker. If the creator of the universe was a special forces operative, creating a way through the wilderness, scientists would be the equivalent of an "observe and report" rent-a-cop at a fledgling strip mall. All they did was observe, discover and reverse engineer things already present in nature.

Einstein may have just been a product of his community biases, language limitations, and formal education. Albeit he was particularly known for being unorthodox and dropped out of school at the age of 15. It seems Einstein himself had already figured out that there was an issue with the formal structure of human education, which perhaps lends credence to the point I'm making. My only caveat here is that Einstein didn't get as far out of the societal machine as he thought he did. He escaped, but the damage had already been done. There were still layers of consciousness outside of his thought process onion for him to ascend to. He just died before ever realizing it.

The point I'm trying to make is that the way we structure information in our society is problematic. Mathematics, Science, Theology, History and Philosophy are not actually separate fields. They are alternative perspectives of the same field of existence: The study of life, and all that includes. There are concepts of this already out there, such as "allology" and "omniology" but they are definitely not mainstream and honestly quite unimpressive in their current form.

The communication gap which is causing the problem is a consequence of academia compartmentalizing the black boxes of each field, without first setting up proper input and outputs between them. It's essentially poor project management. It's the digging of one deep "I'm an expert" whole rather than a thousand "We are all human" holes. The mental framework itself that you use to process data is a societal machine configured by an invisible system, the motives of which you're not really allowed to question.

The problem is that we've gone so far into separating out these fields of study that they have become different languages in the same conversation, or incompatible ways of describing complimentary ideas. Bricks we have used to build an intellectual Tower of Babel, with arrogance as the mortar holding it all together.

It's not a bad idea to caramelize onions separately in a sauté pan. There's nothing wrong with isolating the ingredient from the others, processing it through a specific method (at a specific heat and for a particular amount of time), and using a specialized instrument. But in the end, it was always intended to be added back into the main meal for the final amalgamation. It was never meant to burn, wilt and rot in the sauté pan, losing its structural integrity from over processing.

We have unraveled the blanket of life, color-coded the individual threads, put them back on their own spools of specialty and called it progress.

We have segregated our knowledge at the expense of unifying our understanding. And as a result, we are at an impasse, a cold war armistice of arrogance between religion and science, with philosophy as the "no man's land" battlefield between them. No progress is being made, only the occasional suicide bomb of "you're wrong" and the cyanide pill of "I'm right."

Perhaps this is what Ludwig Wittgenstein (the most famous philosopher of the 20th Century) meant when he said "The sole remaining task for philosophy is the analysis of language."

On the last page of his book "The Theory of Everything", Stephen Hawking explains:

"Up until now, most scientists have been too occupied with the development of new theories that describe what the universe is; to ask the question why. On the other hand, the people whose business it is to ask why, the philosophers, have not been able to keep up with the advance of scientific theories. In the 18th century, philosophers considered the whole of human knowledge, including science, to be their field. They discussed questions such as 'does the universe have a beginning?'

However in the 19th and 20th centuries science became too technical and mathematical for philosophers or anyone else except a few specialists. Philosophers reduced the scope of their inquiries. What a come down from the great tradition of philosophy from Aristotle to Kant. However, if we do discover a complete theory, it should in time be understandable in broad principle by everyone, not just a few scientists. Then, we shall all be able to take part in the discussion in why the universe exists. If we find the answers to that, it would be the ultimate triumph of human reason. For then we would know the mind of God."

Hawking's arrogant assertion that everyone else needs to catch up to him and his chosen language may be the textbook example of the Dunning-Kruger Effect, in which idiots think they are brilliant, while brilliant people second guess themselves into a self induced analysis paralysis.

Calling Stephen Hawking and Albert Einstein idiots in the first chapter of my first book will probably age better if I clarify that they were intellectually distracted, spiritually blind, influenced by their communities, motivated by protecting their sin lives and illiterate to love.

The reason Hawking didn't understand the Bible is the same reason he claims philosophers don't understand science. He didn't speak the correct language. Scientists are too busy thinking to stop and ask themselves if the brain is even the correct organ with which to "understand the mind of God" in the first place. The cosmic fool's errand.

It seems like scientists are all still waiting for their messiah to return and reunite the fields. I am definitely not God, but perhaps I could be Hawking's messiah.

Someone needs to sit everyone down and explain:

- To Ekhart Tolle that "pain bodies" are just demons,
- To Richard Dawkins that "memes" are just rocks in the field from the Parable of the Sower, and
- To Sigmund Freud that the "Id, Ego and Superego" are just the Body, Soul and Spirit.

We are all so concerned with creating something in our own image, for our own glory, that we fail to realize that everything out there was already created in the image of God, for His own glory. There is nothing new under the sun. We are just playing legos with our Father's building blocks.

Everyone's "theory" is just Biblical literary theft. Everyone's book is exactly 2000 years too late, mine included. And if I do my job correctly, you will understand, in the end, why you never needed my book in the first place.

CHAPTER 2

The Language of Love

There is no word for "love" in North Korea.

In South Korea, the word "사랑" (pronounced "sarang") means "love", but not in the North. As such, North Koreans struggle with demonstrating public affection for one another in their day to day lives, while South Koreans do not.

The absence of the word in their language seems to have manifested into a general inability to understand the concept of love itself. They don't know what they don't know. In much the same way, the language in which we structure our worldview becomes a limiting factor to us as well.

Meanwhile, in Greece, there are 8 words for love:

- Eros: Erotic Love
- Philia: Affectionate Love
- Storge: Familial Love
- Ludus: Playful Love
- Mania: Obsessive Love
- Pragma: Enduring Love
- Philautia: Self Love

Sit a Greek and a North Korean down and tell them to discuss the meaning of life in English. How well do you think that will go?

The North Korean would say love cannot be the meaning of life because love doesn't exist. It's a fallacy for the weak.

The Greek would lose his mind and say, "What are you talking about!? Just because you don't understand it does not automatically mean it's wrong. Just because you're confident, does not mean you're right. Just because you can't measure it does not mean it doesn't exist."

Notice that they both speak English as a second language. The fact that English has a word for love, creates an omission handicap for the North Korean, because he is now communicating in a second language which includes words which don't exist in his primary language.

But while English does have a word for love, it lacks the variety of words to describe different types of love that the Greek speaker is used to. This creates a limitation handicap for the Greek who feels unable to fully express himself. Both of them are limited as a result. Both are thinking in their base childhood language and trying to express ideas in a secondary limited language.

Out of the 7 Greek words for love I have mentioned above, the language of love I am referring to that will connect us all, is not on the list. The 8th and final Greek word for love is "Agape." It is the highest form of love. It requires faithfulness, commitment and sacrifice without expecting anything in return. It is unconditional.

Agape is a step in the right direction but also falls flat in the end. The love I am referring to does not have a meaning in any language you currently understand, which is why it's going to take me an entire book to explain it. Essentially, I see many of you as North Koreans who have lived their entire lives without even the true concept of love to rely on. I know this because I have just escaped the trap and come into the understanding of it myself.

This phenomenon of your limited language affecting the way you see the world is called the Sapir-Whorf Hypothesis and there are 2 versions of it:

- The strong hypothesis says that our language determines how we see the world, and
- The weak hypothesis, which is more accepted, says that our language simply influences how we see the world.

It sounds insane that there could be a language with absolutely zero concept at all of love, or that someone would willingly form their entire world view in such a language. But then you realize you are actually one of those people. The languages of mathematics, logic and science are also examples of the same. There is no concept of love in mathematics, logic or science other than chemical endorphin release, which most people agree doesn't quite capture the metaphysical essence of all that love entails. As a matter of fact, love seems to often times defy logic, exceed the bounds of science and transcend the limits of mathematics.

The North Korean telling the Greek that love doesn't exist because they don't know how to process it is the perfect analogy to Atheists telling the Christian that the spirit doesn't exist because mathematics doesn't consider it.

Some tribal languages in Mexico don't have words for left and right, just uphill, downhill and across. This again may sound foreign to you but even in New York City we say uptown, downtown and across town.

Here are some examples of concepts we know but don't have words for in English:

- "Rhwe" (From Tsonga, spoken in Southern Africa): Is the act of falling asleep on the floor while drunk and naked.
- "Pelinti" (From Buili, spoken in Ghana): means shifting a piece of food around your mouth with your tongue because it was too hot to eat, but you impatiently ate it anyways.
- "Gigil" (From Tagalog, spoken in the Philippines): Is the overwhelming urge to pinch something you find extremely cute.

These are all words for concepts we know of, but don't have a word designated for in English. But there are also words in other languages that describe concepts we can't even visualize in our lives. It is hypothesized that perhaps we struggle to comprehend these things because we grew up without a word for them, and that our language therefore influences the way we see the world.

For example:

- "Meraki" (in Greek): Is when you leave a piece of your soul in your work.
- "Fernweh" (in German): Means missing a place you've never been.
- "Je Ne Sais Quoi" (in French): Refers to an indescribable attribute that makes a person or place unique.

Languages can be limited by not having a word to describe a concept. But they can also be limited by substituting a word or having duplicate words that all mean the same thing. All of these can become barriers to communication, not just between languages, but between people who may speak the same language yet have structured their worldview in a limited mindset.

In genetics there are 6 types of genetic mutations that we observe attacking DNA. A mutation is an alteration to data that corrupts it in some way. Some mutations don't cause that much damage. Others are absolutely devastating to the code being altered. The same is true with languages. A language can exclude a word completely (which would be a "deletion mutation"), can add additional words (which would be a "insertion mutation"), can swap a word for another (which would be a "missense mutation"), or cause sentence syntax issues (which would be a "frame shift mutation").

In addition to these examples, the very systems we use to describe things around us are also subject to our chosen worldview language. Here are some examples of how language effects even our perception of color:

- In Russia, they consider light blue and dark blue two different colors (each with its own word), while in America we only have a single word for blue.
- In Japan, they only have one word for both green and blue, and thus consider them a single color.
- Some native tribes in Africa only have 5 words in their language to describe all of the colors that exist.

There is even a popular fringe theory that the color blue was not visible to humans in ancient times and is a color we can only see in more modern times. If that's true, it would be interesting to see if it has anything to do with the modern classification for it, meaning having a word for the color now that they perhaps hadn't labeled back then.

Whether this is true or just a theory doesn't actually matter, it still proves the point. The reason it is hypothesized that blue didn't exist back then is mostly due to ancient authors not mentioning blue very much in their writings. Their omission of describing the color blue, which was probably just because blue inks, dyes and paints were rare and expensive back then, has caused an assumption from our modern reading of their ancient language.

Either way, there are millions of colors that the human eye cannot see and so there are limitations in the language we use to define the colors we can see. Any confidence in a worldview resulting from such limited and subjective data is clearly misguided. The only correct worldview then is humility, which is admitting that we simply don't know, which sets the stage for faith that saves us from death.

The Bible explains this as "the fear of the Lord is the beginning of all knowledge" and describes humility as the decryption key with which to decode the parables and scriptures. This is what it means to say that the Bible is a living Word translated by the Holy Spirit only to those humble enough to receive it.

The thinking man would respond to this with "How convenient. If you only first believe, then you will finally understand." It is logically problematic to say that you have to submit to the infallibility of something before it makes sense to you. It sounds like a cult and it is in a way.

The problem is that science is no different. One of the 4 rules of logical debate is that "The rules of logic hold true". Which is also just a self asserting infallibility clause as a pre-requisite for logic to hold true. Science also allows you to question it... as long as you use science to do so.

Both are cults by that definition. The only difference is that Christian's openly admit to having faith, while science wants to eat its cake and have it too, then gaslight the rest of us that they are the "absence of all faith".

Your worldview is determined by a language you don't understand and only survives in the absence of all information to the contrary.

For example, you probably think the old adage is actually "have your cake and eat it to". But that's just because you've heard it that way a number of times and accepted that mutated quote as the real one. I bet you've said it before and don't even really know what it means, do you? Does it even make sense the way you were taught to say it?

We even get a little dopamine hit from thinking we caught someone saying it wrong. And then when we are corrected and realize we are the ones who were mistaken, we try to justify why we are right rather than simply admitting we were wrong. The correct way to say the phrase is "you can't eat your cake and have it too". Because once you have eaten it, it's gone. There's nothing left to have.

You believe what you believe because it goes unchallenged and if it is challenged, humans tend to reason our way back to justifying that we were really right all along. You could say that human ignorance is resilient. The lesson here is that you don't know what you don't know. Just because you think you know something does not mean it's automatically right. And just because you don't understand something, doesn't mean it is automatically wrong.

It's like a drunk man searching for his car keys under a street light. A cop walks out from the darkness and says, "Is this where you lost your keys?" The drunk responds, "No, but it's the only place I can see."

We form our worldview in the echo chamber of our limited languages. We are drunks searching for our keys in the spotlight. There is hope in education though (and I'm not referring to academic degrees).

We can learn to grasp the missing concepts of a language and open our minds up to a whole new world of understanding. As long as we can be humble enough to break the arrogant resilience of our own ignorance.

This is why pride comes before a fall and humility is the beginning of all understanding. Because without humility, you will never accept the possibility that you could be wrong in the first place, which of course is a pre-requisite to becoming correct in the end. Increased confidence does not equate to increased accuracy.

Science has a version of humility called "Falsifiability" which is supposed to mean nothing is ever nailed down and everything is always possible. But what it has come to mean in practice is "The current thing is always right, until it's not, because the newest current thing is now right". This results in NPC science subscribers who are on autopilot. They have outsourced their faith to the collective consciousness of their celebrity scientists and willingly await the next update from the hive mind.

It's actually quite Orwellian. Whatever Big Brother tells you today is truth, even if it's the opposite of what he told you yesterday. To the contrary, the fact that it's constantly changing is evidence of how progressive it is, and therefore validates you as brilliant for subscribing to it. "Don't question it. Remember, you're a good person and Big Brother loves you. Here, now drink this Kool-Aid. Don't worry, it's got electrolytes."

And if you do question it, use our method to question it. You are free to read anything you want... as long as it's from our community approved scientific reading list of accepted works and authors. Don't worry, everyone else is an idiot anyways. We already vetted them for you.

Scientific Falsifiability is not humility. It is the evil inverse of humility. A counterfeit key the Devil designed to open the same door of life. It is a skyscraper of arrogance built on a foundation that constantly needs to be repaired to support its weight.

Science has figured out that the way to become inevitably right, is to reserve the right to be endlessly wrong. If you were in a relationship with a person who always reserves the right to be wrong, but insists that what they believe currently is always right... that would be considered an emotionally abusive relationship. You would obviously dump that person. So why do you tolerate that sort of nonsense from science?

In every case, except for the scientific community, it's always the one who doesn't understand what is being discussed that is labeled the idiot. Science itself looks down on nonscientists for failing to understand mathematics and advanced academic jargon. Yet, they are somehow also allowed to call people idiots who claim to believe in a soul and spirit, and simply because science doesn't understand what those terms mean. Why are we the idiots based on the fact that you don't know what we are talking about? Atheists have used academic intimidation to usurp a conversation they aren't even in.

One of many reasons I'm a Christian is because it's been the same core message since the beginning. God is never changing and I found identity and stability by standing on a rock that never moves. It's easy to write a doctrine that can bury its failures, and update its inconsistencies, as it goes. As a matter of fact, science finds virtue in admitting it's never going to be right, and uses that as another outlet with which to punt the need for an answer even further down the road. Science has convinced you to: "Live and die by what we tell you, because someday, long after you're gone, we will probably be right. And by 'right' I mean 'slightly less wrong'".

But try being a 2,000 year old book describing thermodynamics, string theory and quantum mechanics using goat and sheep analogies, that is not allowed to change, or be wrong. And yet it's still the number one book ever sold and has convinced the vast majority of the world of its truth. Now that's impressive.

The scientific community is the academic equivalent of the weatherman. You know they are wrong, but you keep listening to them anyways, because at least they are telling you that tomorrow is going to be rainbows and sunshine. But tomorrow comes and it's still just rainy and overcast. And so you tune back in for your daily dose of hivemind hope. Talk about living on a prayer. This is problematic because this false hope is coming from the community that is feeding you the "facts" which make up your worldview.

To avoid this, many people simply revert to the idea that truth is relative, and therefore just because someone else's worldview is more accurate, doesn't mean their less accurate worldview is necessarily wrong by default. But this fallacy breaks the definition of truth itself. Truth denotes a singularity. There is only one truth. It is not relative or open to interpretation. That's what "truth" literally means and how it is distinguished from "opinion".

There is truth, and there is your wrong opinion about it. Notice how familiar words and phrases actually have a deeper meaning than you may have originally thought, hiding in plain sight.

To further illustrate this, let's go over some medical terminology:

- Vitamin means "Vital Amino Acid".
- Adrenal means "Adjacent to the Renal (which, renal means kidneys)." It refers to the anatomical position of the adrenal glands, in relation to the position of the kidneys.
- Gastritis means "Inflammation (itis) of the gastrointestinal system."
- Pap Smear is named after its inventor "George Papanicolaou" but this is often confused with having been named after the "human papilloma virus (HPV)" the cellular damage of which a Pap Smear is testing for. Words named after their inventors are called "eponyms" (epi=upon, onoma=name).
- Thyroid means "Resembles a Shield". "Thyro" means "Shield" and anything that ends in "-oid" means "resembles". Like "human-oid" means "resembles a human". The thyroid gland is shaped like a shield and so again we see that the name is part of the definition or one of the attributes.

Pretty cool huh? When we understand how a language works and we properly define all of the pieces along the way, many deeper meanings emerge.

Let's try a little harder word:

"Pneumonoultramicroscopicsilicovolcanoconiosis."

I know, I know. Calm down, we will do it together (reaches hand through the book to hold yours). The first thing to do is fracture the term down into its pieces:

Pneumono / Ultra / Micro / Scopic / Silico / Volcano / Coni / Osis

Notice how recognizing familiar patterns has already reduced a bit of the intimidation. Academic intimidation occurs when we feel out of control.

The next thing to do is define each individual word part correctly. If we screw up the meaning of a single word part, the entire concept becomes hazy:

- Pneumono: Lung
- Ultra: Beyond
- Micro: Small
- Scopic: View
- Silico: Silicon Carbon
- Volcano: Volcanic
- Coni: Dust
- Osis: Medical Condition

Then put it all back together in a definition: "Lung Beyond Small View Silicon Carbon Volcanic Dust Medical Condition." This is the literal meaning. But that still doesn't make sense, does it? You have knowledge of the word components, and yet it still might as well be encrypted.

Oddly enough, many words in our language only make sense when you read the definition backwards (with a little fine tuning):

"Lung Beyond Small View Silicon Carbon Volcanic Dust Medical Condition" actually means: "A condition of inflammation caused by inhaling small volcanic dust particles that scar the tissue of the lungs."

This is the actual meaning (understanding what the content means) versus the literal meaning (knowing what the content says). You can have knowledge of the literal meaning of a word, and still not understand the actual definition of what it means.

This is how an atheist can read the Bible and know what it says but still fail to understand what it means. It's the difference between conceptualizing knowledge (which always leads to increased arrogance, confidence and a sense of personal achievement) versus understanding wisdom (which always leads to increased humility, submission and reverence to God).

Forming your worldview in a limited language is the same way. Let's look at a real world example. Listen to how Richard Dawkins explains the meaning of life at the end of his book The Selfish Gene:

"Our genes desire to live forever but will dilute within 3 or 4 generations no matter what... When we die there are two things we can leave behind us: genes and memes (meaning we live on in legacy and in the memory of others). But if you contribute to the world's culture, if you have a good idea, compose a tune, invent a spark plug, write a poem, it may live on long after your genes have dissolved in the common pool.

The point I am making now is that, even if we look on the dark side and assume that individual man is fundamentally selfish, our conscious foresight (our capacity to simulate the future in imagination) could save us from the worst selfish excesses of (our unconscious genes). We have the power to defy the selfish genes of our birth and, if necessary, the selfish memes of our indoctrination.

We can even discuss ways of deliberately cultivating and nurturing pure, disinterested altruism (something that has no place in nature, something that has never existed before in the whole history of the world). We are built as gene machines and cultured as meme machines, but we have the power to turn against our creators. We, alone on earth, can rebel against the tyranny of the selfish replicator (genes)."

Dawkins doesn't realize that he is essentially summing up the salvation message of the Bible more insightfully than most Christians. Here's a translation of what he is saying:

"Something deep inside our core desires eternal life (because we were originally designed to live forever before death entered the world through sin) but despite our best efforts, we cannot save ourselves. The wages of sin is death and death will revisit us to the 3rd and 4th generation. The best we can hope to do is rebel against our innately selfish nature, repent and sanctify."

Dawkins is hilariously saying that the meaning of life is to become a Christian. He just uses words like "forced altruism" in place of "sanctification".

Even more hilariously, he is fulfilling Biblical prophesy in his fruitless attempt to disprove the Bible. He read the Bible's literal content, but he clearly missed its actual meaning. He is essentially saying that the meaning of life is love, sanctification and to become more Christlike.

What he is sensing is accurate although he does not do a good job of describing it. The language in which his field has chosen to describe the meaning of life is limiting his ability to sum up his point. Not because the English language lacks the necessary terminology to describe the concept, but because the concept itself flies in the face of his arbiters. You know who owns you by who you're not allowed to offend.

Think about it. Dawkins is literally restricted to a subset of the English language by the biases of his own community. He is socially not allowed to use English words like "sanctification" without being shocked by his captors like a rat in a cage, a prisoner of his own community. Even though he is describing sanctification, his handlers would be outraged if he used that word.

In this case, the word exists in the English language but it's locked out from use by his own social restrictions. And therefore still a limit of his worldview language. It's possible that the reason he doesn't see these ironic correlations is because his worldview language (limited by his social constraints) is missing terms like "sanctification" and so the concept itself is lost on him.

It is said that the English and Americans, as well as the Spanish and Mexicans, are divided by a common language. Americans literally speak English and Mexicans literally speak Spanish, and yet there are nuances when communicating with each other. Interestingly enough, while an American and Englishman can work their way through a spoken verbal conversation with a bit of nuance in the slang, a def American and def Englishman cannot communicate well at all because US and UK sign languages are not even based on the same framework.

The language of mathematics on the other hand is technically a universal language that bridges the gaps of countries and cultures. A Spanish speaking mathematician can build a rocket with a German engineer, because they both use the same numbers and rules in their mathematical calculations and formulas, yet they can't go out to lunch together on their break and discuss the weather or their hobbies.

This is why the field of study that deals with human to human transfer of information is called "communication" and not "linguistics". Because our ability to communicate is both limited by, yet not limited to, language. Everyone is divided by a common language, but they are also unknowingly united through a lost language. The language of love. And this is the language that the password to the eternal tree house is written in.

As a matter of fact, language itself is not really what is skewing your worldview. Language is just the symptom of the deeper disease, not necessarily the cause of the pathology. The one who controls the language, defines the terms, and therefore controls you by proxy. The words are just the chains of your slavery. Breaking the chains is not enough. As long as the slave trader lives, he can always just chain you back up with a stronger lock. The words themselves are just fruit from the poisonous tree. The real enemy you are actually fighting is the one who is intentionally poisoning the roots in the first place.

Both North and South Korea speak the same general language of "Korean". It's only the nuances between them (that are intentionally manufactured and maintained by the North Korean government) which cause the word "love", and therefore the concept of love, to be omitted. Perhaps, "banned" would be a better description.

Again we see two cultures divided by a common language, but it is actually the political rulers of those governments who are using language as a weapon, with love literally held hostage in the war between good and evil. To truly understand The War Within, we must learn to do more than simply swim against the current and curse the water. We must learn to resist the one who is flushing us down the toilet in the first place.

If you trace the hand on the handle back to it's source, you will find it's attached to your own shoulder. It is your own hand flushing your own self down the toilet of life. Likewise, the hand that fed Eve the apple was her own. You are the author of your own damnation. But, the enemy behind the enemy is the one who convinced you to commit suicide in the first place. Your worldview language is important to understand, but this is not because it is the ultimate problem. Rather, it is only a symptom of the problem.

We have to zoom out to layers of higher consciousness and see the bigger picture of the one who is whispering that language in our ear to begin with.

And this my friends, is what the Bible means when it says in Ephesians 6:12: "For we wrestle not against flesh and blood, but against principalities, against powers, against the rulers of the darkness of this world, against spiritual wickedness in high places."

This entire war is a word game. When we ate from the tree of the knowledge of good and evil, we used that knowledge to redefine the definitions of good and evil for ourselves.

We used these new definitions to create new and subjective standards of goodness, and then held ourselves accountable to them, instead of God's standard (The 10 Commandments). As such, we became righteous in our own eyes.

Words are the weapons of the war within. World War 3 has already begun, and information is the game. The definition of death in this war is to become a casualty of cancel culture. Rather than your body, it's the idea of you that dies.

On Judgement Day, we will not be judged according to these false standards of goodness that we have created. We will be judged according to God's standard. The Bible is many things, but perhaps above all, it is a dictionary preserving the original definitions of what these terms mean according to God, and not according to us.

This life is a language class. Judgement Day is a vocabulary test. And the Bible is the dictionary. You might want to start reading it.

CHAPTER 3

The Silence of Slaves

The Bible does in fact condone slavery, just not the type of slavery you're thinking of. Jesus freed us from the slavery of sin (which is "my will be done"), so that we could become slaves to righteousness (which is "Thy will be done"). Salvation is not freedom. It's freedom from freedom. It is slavery on the Salvation Plantation.

I went to medical school in the Caribbean. A small tropical country named Belize. In Belize they speak a language they call "Creole." Technically, Creole is not a language of its own, it's a dialect or an intentional encryption of a larger language so that you can pass through the literal content of what's being said to the person meant to receive it, while hiding the actual understanding, from anyone else listening in. In other words, a Creole (or "argot") of a language is the slang of that language.

Kids speaking to each other in Pig Latin so their parents won't understand the latest playground gossip, is a Creole of English. Encryption is basically just separating the literal and actual meanings and sending them to the recipient in different packages. It's like mailing a lock and a key to a friend in two different boxes, so that any would be thief would need to steal both boxes in order to crack the lock.

To convert English text into Pig Latin, kids will move the first consonant of each word to the end and then add the suffix "ay" to form a new word. I think of it like how Canadians always say "ay?!" at the end of their sentences: "It's a lovely day to repent of our sins... ay?"

Then the kid hearing it will reverse the process to decrypt the secret message.

For instance, the word 'pig' would become igp+ay, or "igpay." So "ixnay on the igpay" would mean "Nix the Pig". The process of converting an English word to Pig Latin, and the set of rules that govern that conversion, is called an "algorithm".

The more complex the encryption algorithm, the harder it is to break. Meaning the more rules there are for converting the text, the harder it is to decode it into something meaningful. This is how crypto currencies work as well. In this case, the algorithm would be intentionally superfluous and difficult to crack. That's what crypto mining is, cracking difficult algorithms.

There are many forms of Creole around the world and they usually are mentioned with the predominant language they are a bastardization of. For example, in New Orleans they speak a French-based Creole. And in Belize, they speak more of a Jamaican-based Creole. I still remember my friends' excitement when I became proficient at speaking it. They said I was officially "no longer a tourist."

There's something wonderful that happens when you can communicate with someone for the first time in their own native language. It intensifies the friendship and opens up all sorts of new doors. I remember the first time I had a dream in Spanish. The way I began to view the world changed with each country I went to and each new language I learned pieces of.

Creole was said to have been formed by slaves who wanted to be able to speak in front of their masters, without their masters knowing that they were encrypting their communication. If they spoke in their native tongues, the slave owners would know they are trying to communicate privately and would punish them. They were forced to speak in English to avoid being able to secretly plan a mutiny or escape.

To solve this dilemma, the slaves brilliantly used English words to make their own unique language under the guise of being too stupid to speak the language properly. And thus Creole was born. The success of Creole was not just reliant on the intelligence of the speakers, but the ignorance of the listeners. It only works because the slave owners wrote the slaves off as idiots and thus opened the door for their own demise.

We do the same thing with God. We try to hide our sin life from Him as if the master cannot understand the truth that is written on our hearts and minds. And so we confidently live our lives like this, only to find out on Judgment Day that He knew the decryption key all along, and He wrote down everything we ever said, which we fooled ourselves into believing was private. Maintaining secrecy is reliant upon your master being an idiot, but God is no fool. There is no expectation of privacy in your sin life.

An easy way to think about Creole is how Yoda talked in Star Wars. But imagine if he spoke like that on purpose to intentionally encrypt his communication so only certain people could understand him. That would be Creole.

Think of an English sentence as made of little word legos. Yoda is just rearranging the legos. Creole is the same way. It is basically an algorithm that shuffles the sentence legos around and maybe pronounces a few words differently to disguise the actual meaning of what something truly is.

The reason this is so important to understand is because the Devil is in the details. Satan does the same thing when he convinces you that the Pursuit of Happiness is actually the Seeking of Righteousness and lust is actually love. The subtle nuances hide the insidious deception.

This is how you can always spot a person pursuing happiness because they will tell you all about how righteous they are. And a person who is seeking righteousness, because they will tell you all about how big of a sinner they are. They think they are on the opposite path because they trusted the signs, but the signs are switched. The road to hell says "happiness!" and the road to heaven says "accepted suffering".

Learning to spot the algorithms of sin so you won't be a slave to them anymore, is called "discernment". And discernment is something that takes a lifetime to become proficient at.

Creole uses most of the same words of the parent language, but changes the sentence structure to hide the meaning. For example:

- In English you would say: "Hand me that remote control." But in Creole you would say: "Make I get the remote."
- In English you would say: "I'm going to go use the bathroom." But in Creole you would say: "I will bust a piss!"
- In English you would say: "Hello miss, I think you're beautiful. May I get your phone number?" But in Creole you would say: "Girl, how that baggy poke stand?"

Did I mention it's a "colorful" language? Once you add in some slurs and say it fast, it's almost unrecognizable:

- "Make I get the remote" would be pronounced, "Mek-a-get-deh remote."
- "Girl, how that baggy poke stand?" would be pronounced, "Gail, how deh beggy poke sten?"
- "I will bust a piss!" would be pronounced, "I wa bus wa piss!"

The key to decrypting the message would have been humility. Think about the mentality of the slaves who figured this out. Constant self control, self denial, patience and submission had to become a permanent way of life in order to avoid imminent death. They had to simultaneously market their own faux-stupidity while downplaying their own actual brilliance.

For this to work, the slave owners had to remain so arrogant in their false belief that they were smarter than the slaves, that they became the fools themselves. The slaves would have constantly had to compliment the masters, investing in their delusion by depositing in a currency of arrogance. The masters would have also reaffirmed themselves by signaling to each other the false reality of their own brilliance and virtue.

The masters would have never accepted they were in a systemic delusion, even if you convinced them to believe it. To admit that you are in a prison of your own making, in which you are both the guards and the inmates is humiliating. It's easier to fool someone than it is to convince them they have been fooled.

This is the state of the unrepentant sinner as well. You are trapped in a self induced system of sin. Willfully blind because as long as you play along, you get what you want: justification for sin. Deep down the slave owners knew something was wrong. But there was an incentive to ignore that intuition. They became addicted to the delusion and flattered by the compliments that where enslaving them. They were happy. Why rock the boat? After all, happiness is the meaning of life, is it not?

A worldwide conspiracy does not happen by hiding the truth, it happens by telling everyone the truth but giving them an incentive not to act on it or believe it. We all know Santa Clause isn't real. And yet you lie to your child that he is. That's a worldwide conspiracy that you are a part of. You know the truth, but if you said it out loud everyone would hate you for ruining their kid's childhood. You have a social incentive to not speak the truth, not care about the truth and not want the truth to be true.

The same is the case with sin. Everyone already knows they are sinners. But they will hate you for ruining the fun if you try to tell them about it.

When you tell someone they are a sinner, their response is rarely: "Really?! Gee. Thank you! This is new information. I had no idea!"

That's because they are under no actual delusion that they are good people. They are just willingly lying to themselves and others. It actually takes a lot of effort to remain willfully blind. You have to attend the false delusion constantly. Your sin life is like a sick man you have to endlessly feed virtue soup to, in order to sustain.

When you tell them they are a sinner, their reaction is more in line with, "I know I'm a sinner you asshole! I'm not stupid. I'm actively trying to forget. I've managed to balance a cease fire arrangement with my conscience by paying it off in 'I'm a good person' points, to shut up for a while, so I can go sin in peace. You're screwing up my little system. Leave me alone and stop bringing it up!"

In this case, they are both the kid being deceived and the adult keeping the secret... from themselves.

The biggest offenders of this are obviously so called "atheists". But also surprisingly agnostics who believe in God and perhaps even in Christ, but who have lost family, friends or loved ones who may have gone to hell under Biblical law. And so they stay somewhere on the fence as a defense mechanism to not have to face the fact that they may actually never see them again, not even in heaven.

I have a close friend who is a chronic victim of this. She cannot face the possibility that her own mother died a staunch Catholic, insistent that she was a "good" person. And so, my friend has warped her theology and avoided the Bible for years, in order to allow heretical beliefs like reincarnation to coexist alongside her faith in Christ. At its core, she is terrified to face the reality that perhaps her mom didn't make it to heaven.

For these people, I usually tell them that the way they feel about the person they lost, is the way I feel about them. My heart breaks for them, like their heart has already been broken. I cannot say whether or not their loved one is in heaven or hell. All I can say is that the larger tragedy would be if they also end up going there to join them. Or perhaps if their loved one is in heaven but they themselves end up going to hell, preoccupied with a wasted life of grief fueled indecision, like some sort of spiritual version of Romeo & Juliet. It's a hard truth, but it is in fact truth.

The reason everyone already knows they are sinners is because of the conscience. Did you ever notice the word "science" is in conscience? "Con" means "with" and "science" means "knowledge. So, "con-science" means "with-knowledge". But with knowledge of what? The Bible says it means "with-knowledge [of sin]". The conscience is God's law written on your heart and mind, that brings to life the knowledge of sin and therefore makes you aware of your need for repentance. That's why you're constantly exhausted. Because you're literally fighting God, and it's a battle that He already won before He ever made you..

Thats also why you still feel oppressed in a world that is actually celebrating your sin. Because the voice you're trying to get to shut up, is coming from the inside. It always has been. It's like you grab your hair, close your eyes and scream at the top of your lungs "SHUT...UP!!!" And then you open your eyes and look around but there is no one there actually oppressing you. And so you become hypersensitive and go out in search of someone, anyone, and accuse them of oppressing you. To which they act bewildered and you feel gaslighted.

That's why you have to work so hard to prove that you're a good person. But you're not just marketing your own virtue to the world. You're not even trying to prove it to yourself, since you already know it's not really true. The reason you are constantly signaling your own virtue, is because you're practicing the speech you're going to give to God on Judgement Day as to why He should let you into heaven. The thing is, He's listening to you practice your little speech right now, and that day is not going to work out the way you think. You will plead ignorance and He will play back all of the speech rehearsals throughout your life that you thought were private.

If this pisses you off, take some solace in the fact that Christians do the same thing too, when they try to explain why they never evangelize. They have all of these justifications about being an elbow or a kneecap in the body of Christ, not the fingertips reaching into the darkness of a lost and dying world, as they are commanded to be. But they too aren't trying to convince anyone really. They already know in their conscience it's wrong. They too are just practicing their speech for Judgement Day to try to convince God that they should be granted grace based on plausible deniability, that God won't particularly find all too plausible.

If the slave owners would have humbled themselves to see what was right in front of them, and considered that perhaps they weren't as brilliant as they thought, they might have been able to see what was obvious to everyone else. In a sense, the masters had become the slaves, chained up and shackled in their own arrogance.

They accepted a version of truth that was false. They created a worldview based on an inadequate language and the assumption of relative truth. They were self deceived and the beginning of their awakening would have needed to start with them humbling themselves to see the actual singular truth.

In a sense, the masters were plugged into the matrix of their own thought life, while the slaves were the agents making sure not to shatter the illusion. This is what René Descartes meant when he said "I think, therefore I am." This is what Plato was illustrating in the Allegory of the Cave.

The crazy thing about this is that the masters were actually resiliently ignorant. Even if the idea had crossed their mind that this was happening, it was in their own perceived best interest to dismiss it as impossible. Because for it to even be possible, they would have to admit that they had momentarily been wrong and outsmarted by a slave. There would have to be an entire conspiracy going on that they are unaware of and their entire life would therefore be a lie.

That simply couldn't be true because that would mean they were idiots. And they already knew for sure that the slaves were the idiots. There was so much evidence of it because all the other masters agreed that the slaves were stupid. Even the slaves said they were stupid. And so the illusion was self propagating. The masters' collective ignorance and shared delusion became resilient because it would just be too illogical and inconvenient for any other possibility to be true. At some point they would rather just be wrong and run with it than eat humble pie.

The Bible describes this scenario in verses and phrases such as:
- The first is last,
- The least of these is the greatest in the Kingdom of God,
- The meek (meaning a warrior in the garden) shall inherit the earth,
- Slaves, submit to your masters,
- Blessed are the poor in spirit,
- Blessed are those who are persecuted for righteousness sake.
- Etc.

In the end, the masters were dopamine drug addicts. Every time they convinced themselves the slaves were stupid, the masters felt smart in comparison. Feeling smart released a dopamine hit and they became addicted to those trips. This is the same thing that happens in society today when non-believers protect their sin lives. The implications would be terrifying if the Bible is actually true and that's just too drastic of a change to accept and so it's easier to reaffirm your own virtue in your social circles and preserve the matrix because sin is fun, sanctification sucks and ignorance is bliss.

The slaves ability to keep the language secret was based on a delicate balance of their own humility and the masters arrogant stupidity. The slaves had to fight the desire to rub their intelligence in the face of the master who assumed they were stupid. If even one of them got mad and said, "You're an idiot! This whole time we've been playing you and your own arrogance has been your downfall," the cat would have been out of the bag. Humility was needed to hold it all together. If the slave owners had humbled themselves, or the slaves had stopped humbling themselves, it would have fallen apart.

What I think most Christians miss is that Jesus did the same thing when speaking in parables. He was not making it easy for everyone to understand. He was making it confusing to hide the meaning from those too proud to receive it. He intentionally encrypted the message. And humility of heart was, and still is, the decryption key to understanding.

The Romans and Pharisees were present in the crowd when Jesus spoke and they wanted to catch Him in a quote they could use to justify killing Him. Also watching on was the devil himself, trying to figure out the game plan so he didn't fall into the trap Christ was planning for him (which he inevitably did in killing Christ).

If the Pharisees would have humbled their hearts, they would have understood the meaning of the parables, but then they wouldn't want to kill Him anymore as they would have already laid down their pride. Since they only wanted to kill Him to preserve their pride matrix in the first place. And so the problem would have solved itself. They couldn't eat their pride and hate Him too. Likewise, if the devil wanted to understand the meaning of the parables, he would have had to do the one thing the devil can never do, humble himself before God. The brilliance of Christ cannot be overstated in this tactic.

Jesus encrypted the parables by separating the literal and actual meanings. He then shipped the literal content to their minds, and the actual meaning to their hearts. Only the people whose hearts and minds were of one accord could recombine the literal and actual meaning. But those hardened hearts grew confused and frustrated because they couldn't obtain the actual meaning from the literal content.

This is what happens today as well when reading the Bible.

The oral tradition of the Bible is typically seen as some sort of ancient game of telephone, where the story was passed from one generation to another, and changed in each transmission. This myth is usually perpetuated by the same people who then attack the literary preservation of the written Bible anyways. At some point, if they are attacking both the oral tradition and the literary text, you have to start to question their motives in wanting it to not be true in the first place.

But in fact, the oral tradition was actually more accurate than the written. Aside from the fact that the oral tradition only required 7 people to pass the story along before it was penned into literature (Adam to Methuselah, to Noah, to Shem, to Isaac, to Levi, to Amram (Father of Moses), and finally to Moses (who penned the Torah), this idea that the oral tradition was inaccurate is simply not the case.

Firstly, this is an assumption based on the current memory capacity of modern day humans. The Bible seems to indicate that we are getting stupider, not smarter.

But even aside from this, when a father would pass the oral tradition down to his son, he would make him memorize the exact sentence and then also ask him the interpretation of what it meant. If they didn't agree on meaning, the father wouldn't teach the son the next sentence. This happens to Christians as well to this day, where the Bible will not let you advance in understanding, until you have agreed upon the basics first. This is called "drinking the milk of Scripture, before chewing the meat of Scripture".

And so both literal and actual meanings were preserved in the oral tradition.

Once written, the Bible's actual meaning was lost and only the literal meaning was passed through. Thus the written Word became less accurate than the spoken Word. Another way to say it would be that God encrypted the Word.

One way to restore the actual meaning of the literal content is for the reader to intellectualize what they think it means. But the Bible says, "Do not lean on your own understanding".

Another way is for the reader to emotionalize what they feel it is saying. But the Bible says "Your heart is deceitful above all things".

And so, the Word of God is not about the written word. And it is not about the spoken word. It is about the Living Word.

The Bible will not unlock its meaning to you, unless your heart and mind are in one accord in submission to God, which the Bible calls "humility".

Then, in all humility, you read the literal words, and the actual meaning is given to you in real time by the Holy Spirit.

The literal meaning results in you knowing about God. The actual understanding is knowing God. It's a relationship building exercise between you and God. And since you are a son of God, the process is still the same as the oral tradition. It's still a Father telling His son a story, as it has always been.

Jesus did not come to start a religion called "Christianity". He called it "The Way". And along the way you have a map (which is the Bible), and a compass (which is the Holy Spirit).

The map alone is a dead document. But the compass makes the map relevant to the real world.

But if you just use the compass, because one leg is always longer than the other one, you will walk in circles.

You have to hold the compass accountable to the map, and this guides you along "The Way".

This is what it means to say that the Bible is the Living Word of God. You don't read it. It reads you.

God is our Father. We are His children. The Word is spiritual food. This life is a Father feeding His child. But the child will not eat, and is just playing around with the food instead, and then complaining about why they are always malnourished.

And so the Pharisees, Romans, and the devil couldn't outsmart Christ by pretending to be humble to grasp the meaning, while still holding on to their actual intent. To truly understand, they would have had to fully surrender their evil intent. This is why true humility eventually casts out all ignorance as perfect love casts out all fear. God is never fooled by their shenanigans, and this one concept alone sums up pretty much all of humanity. We want understanding but we will not let go of pride. We want salvation but we will not let go of sin.

What I think most atheists miss is that they have formed their world view in a language (mathematics) that excludes concepts that are needed to define the meaning of life. On top of this, they have designated their mind as the primary organ of understanding rather than the spirit. If you don't understand what I mean by this or what the spirit even is in relation to the mind... well... exactly. Case and point.

You're a victim of what I'm describing and this book is going to change your life if you will humble yourself enough to question everything you think you already know. Otherwise, have fun living in the matrix, but don't say on Judgement Day that no one tried to warn you.

The lesson we take away from this is to be careful about forming your worldview in a language that is actually limiting your understanding. If your language doesn't have a concept for love, you are excluding love as a possible answer to the meaning of life. Also, be careful when thinking you understand anything. Knowing the literal content does not mean you understand the actual meaning. And above all, be careful when you think you're the winner. Your own arrogance will become your downfall. The devil loves to convince the lost that they are saved and Christians that they are lost. If you find yourself in the majority, it's probably time to stop and reevaluate your life.

Humility is the key to understanding. This is why the Bible says pride comes before a fall but the fear of the Lord is the beginning of all knowledge.

In the famous novel series The Hitchhiker's Guide to the Galaxy by Douglas Adams, the question is posed to a super computer called Deep Thought: "What is the answer to the Ultimate Question of Life, the Universe, and Everything?"

The computer processes data for 7.5 million years and comes up with the answer "42". While Adams claims it was a randomly picked number, it is an interesting choice nonetheless.

In ASCII (the most basic binary computer coding language), "42" is the designation for an asterisk*. And in that computer language an asterisk denotes an infinite variable. For example, if I wanted the web address www.TheWarWithin.me and ww.TheWarWithin.me to both go to the same website, regardless of if someone accidentally typed only 2 w's, I would set the domain name to *.TheWarWithIn.me, and therefore someone could type any gibberish they want in front of the web address, like "(y(3-8+7)z(21)x)/xyz.TheWarWithin.me" and it would still take them to the correct website. The asterisk means: "Anything you want it to be".

So, when Deep Thought was asked what the true meaning of life was and it answered 42, what it was really saying was the meaning of life is "Anything you want it to be!" In other words "Truth is relative, not absolute". The reason this is so important is because this is the foundation used to support the inevitable justification that "sin is just a perspective of truth, not an absolute".

This is what the Bible means when it says the lost will have itching ears and will gravitate towards teachings that reaffirm what they want to believe. In other words, people like confirmation bias. They enjoy any teaching that allows them to further protect their sin life. And they detest any teaching that induces cognitive dissonance. No one actually wants to hear your opinion. They want to hear their own opinion, coming from your mouth.

The meaning of life is not "Anything you want it to be". The meaning of life is the Seeking of Righteousness, not the Pursuit of Happiness. But when Deep Thought responded with "42", it was providing a coherent answer, even though the scientists didn't understand it.

It's also important to note that "42" is an answer which is valid and coherent in all languages across the earth, not just the language in which the question was posed (English). If the scientists would have asked the question in German, the answer would have still been "42". The digits of 4 and 2 are universally recognized as symbols (which is literal content), and yet it would be universally misunderstood as an invalid answer to the meaning of life (due to an encrypted actual meaning).

The question they asked Deep Thought was the correct question. And the answer returned was coherent. But the language that the computer answered in was not human readable. It was a computer language (ASCII mathematics). As a result, the actual meaning to life was literally lost in translation. The problem wasn't the wrong question or an inconceivable answer, it was that the question itself was answered in a language that didn't exist anymore, and therefore didn't translate to what could be understood by those receiving it. It was encrypted and they didn't have the decryption key.

In the 7.5 million years that it took for the answer to return, society, linguistics and computer coding languages had advanced so much that the ancient computer language that the original question was asked in, had been forgotten. Their own advancement had become their downfall. Their own arrogance had become the encryption algorithm obscuring the simple truth. This is why humility is the decryption key, because often times arrogance is the encrypting algorithm.

The Bible is the same way. In our case, "Love" is the answer being returned, but it requires humility to be received. Make sure you have not become too sophisticated to understand a simple truth that will save your soul.

Truly I tell you, the simplicity of the Gospel is an affront to the arrogance of man.

CHAPTER 4

Deathbed Diaries

India. 2018. The wind rushed through my hair as my leg dangled out the door of a speeding Bombay train.

After the British occupation of India, the Queen was nice enough to leave them a few beautiful gems, some fancy buildings and a fully functional rail system stretching across the country. I guess thats a fair trade in exchange for a century's worth of stealing all of their natural resources, crippling their economy on the world's stage and whitewashing their proud Indian culture to be replaced with their own British heritage.

One thing that must have gotten lost in the exchange however was doors on the side of the train cars. In India, the doors stay open while the train is in motion and one of my favorite local pass times was to hang out the door as the trains hurled through the city. A common habit among the other 22 million people who ride the trains each day throughout the nation.

A young Indian man at the next door opening in front of me turns his head to spit out the juice from the tobacco chew in his mouth. He looks back at me and nods his head reassuringly in the stereotypical Indian "head bobble", a signal that he is not going to spit into the wind and hit me in the face. I bobble back to acknowledge and say a silent thank you. He seemed like a nice and respectable kid. I couldn't help but feel I had just made a new friend.

The young man leans out the door a little farther to project the spit beyond the wind. He turns his head back to spit and a loud "ding" rings out as a passing steel pole crushes the back of his skull into his brain. I watched his deep brown eyes bulge seemingly out of their sockets as if in slow motion. Instead of his tobacco chew, my new friend's blood now covered my face.

He stood up straight and faced forward as if nothing had happened. As he turned, I saw that the back of his skull was indented deep into his head. But for a moment, he just stood there. Maybe he was alright? And then he let go of the handle, went limp, fell off the train, and tumbled along the tracks below my feet. And then he was gone.

Did I really just see that? Was I the recipient of his final unspoken words? Was he dead? Was it my fault?

No one cared. The man standing at the door beside me said, "Did you see that?"

"Is he dead?" I asked.

"No one could survive that." He responded decidedly, putting his earbuds back in.

A flood of memories hit me all at once:

- I was 16 again, holding my dying grandmother in my arms, as she looked up at me, said "I love you" one last time, and left this world.
- I was 18, a firefighter crawling under the truck on that cold February night, freeing Valery's leg from the wreckage while the paramedics performed CPR to try to keep her holding on.
- I was 22, an EMT covered in the blood of a man whose sutures from a recent heart surgery ripped open under the force of my chest compressions, causing blood to pour like a fountain from his mouth, as his family watched on in horror.

As we pulled up to Santa Cruz Station I jumped out of the door, over the fence divider, and onto the parallel tracks. I climbed on top of the platform and waited for the next train to take me back. When we passed the place where the young man had fallen, his body was gone, just a puddle of blood remained.

Pulling up to the station, I saw a large group of people in a circle and pieced together that they must have moved him. I ran up to the crowd but no one would open a path.

"Let me in! I'm a doctor!" I yelled.

Instantly a tunnel formed through the crowd, and the people grabbed my arms to pull me through. I was shoved stumbling into the middle of the crowd and looked up to see the young man laying on a stone bench, bleeding out, and gasping agonally for air. I looked up at the crowd staring back at me as if to say "Ok. You're a doctor. Save him!"

In India, doctors are worshipped as demigods. This is really convenient if you're trying to hit on a girl or for day-to-day interactions with grateful people on the street. But if the patient dies on your watch, it's not unheard of for the crowd to turn hostile against you, determining that you had some magical power to save them but for some reason chose not to. If this guy died today, it was a decent possibility I'd be dying with him.

"Has anyone called an ambulance yet?!" I yelled.

"Yes, it's coming!" A girl in her early 20's responded.

I looked back at the young man and thought about what I could do for him. When your adrenaline is pumping, you have to learn to focus the flood of information overwhelming your brain:

"There are 2 irreversible enzymatic steps in the catabolic glycolysis pathway!" My brain shouted, recalling a piece of useless biochemistry theory from med school.

"No. That's too theoretical!" I thought.

My brain scrambled to another folder of related knowledge: "Set up 360 security! Pop smoke and call in a 9 line medevac!" My brain yelled!

"No!" I responded. "This isn't the Army. This isn't combat. Focus."

"Perform a vent enter search around the perimeter of the room, using your Halligan to sweep into the center for survivors." It yelled.

Damn it! This isn't the fire department either. Focus Mike. Calm down. Breathe and focus.

"Check his ABC's." My brain said calmly, finally tapping into my basic EMT skills. "If the face is pale, raise the tale. If the face is red, raise the head!"

"Bingo!" I thought. "Airway, breathing and circulation! Keep it simple."

I approached the patient and checked his airway, respiration and pulse. He wasn't choking, was breathing the best he could, all things considered, and he had a palpable heart beat. Essentially, that means there wasn't much I could do for him.

My particular skills tend to kick in when someone is actually clinically dead (which means there is no breathing or heartbeat). And my skills are only relevant until the patient begins to biologically die (which is the cellular death of the tissues that make up their organ systems). The only thing I could do in the mean time was slow the bleeding and wait for the ambulance to arrive.

If I elevate his legs it may cause blood to rush to his brain, which is already under a lot of intercranial pressure from the trauma and inflammation soon to set in. But if I elevate his head, it may reduce blood flow to a section of his brain already struggling to perfuse oxygen and expel CO_2 from the tissue. All and all, moving him now would just increase the likelihood of further spinal injury. I decided to leave him in place.

Having seen the injury occur, I was already pretty sure where the majority of the bleeding was coming from. I felt behind his ears and traced my fingers gently to the back of his skull to assess the amount of damage. As my fingers reached the back of his head, I could feel his skull caved in where the pole had hit. If I stuck my fingers any deeper, I would have touched the lining of his brain. The blood coming from his ears was thin and milky from being mixed with cerebral spinal fluid.

I took a bloody shirt that someone had laid next to him and packed the wound externally, being careful not to apply any more pressure than was needed to slow the bleeding. As I stood there, watching him die, I flashed back again:

I was 24. A Certified Nursing Assistant in a hospice ward:

- Mr. Carter, a retired Baptist preacher, was telling me how he regretted not breaking up his high school sweetheart's wedding to another man 75 years earlier.
- Captain Sanders was laying on his deathbed in a quarantined MRSA room, telling me World War II stories of flying bomber missions over Nazi Germany half a century before.
- Mr. Craig, a former NASA engineer, was telling me that his career was meaningless and how he wished he had spent more time with his kids who now never come to visit him.

"They're here!" The girl from the crowd yelled, "the ambulance is here!"

Two men stood before me with a primitive stretcher to carry the patient. Another man approached the patient's head to lift him.

"No!" I yelled. "Don't touch him. I'll take the head."

The man looked at me puzzled, not understanding my English. I guided him out of the way and stood at the patient's head. The person at the patient's head calls the shots, as they are the guardians of the spine. They are the one who counts down to move the patient, lest everyone try to lift at different times, twisting the patient's neck and spine in a manner that exacerbates the injury.

I told the man to go to the patient's feet, called over two more people and motioned to the guys to bring the stretcher closer.

"We will lift on 3!" I yelled. But all I received was puzzled looks back. Realizing there was a language barrier, I yelled "Ek, do, teen!" (which means "1, 2, 3" in Hindi). We all lifted and moved the patient as I tried my best to stabilize his head and neck.

As they began to go up the steps, they tilted his body and the blood rushed to his head. He began to violently vomit and I yelled to them to try to keep him level, but no one understood. They took him away faster than I could keep up through the dense train station crowd, all trying to get a glance of the carnage.

When I got to the other end, they had already loaded him in the back of the ambulance. I looked in the back window and the medic was wiping the vomit off of the patient's face with a wet wipe.

"What are you doing you idiot! Hook up an IV or something! Stabilize him!" I yelled trying to open the door. The medic looked at me unconcerned as a colossal police officer grabbed me by the shoulder and the ambulance pulled away.

"We'll take it from here," he said, towering over me.

"I saw the incident and treated the patient. I can help you with the report." I explained.

The police officer looked down at me and chuckled. "A man died on a train. I got it," he said coldly. "This happens 6 times a day here," He said closing his notebook and walking away.

As I watched the ambulance disappear into the crowded Bombay streets, knowing I would never see that young man again, the memories flooded my mind once more:

- I was 26, back in med school, watching the autopsy of a pregnant mother who had been shot in the face four times. We were pulling the nearly full term baby out of her womb, and laying its gray, suffocated, lifeless body on the table next to her. A child now reduced to little more than a piece of evidence with which to convict its father.

I walked back to the train platform and the girl who had called the ambulance walked up to me respectfully, as if in a state of grateful awe.

"Thank you for helping my cousin," she said. "Please tell me honestly, do you think he will live? His mother is on her way here now and I don't know what to tell her."

I looked her in the eyes, wanting to give her some semblance of hope. "I am so sorry. But I don't think he will survive. He..." I stopped, not sure whether I should tell her that he was only dead because he had tried to perform an act of kindness towards me.

"I understand. Thank you." She said giving me a hug and walking away.

Some of the people who had been in the crowd began to clap, but all I could do was run back through the scenario thinking about all of the mistakes I had made and how I could have done more if I had studied harder or been more prepared.

A train pulled up. I jumped on, not knowing or caring where it was going. At this point I figured all trains were heading to my desired destination, which was anywhere but here.

As it whisked me away into escapism from the chaos, I felt fear grip me as I habitually leaned out of the door of the train again. The air rushing past felt colder now, as I realized that young man could have easily been me. Considering my options, I decided to lean out of the door all the same, lest I let fear control my life from that point forward.

A few years later, I was in Pokara, Nepal, on the border of China, while the COVID-19 outbreak was ramping up around the world. I was finishing up my final year of medical school, working in the intensive care unit. It was a typical day. Nothing particularly interesting.

All the sudden the ICU doors fly open and a man on a cart is pushed into the room with Dr. Klara on top of him doing chest compressions. They park his bed in the medical bay and begin hooking him up to oxygen tubes and a heart monitor.

Dr. Badri motions me to take over chest compressions. I climb up on the bed and begin to pump his chest. And my mind went into adrenaline mode:

"CPR stands for Cardio, Pulmonary Resuscitation (which means 'heart and lung revival')". My brain regurgitated, trying to be helpful. Having a selective photographic memory is a blessing in many ways. But not when you're in the middle of a life and death situation and need to perform.

"When you compress the patient's xiphoid process, you are breathing for them and causing the heart to pump blood through their body." My brain continued, as I rhythmically pumped the patients chest.

"When the patient inhales, they are breathing in 21% oxygen, 78% nitrogen and 1% all other gases, but the hemoglobin in their blood is only carrying the 21% oxygen to their cells. When they exhale, their blood is carrying 16% oxygen and 5% CO_2 from the KREB cycle away from the cells and back to the lungs to be blown out of the body. This is also how 85% of the fat we "burn" in weight loss leaves our body. We breathe it out. If we had a nitrogen receptor cell in our blood, like hemoglobin does for oxygen, we could get nitrogen from the ambient air and wouldn't need to eat protein in our diet. Oxygen is the final hydrogen acceptor at the end of the Electron Transport Chain. If there's no oxygen in the cells, there is nothing to bind to that hydrogen. "pH" stands for "Potential of Hydrogen" and so if hydrogen builds up, the patient's body can turn acidic. Or if we hyperventilate them, they can go into respiratory alkalosis, which is why we give a hyperventilating patient a paper bag to breathe into and..."

"He's already gone." A junior doctor whispered to me, interrupting my train of thought. "Look at his eyes." He said shining a flashlight on the patient's face. He lifted his eye lid to reveal a heavily dilated pupil.

"See how his eye looks like a fish? Once the pupil is dilated, the brain is dead." He said. "Just put on a show for the family. Try to give them some closure. But he's gone."

As I looked at the patient, I noticed a red dot on his forehead. He was Hindu. He believed that if he was a good person, he would go to heaven. The medical team called time of death and told me I could stop compressions. As I got down off of his lifeless and abandoned body, I almost slipped on the tubes and packaging wrappers laying on the floor all around his bed from working the code. I walked past his family standing at the doorway, looking to me for some sign of hope.

In her hands, an elderly woman held a book, the Bhagavad Gita (which translates to "The Song of God"). It's not technically the Hindu Bible, since Hinduism is considered more of a way of life than a religion, but you could think of it as the Hindu Bible.

As I left the hospital that day, it hit me for the first time that I would someday lay in that bed myself. My father, my mother, my brother and my sister would all lie there too. I asked myself if I was ready for that day and if I understood what really saves a soul. If I really was a Christian, did I believe that I just watched that man's soul go to hell just because he didn't believe in the same God as I did? Was I really ready to say that this harsh reality was my actual worldview?

And if I really did believe that, what the hell was I doing with my life? I should be out there in the streets trying to save every last one of them. The truth is that the Bible is real, and unless God gave that man a chance right before death, he is in fact in hell.

We are not good people. We cannot save ourselves. At the end of the day, I figured there was no greater love I could give and no better way to honor my Hippocratic Oath than to spend my life being a doctor of my patient's eternal soul, rather than just a mechanic for their temporal body. After all, Jesus was the Greatest Physician and He spent His days on earth serving and saving souls. If it's good enough for God, it's good enough for me.

It's true that Jesus physically healed the sick. He made the blind see, the crippled walk and healed leprosy. But all of these are physical mirrors of the spiritual work He was actually there to do. A leper was not allowed to get within 6 feet of anyone. 6 feet is how deep we bury the dead. These people were dead to the world in their leprosy. And yet Jesus entered their death to take their place and pull them out.

We are the lepers, spiritually speaking. Sin is spiritual leprosy. We are spiritually blind. We are spiritually crippled. Jesus took our place and gave us life as a result. We were dead in our sin, and the One who knew no sin, became sin, that we might become the righteousness of God.

When I look back on my life, it's not the lives I've saved nor the ones I've lost that keep me up at night. I lay awake to the sound of the lost beating their chests in arrogance. Because I know it will soon turn into the sound of them beating on the side of the Ark as the waters rise. At the very least, when I hear it on that day, I hope I will have lived my life in such a way that I can take solace knowing that I used my time wisely to save as many as possible.

You shouldn't be mad at God for drowning the world. You should apologize to Him for the pain it caused Him to have to do it. He only did it because we forced His hand. It breaks His heart to watch His own children drown, then and now. At the very least, don't make Him watch you die twice. When the Bible says there will be no more tears in heaven, perhaps it's also talking about God's tears as well.

My greatest life achievement is not the burning buildings, the raging rapids or breathing in the brisk Himalayan air of Everest. The greatest thing I've ever done, my daily hope and my crowning joy rests in the souls who are now heaven bound because God used me to reach them.

There are people out there right now who I'll someday see in heaven because I loved them enough to share my cup with them. Each one of you are the most precious things I will ever do. If I died today, it will have been worth it.

Tears fill my eyes and warmth floods my heart when I think about you Conor, Vince, Ina, Britan, Brandy, Steve, Michael and all the rest. I love you. I am still praying for you BJ, Adam, Brandon, Tara and all the rest. There is no greater honor on earth and no greater calling than to be about our Father's business. I am still in awe that He would let me be even a small part of the wonderful thing He is doing. I only hope that as many as possible might make it onto the Ark before the door is shut and sealed.

If that's you, I am pleading with you. Please repent. I think God is showing so much mercy here and now, because there will be none left to give on Judgement Day. This is not a game. It is not a joke. I've watched many, many die. And I promise you, you too will lay in that bed. Repent of your sins, take up your cross and follow Christ.

CHAPTER 5

A Tale of Two Toddlers

Science and Religion are two warring toddlers throwing factual feces at each other in the sandbox of Philosophy. Both of them are faith based religions with different answers to the same questions.

As I studied the religious books, world cultures, human histories and hard sciences, I began to realize that humans have been trying to answer the 7 questions of existence since inception:

- Who am I?
- What am I supposed to be doing?
- Where did we come from?
- When did creation begin?
- Why are we here?
- By whom were we created?
- How did we get here?

The most notable contributions to solving the meaning of life have been made by 3 communities: Theists, Philosophers and Scientists. You can think of Science as the "knowledge of how", Philosophy as the "wisdom of why" and theology as "an intellectual desire to commune with God". Most of the work done in these fields of study mainly occurred during 3 periods of human history specifically:

1. Philosophy is Born: The official journey for "why" largely started about 400 years before Christ with the birth of Greek Philosophy (Aristotle,

Socrates and Plato). I suppose if you were gang raped by an entire barracks of battle hardened men (as was a customary rite of passage in ancient Greek culture), perhaps you would grow up deeply contemplating the meaning of life as well. We may be romanticizing philosophy to the extent of overlooking the underlying traumas which may have sparked it.

2. Philosophy Births Science: From the time of Christ (at 4 BC), there was roughly a 1300 year dark period until the rebirth of philosophy in the Italian Renaissance (with Descartes, Machiavelli and Da Vinci). Of which my Great... Great... Great Grandfather, Giuseppe Cocchini, was a key player (he was the Publisher & Illustrator of the House of Medici, Sir Robert Dudley, Lorenzo Magalotti and the students of Galileo himself). One of his most famous works, The Circle of Giuseppe Cocchini, is still on display today at The Metropolitan Museum of Art in New York City.

3. Science Leaves Philosophy Behind: And finally, the official journey for "how" began with the advent of modern science in the last 300 years (with Galileo, Newton, Darwin, Einstein, Dawkins, Michio Kaku and Hawking). This was likely due to compounding advances in technology, as well as increased speed of communication. Rapidly developing technologies improved the documentation of scientific discoveries and made peer revision of those theories more efficient and brutal. You can think of modern science as a competitive evolution of ideas, which Dawkins called, "memes".

These 3 periods of history helped shape the world we live in today, and this is not a compliment. But it's the space in-between these 3 time periods that is most interesting. Officially, the Dark Ages occurred between 476 AD to 1000 AD. But in general, the entire space of human history outside of these 3 periods of enlightenment is more or less considered today to be mindless, superstitious and barbaric by many scholars, historians and laymen alike. And for good reason. The unenlightened voids between these proverbial periods of progress were filled with pointless war, rape and pillaging, and all in the name of some ruler, ideology or god.

During the 1300 years between Christ and the Italian Renaissance, many religions sprung up around the world. There had long since been many polytheistic pagan religions, as well as variants of the Jewish monotheistic Abrahamic religion.

But all of the so called "holy books" relevant in the world today (such as: Christianity, Islam, Hinduism, etc) were penned from oral tradition and/or compiled during this time period, minus The Egyptian Book of the Dead (written in 1650 BC) and The Book of Mormon, which was written in 1835 AD, but describes events that supposedly occurred 600 years before Christ in the early, unsettled days of what we now know as North America.

Like Muhammad, Joseph Smith claims an angel told him these events, which he then wrote down. Both Joseph Smith and Muhammad were said to be illiterate when they wrote their books, which sets up a sort of "How could it not be divine?!" type of argument, in support of their legitimacy. In comparison, in the Bible, we see a trend of God publicly convincing intelligent skeptics of things that are observable and testable. And conversely, in other holy books, we see so called "angels" privately preying upon the uneducated and impressionable regarding things they couldn't possibly know, refute or verify.

This goes back to a deeper theme I noticed when reading the holy books of the world. All of these books seemingly tried to persuade me of their truth, as if marketing themselves to me as a vessel they could live on inside of. Over time, the trick started to become obvious. This was the same way the Bible describes the Devil deceiving Eve as well. They were all pointed at my intellect, not my spirit. I also noticed that I was excited about reading the other books but hated reading Scripture. It was like my flesh was rebelling against it, which is what the Bible says would happen.

While these other books were trying to convince me, The Bible didn't seem to care if I believed it or not. It was written from God's perspective, not mine. As a matter of fact, it seems to be intentionally ridiculous for the sake of you not believing it, unless you're willing to humble yourself. These angelic gospels where also foretold by the Bible itself. Paul writes in Galatians 1:8: "But even if we, or an angel from heaven, should preach a gospel other than the one we preached to you, let them be under God's curse!" I noticed that the Bible always outer enveloped all of the other books.

It reminded me of how the philistine god Dagan bowed to the Ark of the Covenant, in the book of 1st Samuel. These other books all seemed to be ruled by the over arching authority of the Bible. In the Quran, for example, it is written "He has sent down upon you, [O Muhammad], the Book in truth, confirming what was before it. And He revealed the Torah and the Gospel." (Quran 3:3).

The Quran also says of Jesus, the Torah and the Gospel:

"[The Day] when Allah will say, "O Jesus, Son of Mary, remember My favor upon you and upon your mother when I supported you with the Pure Spirit and you spoke to the people in the cradle and in maturity; and [remember] when I taught you writing and wisdom and the Torah and the Gospel; and when you designed from clay [what was] like the form of a bird with My permission, then you breathed into it, and it became a bird with My permission; and you healed the blind and the leper with My permission; and when you brought forth the dead with My permission; and when I restrained the Children of Israel from [killing] you when you came to them with clear proofs and those who disbelieved among them said, "This is not but obvious magic." (Quran 5:110)

Both the Book of Mormon, and the Quran are "latter day" additions to the Bible, rather than stand alone books. Conversely, the Bible does not pay homage to any other book. Instead, it tells you to burn them and puts a curse on anything added to, or taken away from, "God breathed Scripture", which defeats the purpose of writing a latter day addition in the first place.

For example, the Bible describes God cursing man and the earth in Genesis 3. And then, the other religions describe people worshiping gods to alleviate the symptoms of the Biblical curse. God said in the Bible that the earth will be hard to work, people will die as a result of sin and love will wax cold. And so we see in other religions they have gods of harvest, longevity and fertility that they pray to in order to make the ground easier to work and get food from. The smaller gods (which, by the way, "demon" means "lesser spirit" and refers to fallen angels), only promised to midigate the effects of God's Biblical curse, not permanently rescue humans from it. It stands to reason that they couldn't do such a thing, because they don't have the authority to in the first place, which is what the Bible says.

I also noticed that there were really only two religions not openly considered "mythology". That's Christianity and Islam. It's like God had already crushed all of these other false religions over the years and forced them to admit, even unto themselves, that they are lies. Which, again, the Bible says God will do. Islam is not yet considered mythology, but the Bible also, again, outer envelopes it and explains it's origins.

The Bible seems to say that Islam comes from Abraham's first born son Ishmael, born to him by Hagar the Egyptian. This is not even a contention between Christians and Muslims. It's mutually agreed. Ishmael is recognized by Muslims as the ancestor of several northern prominent Arab tribes and the forefather of Adnan, the ancestor of Muhammad. Muslims also believe that Muhammad was the descendant of Ishmael who would establish a great nation: The "Nation of Islam".

This was always odd to me that Muslims would openly admit to coming from Ishmael, since he was clearly regarded as Abraham's shameful and illegitimate son. It stands to reason, especially given the way God is described in the Bible, and even Allah is described in the Quran, that any illegitimate bloodline would result in no inheritance (heaven).

Many other false gospels of Jesus Christ, as well as renditions and spin offs of other holy books, were also written but later burned by the Roman Catholic Church. It's worth noting that the actual dates which all of these religions started, and their books were penned, are controversial and hotly debated. Everyone seems to pick the date which best suits their current narrative (myself included). I will say though that I tried to be fair and conservative with the dates I used. But more so to "steal man" the opposing argument, rather than simply defeat a straw man.

Everyone wants to believe their religion is the oldest somehow, since this would seem to indicate, based on linear human level logic (despite a limitless God outside of time), that the oldest religion would be the first one, and therefore the predecessor of all others. These types of spiritual shenanigans have been going on since the beginning of human existence leading up to modern times.

In the search for truth, you can automatically disqualify any religion that openly claims to be mythology. It's like they're doing the hard work for you. You go to research their religion and they stop you right up front and say "Hey by the way, we don't actually believe any of this. Our gods aren't real and all the stories never happened. We're just kind of playing around because it feels good and this is how we were raised. We don't take ourselves seriously, and neither should you." And so, you can immediately throw that way of life right in the trashcan.

When you narrow down to only the religions who actually take themselves seriously and claim not to be based on lies, which is what calling your beliefs "mythology" is openly saying, you end up at the Abrahamic religions (Judaism, Christianity and Islam). You can kind of exclude Judaism as well because they openly claim to be based on tradition, mythology and folklore. For example they believe that there was a woman before Eve named Lilith. Catholics believe in a lot of extra-biblical stories too, like the apparition of mother Mary at Fatima, but they claim this is evidence based truth, not just tradition, mythology or folklore.

And so you really only come down to Islam and Christianity. Islam is governed by a book (the Quran) secretly given to an illiterate man by an angel and openly submits to the Gospel and the Torah as the original larger truth that it is expounding upon, or rather "correcting", as they believe it's inaccurate and corrupted. It also claims that Jesus performed miracles like raising people from the dead, with God's permission. The main difference is that they believe Jesus was a mere man, and not God wrapped in flesh. The problem here is that they now worship a God who has never suffered along side them, doesn't understand their struggle and is openly commanding them to do something He Himself never did first. If Jesus is not God, then God is an impersonal God, a hypocritical Father and a poor leader.

The New Testament of the Bible was also written 500 years before Islam was ever created, and goes back about another 4,000 years in oral tradition before that. In comparison to the Quran, the Bible was publicly written by God through about 40 independent intellectual skeptics, of diverse backgrounds.

Both religions have martyrs willing to die for their faith, but only the Christian martyrs died because they refused to recant sworn testimony of eye witness accounts they personally experienced. Muslims who die for their faith are dying for their belief in a God they never met, miracles they never witnessed and a book that is just an amendment to the Bible.

There are really only three groups that actually take themselves seriously in this debate, and that's Christians, Muslims, and Atheists. All of which claim to be based on truth, accurate history and scientific evidence. Between Christianity and Islam, I don't really see why anyone would choose Islam. Unless of course you were raised that way, were discouraged from asking questions to outsiders and only read the Bible as a notch on your belt, while closely monitored by your family peer pressuring you into choosing a fallen angel fallacy over God breathed Scripture. And so the real battle, in my mind, is that of the Atheist verses the Christian.

Atheism, as a religion, avoided the "mythology" label by openly embracing being endlessly wrong as their actual qualification for why they are ultimately right. A genius tactic, if ever there was one. I must say so myself. The irony is hidden right in plain sight: "Question everything! ..Except us". But viewed through the same lens as they use to examine religion, Atheism would be the youngest, most laughably inaccurate religion of all. Even what they currently accept as true today, they openly admit will probably be wrong tomorrow.

It's pretty easy to move your goal post when you never stake it down to the ground in the first place. Atheists love to accuse Christians of "throwing darts at a board" and then "counting the hits". But what is science other than exactly that? They throw a clump of intellectual oatmeal at the wall, see which theories stick. And then run with it until something else sticks a little harder. Again, this is the way the Bible describes the devil developing false theologies as well.

Half the stuff I learned as fact in med school has since been proven wrong. Yet, nothing the Bible ever told me has ever been wrong. And that is medical information that was used at the time to make decisions that might literally kill someone. The only thing science can accurately say for sure, is that something they currently believe as fact will soon be proven wrong. The only thing they are right about is how wrong they are. They can't even go 24 hours without being wrong about something. The Law of God, in comparison, was literally written in stone millennia ago and still stands to this day.

There's a reason it's called "the practice of science". It's not that hard when you have an unlimited "undo" button, and you actually view it as somehow virtuous every time you click it. Try being a book that was written 2000 years ago, boldly defines truth that's not allowed to change, and it is still somehow the number 1 book of all time, with a 3rd of the world's population captivated by it.

Now imagine being science, with absolutely zero burden of truth, and still getting your ass kicked by this old ass book that just won't go away, complete with talking donkeys, bread falling from the sky and women being told to submit to their husbands in all things.

Many people don't seem to realize that modern science, as they know it today, is only 300 years old and rests on a bed of heavily subjective philosophy, from which it was birthed. For example, the scientific field of atomic theory, flushed out by physicist John Dalton in 1808 was first conceptualized in Ancient Greece by the philosophers Leucippus of Miletus and Democritus of Abdera, 430 years before Christ.

The word atom in Greek means "indivisible" (I know, I know... it was coined before they were trying to smash atoms at CERN). The original Greek concept of an atom was that if you cut an apple in half, and then cut that in half again... and so on and so on... eventually you would get to a piece of apple so small, it cannot be made any smaller. At some point, the piece of the apple would be smaller than the width of the knife you would cut it with. That piece of apple would be indivisible, and that's where the term atom comes from.

Now, imagine that tiny piece of apple... Anything smaller than that indivisible atom, is what we refer to as the quantum realm, the space smaller than an atom. And that is why there is so much concern that smashing atoms could cause all sorts of quantum anomalies, like multiverse cracks, if that's even a thing.

It was Aristotle himself, in Ancient Greece, who critiqued the earliest versions of the Big Bang theory with his quote "Nothing comes from nothing" in his book "Physics". Yes, the first Physics book was written by a philosopher, 2000 years before the advent of modern physics by Galileo and Newton. And the man who conceptualized the Big Bang Theory in the first place, was a Catholic Priest named George Lemaitre in 1920. The fields of theology, philosophy and science being distinct from one another is a very, very new thing.

Modern science can be thought of as the next evolution of philosophy, but like all evolution, it lost information, not gained it. Science did not expand the horizon of philosophy, it narrowed the purview from "why" to "how" and baked into its foundation the presupposition that "If we can figure out 'how we got here', we can then derive 'why we were put here'". And then somewhere along the way they forgot the original mission in the mountain of minutia and arrogance of oh how smart they had become. Or perhaps it was planned all along.

The field of Psychology (Freud, Skinner, Pavlov, Maslow and Jung), which we will discuss later as a subset of science, is even younger still. Less than 150 years old.

Originally, philosophy and science were the same field. But at some point science became distinct from philosophy in that the specialties became so mathematically advanced that the people asking "why" (philosophers) were left behind in their ability to understand the language of those explaining "how" (scientists). At some point, each person had to pick their proverbial poison and respect the boundaries and limitations of their craft. The problem then became communication between the 2 groups, with the language of mathematics becoming the barrier.

Isaac Newton was probably the final true mix of all 3 disciplines (Theist, Philosopher and Scientist). As a Christian, albeit an unorthodox one, Newton carried on the work of Galileo (A Christian who created the Scientific Method we use today). Newton is considered one of the greatest philosophers and mathematical scientists to ever live.

It was Newton who created (or rather, discovered) the mathematical language of Calculous to describe forces, and began leaving the less technical minded philosophers in the dust. Newton first asked "If an apple falls, does the moon fall as well?" But instead of asking the question and debating it for the rest of his life, he created predictions, tested them and found them to be reliably accurate. And thus modern science was born.

I would describe my own attitude in this book as a Newtonian type approach. A return to the multidisciplinary attitude of the philosophical yet scientific theist. Not to compare myself to Newton in any other way than our shared modality. I make no claim to greatness and if it comes to pass that I someday see further than him, it is simply by standing on his shoulders.

Everything before, during, after and in between these 3 growth periods of history (Greek Philosophy, Italian Renaissance and Modern Science) has been occupied largely by religion, or politics... or both. I would define politics as mass manipulation for the sake of individual ambitions. And let's go ahead and define religion as the exact same thing, but with the added nuance that God created everything, and anyone who asks too many questions needs to be rolled down a hill in a barrel full of knives (which is one of the infamous 13 Tortures).

During this millennia of universal human ignorance, as various political empires rose and fell, many holy books were written and compiled. For example, the Christian Bible was compiled by the Catholic Church and the Muslim Quran was written by Muhammad. The Gnostic Gospels of Judas, Phillip, Thomas and Mary were also authored and buried in the caves of Nag Hammadi, Egypt and would not be rediscovered until 1945.

During these darker years there were still many great philosophers within the church itself (like Augustine, Ignacios and Aquinas). But these men would have been considered theologians more than philosophers since they largely contained their arguments inside the framework of "Anything is possible... as long as it's God".

True Philosophy must simply suppose "Anything is possible" and walk away. No presuppositions are allowed.

The point is, we can try to classify and simplify the groups and events of human history into neat little packages, but the fact is that everything was chaotically happening all at once. During these 3 periods of time, religion still raged on in steep competition with human governments, philosophers and the fledgling and disenfranchised scientific community.

Furthermore, the lines between these 3 groups themselves were most definitely blurred. Paul, the writer of much of the New Testament, was arguing with the students of the great Greek philosophers (Plato, Aristotle & Socrates) when he was preaching The Gospel to them in Biblical times. Many of those student philosophers converted to Christianity as a result, still belligerently holding onto their truth seeking mentality of "Anything is possible... Period!"

When these Greek philosophers accepted Jesus as their Lord and Savior, it was not through ignorance or weak minded blind faith. After weighing the evidence, they came to the logical, socratic and philosophical conclusion, that Jesus is truly God, and all of this before the Bible itself was even written.

The Catholic Church also force converted many pagan cultures at the edge of a sword but allowed them to retain many of their polytheistic beliefs and rituals. The only requirement seemed to be that they marched under a common banner, publicly professed Christianity and generally directed their worship towards the Christian God and Christ... and of course also paid their bribes... (cough, cough) I mean "tithes" to the church.

The Catholic Church later adopted many of these pagan practices as Christian in origin (a large part of what inevitably led to the Protestant Reformation), which is why the years of our calendar today count up from Christ's birth 2000+ years ago, but the days of the week, and months of the year, are still named after pagan gods and Roman politicians (Thursday being "Thors-Day" and July being named after "Juli[us Caesar]").

The Catholic Church had a "Take whatever we can get" mentality towards evangelism, which makes sense given the fact that the word Catholic itself means "Universal". Perhaps this is why Catholics consider Mary the "Queen of Heaven" (which was originally the name of a pagan goddess). They may have told the pagans that their Queen of Heaven goddess was actually Mary (Jesus's mother), just as Paul had told the Greeks that their "Unknown God" was actually YHWH (The God of Israel) and modern Christians tell Muslims that the Camel of God sent by Allah, is actually Jesus. On one hand, these seem like bait and switch debate tactics, but as we will see in coming chapters, these correlations may have actually been correct.

While all of this was happening, the Catholic Church was also actively suppressing scientific ideas they felt contradicted the Bible. Galileo, a Christian philosophical scientist, was also persecuted for his theories of space by the Catholic Church, the largest organized religious community in the world, then and now. Talk about a conflict of interest. He had to publicly renounce his scientific theories to avoid being burned at the stake. And so the man who created the telescope to see God, who saw further than anyone before him, died blind and alone, silenced by the same organization he was trying to prove correct.

Galileo's vindication may have come in 1950 when Pope Pius XII endorsed evolution and cosmology as the church's official position on creation. The Catholic Church has a history of recanting their mistakes, covering them up and playing the victim. Although it's not officially admitted by the church, there are numerous historical contentions that many of the current church saints were originally martyred as heretics by the Catholic Church itself, and then later canonized as some sort of posthumous "oops".

Galileo may have done better for his legacy by allowing them to kill him. Catholics all over the world right now would be praying to Saint Galileo to help them with their astronomy homework, to find their lost car keys and to not burn their tacos... or whatever it is Catholics pray about. Hindsight is 20/20, they say.

For example, the 13 Tortures I mentioned earlier were said to have been committed against the Catholic Church by political administrations wanting to persecute Christians. But when you visit the actual places (Barcelona Spain, for instance), the local word on the street is that it was actually the Catholic Church who rolled a 13 year old girl ("Saint" Eulalia) down a hill for speaking out against the church. A lot of the history of the Catholic Church, you kind of have to take the church's word for.

If you don't think the Pope was powerful, corrupt or influential enough to rewrite history, you should take a good look at the Gregorian Calendar we use today.

The reason we live in the 20th Century, is because in the 1500's, Pope Gregory XIII retroactively overlaid his own calendar onto the entirety of human history, using the birth of Jesus Christ as the end of the old AD time period and the beginning of the new BC time period. This is where the saying "the year of our Lord [Jesus Christ]" came from. AD is an abbreviation for "Anno Domini" which is Latin for "In the year of our Lord". And BC stands for "Before Christ". AD does not mean "after death", this is a common memory mutation of what the term originally was. All of this only happened 500 years ago, which means in the year 500... it wasn't.

Don't get me wrong, I'm a fan of the calendar switch, but the way it happened was pretty messed up. Back then they used the Julian Calendar (named after Julius Caesar), whereas documents in Biblical times were usually dated from the inauguration date of the current reigning king. For example, let's say you were doing your astronomy homework a few thousand years ago, you would date that document by writing: "It has been 3 years, 5 months and 10 days since... King XYZ took the throne." This is why our calendar today is based on the birth of Jesus, because according to the Bible, He is the current reigning King (sitting at the right hand of God).

Every time you write the date, you are acknowledging Jesus Christ as the current reigning King. This is a small part of how the Bible could rebuild itself from scratch if we all woke up tomorrow with collective cultural amnesia, albeit this would not matter in the case of a complete societal reset where history itself has been erased.

And so we date everything in our lives based on the birth of the current King. This is why everything before Christ (to negative infinity) counted down to Him, and everything after His birth (to positive infinity) counts up from Him. Christ being the Alpha (Beginning), and the Omega (End), which is one of the more bombastic Biblical prophecies, has been fulfilled right before our eyes.

Albeit, being the end and beginning of our calendar is probably not the full depth of what Christ meant when He said in the very last chapter of the Bible: "I am the Alpha and the Omega, the First and the Last, the Beginning and the End." Rather our calendar is probably just another mirror, or foreshadowing, of what He actually meant and what we currently fail to understand.

Another ambitious prophecy would be that we will all worship God whether we know it or not. Did you know you've been acknowledging the kingship of Christ every day of your life? Didn't think so. Prophecy... check!

The hijacking of the modern calendar is a huge point of contention between Christians and butt-hurt scientific atheists, who have feebly attempted to replace "AD & BC" with "BCE (meaning 'Before Common Era') & CE (meaning 'Common Era')" to avoid tipping their hat to the Catholic Church who oppressed their community for a literal millennia. I know "butt-hurt" is not the most professional term to use in this setting, but it certainly does seem to be the most descriptively accurate. The way scientific atheists complain about Christianity comes across as very whiny. They describe Christianity as "the cult that won" and the God of Israel as "The Sky Bully".

The insult to injury is that the Catholic Church's calendar is extremely accurate, and scientifically sound. The reason for this however is, you guessed it: science. The Catholic Church used the scientific philosophers among them to create a ridiculously accurate calendar, all while threatening to burn them at the stake if they got a little too "sciency" for the church's liking. It was kind of a, "You can science when we tell you you can science" type of relationship. You can see how this would build into the contention, malice and resentment for religion that we observe in today's scientific community, especially considering that modern scientists feel they have been largely vindicated as correct, even by the church's own admission.

The history is quite fascinating and tells us a lot about why religion and science seem to be fighting a silent war to this day. They are actually 2 warring religions, both exhibiting the same attributes, community structure and sociological behavior patterns, but only one of them admits that it's faith based. For example, atheists label the organized church as a money hungry monopoly, feeding off the forced tithes of its congregation, which of course it is. But I can tell you that as a doctor and scholar myself, academic grants are the tithes of the Atheist religion. They are both the same. This is a tale of the two toddlers, destined to grow in enmity, and marry against their will. The relationship between science and religion is a dysfunctional marriage that both parties want out of, but no court will grant a divorce for.

CHAPTER 6

The Accidental Ape Theory

If all of human creation was reset right now, and all books, historical records and human memories deleted in an instant, the same basic experiments would be repeated to build scientific literature back from scratch. But what would happen to the various holy books of the world? If all we had to go off of was what we could observe, could the Bible survive the proverbial finger snap of Thanos?

The answer is actually yes and this is the reason science led me back to my faith in Christ. The Bible says that "All creation testifies" and if it is truly the Word of God, evidence strewn across all creation should be able to be used to derive the Bible back to life. If the Word of God cannot be resurrected from death, it's not the Word of God in the first place.

As Paul says in 1 Corinthians 15:13: "If there is no resurrection of the dead, then not even Christ has been raised. And if Christ has not been raised, our preaching is useless and so is your faith. More than that, we are then found to be false witnesses about God, for we have testified about God that he raised Christ from the dead."

Jesus is the Word. And the Word is also the Bible. If the Bible is not evident from all of creation, what's the point?

Actually, the Bible is the only holy book on earth that would survive a complete cultural reset because science is not at odds with the Bible in the first place. Science is a subset under the Bible in fact, but science is so far behind that it's hard to tell. As a matter of fact, this scenario already happened. The Biblical flood was nearly a complete reset of the world. The stories of the pre-flood world (such as the Garden, Adam and Eve, the Nephilim, etc), were preserved through one family in oral tradition and survive to this very day. That's not the same thing as a complete reset, but don't worry, we'll get there.

I am the product of abortion. My mother and father aborted their first child and would have never had me (the youngest of 3) if they hadn't. My mom got saved while she was pregnant with me and I myself got saved at the age of 4 years old. I remember standing in the dining room of our old colonial house in an upstate New York ghetto, welcoming Jesus into my heart and feeling a warm, loving embrace in the form of a protective presence filling the room.

Fast forward a few decades of debauchery and the scene pans into a 27 year old self proclaimed atheist in Caribbean medical school. Enticed with the status a medical doctorate could bring me, I accepted that my parents had indoctrinated me with what they believed and there was no actual scientific evidence of a magic man in the clouds or a homeless dude walking on water. It was just too jagged a pill to swallow to say that "The Bible is true... because the Bible says so." This is known as circular logic and is the bane of any would be logical thinker.

I began to read books by famous atheist and evolutionary scientists like Richard Dawkins, Stephen Hawking, Michio Kaku and Antonio Damasio.

It was actually Richard Dawkins' book, The Selfish Gene, that brought me back to Christianity through the scientific method. Meaning that the things I observed in my daily life and in the world around me today are best explained by the Bible written thousands of years ago. It was in fact "with science" that I found my long lost faith in Christ again.

The Selfish Gene remains my favorite Christian book of all time, other than the Bible itself, of course. That's pretty hilarious considering Dawkins wrote it to try and finally disprove the existence of God once and for all. And so prophecy is again fulfilled that God will make fools of the wise. As we will see, God has a sense of humor. Where else could we have gotten it from?

There are many versions of the evolutionary worldview ranging from Richard Dawkins, to Carl Sagan, and not all Evolutionary Atheists are fans of Dawkins. But we will be using The Selfish Gene as the primary explanation of evolution in this book.

The basic idea is that the micro world (which is the space smaller than an atom), expanded or decompressed into the macro world we know and live in today (which is made of atoms, compounds, molecules, tissue, organs, organ systems and organisms). The study of the origins of the universe is called Cosmology. Think of Cosmology as the evolution of matter, rather than of humans. Cosmology sets the stage for the theory of human evolution and you can essentially think of it in 3 steps:

1. The quantum level (meaning the space smaller than an atom) injected energy into our universe. There is no real explanation as to where that quantum energy came from other than a "multiverse" generator, which sounds a whole lot like the Biblical attributes of God (minus consciousness, an intolerance towards sin and a desire to have a personal relationship with us). The first rule of thermodynamics was always an issue here for me. If energy is not created or destroyed, where did it come from before this point and how could we possibly say with any certainty that it's not God?

2. From that quantum energy, the "Big Bang" occurred. The Big Bang is not an explosion. It is a decompression of infinitely dense matter. Think of it like putting a firecracker into a really hard clump of dried clay, and then the dirt being blasted out from the center as the fire cracker explodes. Now take away the firecracker. It's not about the explosion, it's about the expansion of matter from an area of higher, more organized density to an area of lower, more chaotic density. This process of matter falling apart is called "Entropy", which is officially defined as "a gradual decline into disorder", and it is the second law of Thermodynamics. It's also possible that the matter being expanded in the Big Bang was pulled open from the outside rather than pushed open from its core. Meaning the envelope of space itself may have been stretched open and the matter inside expanded along with it.

3. The framework of the universe is time, space and matter. And all 3 of them are governed by light, or rather they are all relative to the speed of light. Time is a result of matter moving through space. And so time is relative to space, since the speed of matter moving through space can change. Think of it like this: The firecracker in the clay clump blasts the dirt outwards from the center. But if you used a stick of dynamite to

blast the clump of clay open instead of a firecracker, the speed of the dirt exploding would be greater, and it would travel a farther distance, in a shorter amount of time, than if you used the firework. And so the speed at which the dirt flies through the air and the distance it travels through the air is relative based on other factors. What wouldn't change is how quickly you see the explosion. This is because in either case, the light of the explosion would travel to your eye at the same speed. The speed of the molecules exploding outwards, and how quickly they move across a distance, does not affect the speed of light traveling to anyone observing the explosion. Therefore, time and space are relative to light. Einstein's Special Theory of Relativity says that all observers, whether stationary or in motion, must agree on the value of the speed of light (which is a constant). This means that they will therefore disagree about distance and speed (which are variables). Quantum mechanics is the branch of physics that describes the properties of atoms and how they interact with light.

Conversely, the Bible sums all of this up in the first 3 sentences:

"In the beginning (which is time) God created the heavens (which is space) and the earth (which is matter). Now the earth was formless and empty, darkness was over the surface of the deep, and the Spirit of God was hovering over the waters. And God said, 'Let there be light,' and there was light."

The "light" is Jesus, as described in the book of John, Chapter 1. Jesus, who is the light of the world, is described as the King of kings and an unchanging rock, which is why time, space and matter are relative to Him, which is how He manipulates them to perform what we call "miracles". The Bible also says even the sun, moon, rocks and trees will worship Him. This is not the same light of the sun, as the "luminaries" were created on day 3 of Creation. Rather, the Bible is describing what we call "quantum mechanics".

Jesus was not created, but was poured into the vessel of the universe. This is why we observe that light is evenly distributed throughout the universe, rather than still traveling to the edges of the universe from the source of the Big Bang, a phenomenon which science calls "The Horizon Problem". But it's not a "problem" for Christians. It's evidence, as it rightly should be for everyone.

The Bible seems to be saying that the Big Bang happened without light and that the atoms were not decompressed from an infinitely dense single atom, but rather that God multiplied the atoms in the same way Jesus multiplied the fish and loaves. From one came many, like all of us from Adam. Like all of the cells of a mustard plant from a single seed.

I have some deeper theories of how it all works that are a bit past the purview of this book, but I believe the Bible might be saying that the entry point from which this light was poured into the universe, is from the core of each atom, as Heaven is described as already within us, and as Eve was created from Adam, her "stronger vessel". The weaker and stronger vessel concept may be describing the weak and strong forces of modern Physics. Jesus being the weak force and the Father being the strong force.

The Bible says:

- God spoke time, space and matter into existence (which is consistent with String Theory's hypothesis that sub atomic vibrations make up the core of matter). This is what science calls "the Big Bang", but the Bible describes it in Job, Psalms & Isaiah as God "stretching out the heavens like a curtain".
- The Word God spoke was "Jesus" (or whatever His name is in the secret language mentioned in Revelation 19:12). When God said "Let there be Light", the Bible is referring to Jesus, who is the light of the world. The scientific phenomenon of sound converting to light is called "sonoluminescence".
- Then God "held all things together" which is how Adam and Eve were immortal, as it says in Colossians 1:17. When death entered the world through sin, God stopped holding matter together in the curse of Genesis 3, and now everything is decaying (which we observe as entropy).

We will not go any deeper into the 8 epochs of the Big Bang, the 4 forces of the universe or the makeup of matter. For the purview of this book, this explanation shall suffice.

Now that Cosmology has explained the origins of light, time, space and matter, as well as an earth, moon, stars, water, dirt, air, atmosphere, gravity and all the rest... as well as the laws of thermodynamics (which, by the way, seem to contradict the theory of Evolution we are about to go over), from "nothing"... on accident... the theory of Evolution takes us the rest of the way to explaining how we humans got here. And it explains everything... except for our conscience, consciousness, love, hope, depression, sense of humor and everything else that only the Bible provides an actual answer for. But, while evolution fails to actually answer any of these questions, it does do the one thing the Bible will never do, it justifies your sin as acceptable. But I'm sure that's just a coincidence. .

You can think of human evolution in 5 steps:

1. 4 gases in earth's atmosphere sparked by a lightning strike resulted in a primordial soup of amino acids. This is the only part of evolutionary theory that is currently reproducible in a lab today (as evidenced by Stanley Miller and Harold Urey in 1953).

2. A statistically impossible anomaly (what some might call a "miracle") occurred when a single spark of life came from this accidental amino acid soup. This phenomenon of life from non-living material is called abiogenesis. A-bio-genesis means "without-life-creation" or life from death (what some might describe as Resurrection: rising from the dead). It's actually even more ridiculous than resurrection from dead tissue, since abiogenesis describes life coming from tissue that was never living in the first place, not which was once living, died and has now been resuscitated.

3. From there this new life (called an RNA Replicator gene) began creating clones of itself (on accident) that eventually started to compete against each other for resources (also on accident).

4. Because of this competition, variation occurred due to environmental factors, mutations and genes attacking each other in the soup. The genes that evolved to have better protection (such as thicker or more flexible protein walls) survived. As time went on, they developed more and more advanced survival suits... all on accident, without consciousness or design. This chain of events eventually resulted in primitive cells.

5. These primitive cells began to multiply and clump together into organic tissue. And from there, the gene survival suits eventually evolved into all plants, animals and humans we see today. The point at which these

single RNA replicator gene survival machines evolved into male and female, sexually reproducing plants, animals and humans, all across the spectrum, at the same time, on accident, simultaneously losing the ability to clone themselves (against their own best interest, since non-diluted replication is all genes want to do) is ambiguous and, as Dawkins explains, only addressed in advance mathematical models not accessible to the layman.

The government likes to use numbers you don't understand to get you to agree with policies you shouldn't support. For example, "the deficit was lowered this year to 2.9 trillion from 3.2 trillion last year". A trillion is not something the human mind really conceptualizes very well and so to pretend we understand, we just nod and agree.

Atheists do the same thing with the "millions and billions of years" cop-out. When they can't answer your question, they just say "well, I mean, obviously this all happened over millions and billions of years!" And then they start talking about entropic uncertainty, and we sort of just zone out thinking we are the only ones who don't know how to conceptualize what that means, and we submit to believe their explanation without anymore questions.

Academic intimidation is a tactic we intellectuals use to silence dissidents. If I represented the government, and you had the nerve to question a policy I was being paid to peddle, I would just say something like "Great question! Would you prefer I explain the answer using binomial analytical geometry or statistically finite differential equations?"

To a mathematician, that doesn't even make sense, but the average person doesn't know that. All you know is that you feel like an idiot. It's really a language attack. It's not much different than if a guy walks out of a restaurant without paying and you yell at him, but he turns around and says "No Habla Englis!" But in this case, let's say he does speak English and he is lying. He gets away with it because you don't speak his language.

It's important to remember that every single step of evolution I just described (except for step 1) is not only unprovable in a lab today, each step is so statistically improbable, even given millions and billions of years as a crutch, that they can only really be described as impossible.

When you stack them all together, it's more statistically likely that a tornado could sweep through a junk yard and accidentally assemble a fully operational Boeing 747 airplane. Atheists like to discredit this statistic as an ignorant false equivalency. But this quote actually comes from astrophysicist Sir Fred Hoyle who formulated the theory of Stellar Nucleosynthesis and coined the term "Big Bang". That's right. The guy who coined the term Big Bang... didn't believe in it. Rather, he was mocking the theory and the name stuck. Hoyle was an atheist but stated that "a superintellect has monkeyed with physics, as well as with chemistry and biology..."

The main take aways from Dawkins are:

1. Genes "want" to live forever, meaning they exhibit the behavior of trying to resist dilution as long as possible. All genes want to do is procreate to the next generation. While genes exhibit this behavior, they lack consciousness and don't "want" anything. Dawkins is clear that the personification of genes "wanting" anything is strictly for illustration. The problem with this is that the only other way genes could play out this function, if they don't have consciousness, is if they were originally designed as eternal beings, and they are playing out their original design, but something went terribly wrong (namely: sin and death).

2. Humans are not the individual, their genes are the actual individuals of life. The human body is just the survival machine of the genes. Think of your body (consciousness included) as a meat mech suit for your genes.

3. Atheists believe that consciousness, a sense of humor, love (beyond the chemical endorphin rush), the conscience, and any other element that makes us "human" are simply accidental mechanisms given to our survival machines (which means your body) by evolution to further the chance of survival. That's a lot of intelligent design for something that was never intelligently designed in the first place.

The "survival of the fittest" idea would suggest that these designs were not designs at all but that they are simply what survived. The determining factor of what survives and what doesn't is called an Evolutionary Stable Strategy (or ESS) and the interaction between animals that determines which one procreates or not is a game theory concept called The Prisoner's Dilemma.

Think of it as a reiterative tic-tac-toe match of whits between animals. Different strategies and algorithms are seen all throughout the animal, plant and human kingdoms. Imagine a monkey who scratches another monkey's back, and then turns around expecting him to reciprocate with a return back scratch, but the second monkey plays him for a sucker and walks away. That's the Prisoner's Dilemma.

The Prisoner's Dilemma is yet another reason why I am Christian. Atheist somehow missed that Jesus already solved the dilemma. The way He tells us to live (turn the other cheek, forgive 70x7, do unto others as you would have them do unto you, etc) is the perfect algorithm with which to beat the game. He couldn't make it any more obvious either. There were literally 2 prisoners next to him on the cross, faced with the dilemma of whether to choose a reward or a punishment. The scene of the cross is literally a dilemma between 2 prisoners with Jesus in the middle as the banker paying out the wages of eternal life or eternal death. But, I'm sure that's just a coincidence.

We think "they don't build things like they used to" because all we see of the past are the things that survived. We have a survivorship bias because all the poorly made products in our parent's time already broke, rotted and decayed long before we were born. Because all we see of the past are the sturdy things that survived, we thus conclude that everything back them must have therefore been sturdy. This belief is about as accurate as if artificially intelligent robots find an Avengers DVD set in the rubble of a post apocalyptic world someday and conclude that humans went extinct when a group of super heroes failed to save the world from a super villain.

If this theory of evolution is true, imagine what other traits on the level of consciousness we could have already lost. Maybe we could fly at some point and that just wasn't a trait that survived. Imagine if consciousness itself becomes evolutionarily unstable and humanity descends back into the darkness of idiocracy. It's possible that humanity has already reached its peak and now we are declining back into an evolutionary stupor.

The idea is not that genes intentionally designed white polar bears to match the color of the snow, but instead that all colors of polar bears once existed and based on white being the best version of polar bear for that environment, the white ones survived and all the rest died out. Since their trait of having white fur was the most evolutionarily stable for the given environment, they were the most successful at hunting, mating and surviving. They rose to the top of the community and procreated until they were the only ones left. That's what "survival of the fittest" means.

The problem is that this highlights a loss of genetic information over time (what some might call "a gradual decline into disorder") because in order for polar bears not to just evolve back into various colors of fur again, new genetic data would have to be saved in the bear's DNA to let them know that white fur is the best choice (which is not what we observe in studying their DNA). The only other option is that the genetic information that was needed to make a pink polar bear was totally lost and all that is left is the DNA recipe for white polar bears, which is more likely. This is a problem for evolutionary theory because this shows that genetic information is generationally lost over time (not gained), which is consistent with entropy.

Think about it like this. We get chihuahuas from breeding down wolves. But do you think you can ever take chihuahuas and breed them back up to a wolf? Most people would say probably not. This is again problematic because the theory of evolution is that we are evolving from atoms. That since the very beginning we are getting smarter and more advanced due to gaining genetic information, not losing it. Evolution is telling you that a skyscraper can build itself without a blueprint (which would be gain of function). What we observe however is that a skyscraper will never build itself, but it will decay and fall down over time if not maintained (which would be loss of function).

What the scientific community was toting as its greatest strength, falsifiability (meaning the ever changing nature of science through new discoveries), slowly began to reveal itself as a cop-out in practice. It became an excuse to not know, be endlessly wrong and outsource your faith to a community of celebrity scientists. It wasn't all too different than the Catholic Church who would read the Bible in Latin and then tell the illiterate congregation what it said. I guess the scientific community picked up a few tricks from it's big bullying brother after all.

When I advanced to the level of a medical doctorate, I found my credentials endlessly questioned on emotional grounds. Having a doctorate in medical sciences, I was told "You're not an astrophysicist!" when commenting on Cosmology. Or "You're not a Evolutionary Biologist" when commenting on evolution. It didn't seem to matter that the people questioning my credentials on social media had dropped out of high school to sell essential oils on Facebook messenger and didn't know the difference between cosmology and cosmetology.

In the end I realized that believing in evolution and being a Christian are incompatible. One theory is saying we were fully formed and are now falling apart. The other is saying that there were billions of years of death and decay before God said "it is good". How could God say it is good, if there had already been death through evolution beforehand? If death entered the world through sin, how could there have been death before sin?

The Bible seems to be saying that the universe is some sort of cosmic bag that God breathed everything into. Perhaps that's why it's expanding. If you take the Bible literally, God's breath would contain all the elements needed to start the universe:

- Water: From the vapor of His breath,
- Heat: From the warmth of His body,
- Matter: From the vibration of His vocal chords (which is consistent with String Theory),
- Motion: From the pressure of His lungs,
- Time: As a consequence of matter in motion (the speed at which matter moves through space),
- Light: From the Words He spoke (which the Bible says is Christ),
- Gravity: From the weight of His words, and
- DNA: From the saliva of His mouth.

It's a little crazy, sure, but if I had to choose between something that made sense, but was a little whacky, versus something that was completely scientifically impossible... I'll take whacky any day. Anyways, I had already realized that the things of man make sense, but do not work. While the things of God do not make sense, but do work.

The only leap you really have to make is that Science is the disciplined pursuit of failing to explain God's construct. And that the Bible is not a story of old events, but a foretelling of future events, using ancient examples. That wasn't too hard for me to accept. After all, this seems to be the narrative the Bible is hinting at.

Now, in retrospect, I would argue even further still that science is the formal discipline of coming up with any explanation necessary to disprove God, for the sake of justifying sin as acceptable. I say this, as a Medical Doctor, understanding full well that even this single statement will likely render me unhirable for the rest of my life. What choice do I have? Truth is truth.

The Old Testament name for God is spelled YHWH. Modern Christians pronounce this "Yahweh". But it's actually pronounced "YHWH" because they are breathing sounds. YHWY is an onomatopoeia like "boom" or "bang". "YH" is the sound your lungs make when inhaling air and "WH" is the sound they make when exhaling. God was telling Moses that He is the very air he is breathing. There are many references to this and inferences of this throughout Scripture. Here are just a few:

- Genesis 2:7 says: "Then the Lord God formed the man of dust from the ground and breathed into his nostrils the breath of life, and the man became a living creature."
- Job 27:3 says: "As long as my breath is in me, and the spirit of God is in my nostrils."
- Psalm 150:6 says: "Let everything that has breath praise the Lord!"

It also makes sense biochemically. When God breathed into Adam, assuming the atmosphere was also 21% oxygen back then, the 21% oxygen in the air would have went into Adam's body, and accepted hydrogen, at the end of the Electron Transport Chain, allowing his body to start the process of energy creation using cyclic adenosine monophosphate.

Oxygen accepting Hydrogen would have also balanced his pH, since pH stands for "potential of Hydrogen", and the binding of the oxygen to hydrogen would have created H_2O. Literally, the water of life, or living water from God's breath. This would have all taken place in the mitochondria of Adam's cells, which has nonhuman DNA, separate and distinct from the nuclear DNA of the person's body. But again, all coincidence of course.

Did you know that every breath of your life, from the first to the last, has been calling out to God? And taking His name in vain is to take your very breath for granted? Perhaps this is why the Bible says God hears even our "wordless groans" as prayer.

The word "spirit" itself comes from "spirare" or "spirate" which means to breathe, emanate, exhale or inspire. The Webster Dictionary defines "spirate" as: "the action of breathing as a creative or life-giving function of the Deity. And the act by, or manner in which, the Holy Spirit proceeds from the Father or from the Father and the Son. The Bible further expounds on the correlation between God and breath as it describes the death of Christ in the various Gospels:

- Mark 15:37 says: "With a loud cry, Jesus breathed His last."
- Luke 23:46 says: "And when Jesus had cried with a loud voice, He said,

Father, into thy hands I commend my spirit: and having said this, He gave up the ghost."

- Matthew 27:50 says: "And when Jesus had cried out again in a loud voice, He gave up His spirit."

A delusion is defined as: "a belief that is firmly maintained despite being contradicted by what is generally accepted as reality, typically a symptom of mental disorder." Atheists only make up 7% to 14% of the world's population. Everyone else believes in a God, spiritual world and afterlife of some sort. By it's definition, Atheism is clinically classified as a psychological delusion. What some might call a "cult".

Not only is the Bible consistent with the laws of thermodynamics, the Curse of Genesis 3 is where thermodynamics came from. For either God or evolution to create anything against the order of entropy, the laws of thermodynamics would either have to be temporarily suspended, or creation would have had to take place before the laws of thermodynamics ever existed in the first place.

The Bible says:

1. God locked creation (which is where we get the first law from: Energy is neither created nor destroyed),
2. Death and decay entered the world through sin (which is where we get the second law from: Entropy), and
3. Now the warmth of God has left our presence as the world waxes cold (which is where we get the third law from: Absolute Zero).

It's also Biblically possible that entropy preexisted the curse, since the eating of fruit in the Garden of Eden would produce feces that would likely be excreted and decay back into soil. Either way, I came to accept that we are more likely not evolving from atoms, but devolving from Adam. Idiocracy is prophetic, and if you haven't noticed it yet... you're the example.

This all might sound complicated, but you can think of it very simply as this. If asked "Which came first, the chicken or the egg? Science says it's the egg. Christians say the chicken. Science says we are evolving from atoms, getting smarter over time and becoming more advanced. The Bible says we are devolving from Adam, getting stupider and falling apart.

Science believes in the "molecules to man" scenario, whereas the Bible claims more of an "atoms to Adam" model. In other words, God made Adam from the dust of the earth, while Science wants you to believe that the molecules which made man, also made themselves, on accident, from nothing.

Science says you can enjoy your sin life, because there is no meaning to life in the first place. Christians say that you need to re pent of your sins because the meaning of life is not the pursuit of happiness, but rather the seeking of righteousness. Science is telling you what you want to hear. The Bible is telling you the bitter truth.

You will never be able to unhear these words. The choice is now yours as to what you choose to do with them.

CHAPTER 7

Mutant Memes

All is fair in love, war and memes. But what you think of as a "meme"... is actually ironically a mutation of what "meme" originally meant. A meme is not a clever or funny captioned image on social media. Those are examples of memes, but the term "meme" actually refers to any encapsulated idea like a song, poem, quote, quip, joke, script, book or... yes, social media meme. Basically, a fully baked idea that you can easily share and other people can easily remember, is a meme.

For example, the quote: "All is fair in love and war" is a meme. And when I added "and memes" onto the end of it, I mutated the original meme. Does that make sense? The term "meme" was coined by Richard Dawkins in the 1970's to describe the evolution of ideas and comes from the word "memory".

Another example of a meme, is the word "meme" itself. The fact that Dawkins coined meme, and then the general population misunderstood "meme" as being just a social media image (which is only one example of a meme), is a mutation of the original "meme" meme. And when you couldn't figure out how to say it and use to pronounce it "me-me" instead of "meem", that again was a mutation to the already mutated meme.

The history of the mutations of memes over time, is essentially the evolution of human memories. Likewise, the mutation of genes over time, is the evolution of human genetics. And that is the point Dawkins was trying to make. He is comparing genetics to memories and making the point that they both are very similar in how they spread, age, mutate and evolve over time.

As we discussed in earlier chapters, the worldview language you use to structure your thoughts will heavily influence the way you see the world. But this is only an influence. Yes, it creates a layer of inaccuracy, but it does not control the way you see the world, it only skews it.

What is actually controlling your belief system, on an even deeper level than your worldview language, is a worldview government of competing ideas. And in this government of the mind, there are seats up for constant election. The thought politicians (which are memes), that you allow to win those elections and occupy those seats in your mind, subsequently determine your worldview.

In 1642, renowned Norwegian philosopher Bengt Washburn, performed a controversial series of human trials that resulted in the general consensus that humans are gullible. Washburn's extensive work in the field of human psychology unearthed that humans basically believe everything they hear 3 times. This is how you form "facts", by hearing them 3 times. Do you believe me? Or should I repeat it 1 more time?

According to Washburn, in his ground breaking study "The Excessive Inaesthetics of Drollery", the first time you hear something, you reject it. The second time, it feels familiar and you're more neutral to it. The third time, you'll not only accept it as fact, you'll add your own twist onto it. And thus a meme factoid is formed.

For example, Bengt Washburn is a modern comedian, not an ancient Norwegian philosopher. See how susceptible we become to lies, when we allow people a portal to speak into our lives?

Allow me to demonstrate some of the memes you already believe, that aren't actually true:

- Bats are blind,
- Bulls hate red, and
- Gold fish have 3 second memories.
- Our right brain is creative and our left brain is logical,
- We only use 10% of our brain, and
- Men have 12 ribs, while women have 13.

All of those are false. These are common myths you believed because you heard them repeated 3 times and formed them into memes you accepted as fact. The truth is:

- You don't have to drink 8 glasses of water a day,

- You don't have to get 8 hours of sleep a night, and
- Eating more calories does not automatically mean you will get fat. It's the hormones released by your endocrine system that determine what happens to calories when you eat them.

You believed these memes because you didn't really judge them based on the standard of their accuracy, but rather the standard of how memorable, impressive or "cute" they were. If you thought it would be able to be used to signal your virtue, intelligence or authority to someone else, you accepted it as fact. This was not because it was true, but because it might be useful. You didn't feel the need to fact check it, because you knew you would be able to share it with other people who also wouldn't feel the need to fact check it. The idea itself is a form of currency you're trading with other meme merchants and this economy of thought we call society.

A great example of competing memes is when truckers pass each other on the interstate. Some truckers believe the meme that "it's better to hit the gas going uphill and then coast going downhill". While other truckers believe the meme that "it's better to speed up going downhill, so you can coast going uphill". And so they constantly pass each other because they are not all playing by the same rules. And as a result, all of us other drivers are caught in the cross fire of their unintentional meme warfare.

There are also expired memes. For example, you might think that you're not supposed to flush the toilet while someone's taking a shower. But that meme had to do with a type of plumbing system that is now antiquated. So now it's perfectly fine and it's not going to change the water temperature in the shower. But that meme might be tied to a real life experience of someone doing that to you. As such, you may be emotionally attached to that meme, and more inclined to pass this "don't flush the toilet while someone is taking a shower" meme down to your children, even though it's no longer relevant in their generation.

René Descartes said "I think, therefore I am", in which he was saying that you are the some total of your thoughts. Antonio Damasio noted in his book, "Descartes' Error", that we actually make decisions based on how we feel, rather than what we think. Apparently, emotions play a large role in human decision making. In other words, people don't really remember what your words made them think, they usually just remember how those resulting thoughts made them feel.

Another expired meme is the "clump of cells "abortion meme. Even the scientific community doesn't use that terminology anymore. But people on the street arguing about abortion still do, because they don't keep up with the actual science behind abortion. They have just memorized the memes they need to in order to justify sin in their daily life.

At which point do:

- Letters become a Word,
- Words become a Chapter,
- Chapters become a Book and
- Books become a Library?

Letters themselves are memes. And these memes form larger memes (like works), which form larger memes (like sentences) and so on and so forth. They are like legos stacking together to form larger meme monstrosities.

Once a meme is formed, the content inside it becomes more easily transmitted from person to person. Think of it like a letter in an envelope. It's hard to mail a letter without an envelope. And likewise it's hard to explain content to another person unless it's in a form factor they are already familiar with.

The meme form factor also allows content to go viral and become resilient to change. Simply by being labeled a song, book or movie and categorized as music, literature or cinema, your meme enters some sort of protected class of information that is easier for humans to digest, understand, share and preserve.

If you just wrote some words on a piece of paper and started reading it to a friend, they would stop you and say, "Wait a sec. What is this? Is it a song you're writing? Or a poem you like? What exactly are you reading to me". And when you tell them, "It's a song I wrote", they say "Ok cool. Go ahead."

What they are really saying is, "What meme category should I file this under in my mind? What mental process should I conceptualize it with? And what societal standard should I judge it by?" Because it's a song you wrote, they know that they should hear it rhythmically. They also know it might not make perfect sense, but that's ok because songs are allowed to be artistic. And they are fully aware that it might suck, because an amateur wrote it, and so they will judge it against a lower standard than a professional song they hear on the radio.

If you tell them "It's not done yet, but this is what I have so far", you are telling them "It's not a fully formed meme yet, it's still under construction." And if they offer you advice on some better word choices, they are editing the memetic code of what will eventually become an encapsulated meme once it is fully formed. If that song goes viral and some drunk person in a bar someday sings the lyrics wrong, they are now mutating your original song meme.

Packaging content in an accepted meme format would be similar to packaging a product for distribution. And people who become proficient at this craft would therefore become fantastic orators, communicators, writers, influencers, teachers, politicians, lawyers or marketers.

Technically speaking, this means you will die 3 times:

- The first time you die is the death of your physical body,
- The second death is dilution of your genes into the gene pool and
- Your final death occurs the last time someone thinks of your memory (meme dilution into the collective meme pool).

Meme death could also be described as the death of your legacy, which is why at the end of their lives we see the cutthroat business tycoon turn lovable philanthropist. It's not that they suddenly become "good" people. It's that they realize they will die, God will win, they can't take their money with them and the only thing left of value is to live on at least in legacy. And so they spend their wealth to hurl their legacy ball as far into eternity as they can, hoping to beat their rivals in death by being remembered better and longer than anyone else.

But legacy is a lie. A long lasting legacy is just a cheap consolation prize for eternal life. In a sense, you are meme mummifying yourself. Maybe now is a good time to coin the term "memifying" oneself. You are turd polishing your image into a better version of yourself than was ever actually true, and then trying to horcrux the song of your life into the minds of everyone around you so you can live on in them. Meme death is the last time someone sings the song of you or watches the movie of your life in their mind in longing, loneliness or disgust.

As you read this book, meme theory would suggest that I am planting my cuckoo egg ideas (like parasites) in the nest of your mind (like a host) and forcing you to burn your calories, processing power and mental storage incubating my ideas for me. If you read this book and contact me later with some interesting correlation that I may have missed, you will have hatched my eggs for me and raised my meme babies at your own caloric expense. Are you uncomfortable yet? It's about to get worse.

This is why you become an amalgamation of the top 5 people you hang out with. You're being infected with their "memetically transmitted diseases". I doubt "MTD" is already a term, and so I'll go ahead and coin that one too. In other words, you're having thought sex with them. And that's why a stimulating conversation is so satisfying. It's like a little cognitive orgasm, which is why many people describe themselves as attracted to one's mind, which is called being a sapiosexual ("sapio" meaning wisdom).

This is why you hate being around certain people at work. You can feel them infecting you with their MTD's but you can't get away from them because you work together. It's nonconsensual thought sex, or meme rape. The reason they irritate you is because you subconsciously see yourself slowly turning into them and it drives you nuts.

The reason you will eventually "come around" to liking them over time, and perhaps even become friends, is because you will have become enough like them to be able to relate and feel you actually share some common interests after all. You feel perhaps you misjudged them, but the truth is you have become so much like each other, that you now have similarities with which to bond over. This is also another reason why you cannot trust your worldview. You are just a meat bag full of other people's meme babies.

Your parents passed down your genes to you. And so your genes are 50% from your mother's DNA and 50% from your father. But, let's say your father was absent and your mother raised you. Your mom would have passed down 100% of her memes to you, while your absentee father contributed none. And so genetically, you are 50% him, but memetically you are 0% him.

I'm not saying this to impress you, but I am actually a 99.9% DNA match blood relative to King Arthur, Batman and Jesus Himself. The reason I'm sure of this, is the same reason you shouldn't be impressed. That's because you are too. All humans share 99.9% the same DNA. It's the 0.01% that makes all the difference between us. You also share 99% the same DNA with apes, 98% DNA with pigs and 60% DNA with a banana. God made us via templates. We see this in scripture when He made Adam from the dust of the earth, and then created Eve from Adam's rib, rather than create her from scratch.

All seriousness aside though, I really am related to King Arthur (assuming he was a real person), via the Angevin Empire. But practically speaking, even with a DNA test, and a 99.9% DNA match, there would be no similarities between us to link us as relatives. The way gene dilution works, after 3 or 4 generations, your grandchildren and great grandchildren no longer accurately represent you genetically.

Memetically speaking, I am related to everyone who's book I've read or theory I've inculcated. As crazy as it sounds, after reading this book, a piece of me will forever live on in you. It's like we are having thought sex with everyone we listen to. And maybe that's why the Bible tells you to guard your heart and mind. Do not even eat with wicked people. Protect your thought life and fellowship with true believers.

My grandmother lives on in me more memetically than she does genetically. The dead live on in memory as if they are files saved on the hard drives of our minds, and processed through the CPU of our intellect. And so, again, on this earth she will die at least 3 deaths:

- The death of her physical body,
- The dilution of her genes over the generations, and
- The fading out of her memory into the memeverse.

As individual memes bind together and form into higher level meme molecules, those meme clusters are called "meme complexes". When meme complexes group together and form an even larger structure, this master meme complex becomes your worldview. In other words, your "facts", make up your beliefs, which make up your worldview.

Think about it. At which point do:

- Letters become a Word,
- Words become a Chapter,
- Chapters become a Book and
- Books become a Library?

Letters themselves are memes. And these memes form larger memes, (like words), which form larger memes, (like sentences), and so on and so forth. They are like legos stacking together to form larger meme monstrosities.

The outermost meme complex is your worldview.

The problem is, if you believe everything you hear 3 times as fact (which you do), your resulting worldview cannot be trusted. As you can imagine, this opens the door to information warfare where destructive content can now be wrapped in familiar wrappers to enter your mind as a Trojan horse.

Don't think about meme warfare as two worldviews fighting against each other in an arena. Think of meme warfare as two pirate ships, lining up against each other in the ocean for battle. They shoot individual canon balls at each other, to poke holes in the other ship, and eventually cause it to sink.

Likewise, think of meme warfare as two competing worldviews, lining up against each other in debate. They shoot individual memes at each other, to evoke cognitive dissonance, and eventually trigger an existential crisis.

Not all memes are created equal. The structural integrity of your worldview is supported by structural memes. These are memes which you cannot allow to be attacked or your entire worldview might collapse. For example, for the Christian, a structural meme is the infallibility of the Bible. If that meme falls, their entire worldview could collapse.

A few common types of meme attacks are:

1. Neutralize: Make the person apathetic to something. For example: "You know, I used to be Christian... but I'm just so turned off by the church after I watched this documentary. I think it's better to just let everyone believe whatever they want to believe."

2. Oppositional Defiance: Reverse a persons passion for something they once held dear. For example: "I used to love him, but ever since I read that new book, I realize he should be more emotionally available for me and now I just can't stand to even look at him!"

3. Bait and Switch: Pull a person into a familiar idea and then trade it out for a new and nefarious one. For example: "You are Christian, right? Great. Well you know Islam believes in the exact same God of Abraham. We just call him Allah. You are already one of us."

This has far reaching implications in our society. For example, and this is strictly a psychological observation, not a political statement: The reason liberals are criticized for always supporting "the newest thing" by default is because they seem to automatically believe the newest meme coming down the line. This is because they have already accepted the larger worldview meme complex of "I am a good person" and the rest is just a trigger of the "if/than" reflex.

The Democratic Party knows this and packages everything as "If you are a good person... Than you obviously support [insert newest thing]." It's an automatic inference by association that any professing liberal will automatically support whatever the next party issue is.

By going against the grain the individual (which is really just a cog in the collective) risks being excommunicated, penalized or suffering an existential crisis from a resulting worldview collapse. Its safer just to agree with your captors.

I would call this type of tactic an "If/Than" attack. The way to fight this is to question the "if" statement by questioning, "Hmm... Maybe I'm not actually a 'good person' after all. What evidence is there of my goodness? What standard of goodness am I using to make this determination in the first place?" Conservatives have all sorts of meme warfare issues as well, but they are more based on dopamine addiction to doom and gloom fear baiting. More on that later.

Liberals are an easy target because they not only have poor brain border security, they actually think it is virtuous. They believe in open meme borders and call it "open mindedness". This is why "they know so much that isn't so". They are a cesspool for unvetted memes. They are memiscuous little meme whores, having thought sex with everyone they come in contact with and then calling themself "cultured" as a result. But there is no virtue in being weak, and that's what poor meme security is, weakness. To be virtuous, you have to be a monster who knows how to restrain yourself, not a weakling who has no other option. It's worth mentioning that I know this from experience. When I was atheist, I also leaned quite liberal.

Conservatives on the other hand might be described as closed minded and overly strict with brain boarder security. While this is almost just as bad of a problem to the other extreme, I lean in favor of it because at least they have security. The Bible says to take every thought captive and compare it with Scripture before allowing it into your worldview, which is describing meme warfare and mental boarder security. Conservatives may be going overboard, but too much security is better than none at all.

Since liberals already know they are good people, meme acceptance is automatic due to confirmation bias. You just slap a "delivery for good person NPC# 927, 261" label on the meme box and they will take it right in because you are confirming something they already identify with. This get's the insidious new meme through the door, and then you just unpack the Trojan horse once inside.

This is much the same way viruses work. Viruses are recognized by receptors in the human body like a lock and key mechanism and then they deploy their genetic payload to cause devastating effects. This is why we say memes go "viral". Meaning, they catch on or spread rapidly (which is a high morbidity rate). If you remember that idea forever, it has a high mortality rate. How severe of a reaction you have to the idea would be its virulence. Because memes act like genes (as well as viruses), we can use Epidemiology (which is the study of how diseases spread) to discuss their transmission, and Genetics to discuss how they mutate over time.

Do you remember the scene in the movie "Inception", where they try to break into the rich guys mind to plant an idea and they have trouble because he has had mental fortitude training? Because of his training, he recognizes that they are thought intruders trying to plant an idea in his mind. Do you remember thinking that was cool and if it was real, you wish you could do that too? Well it is real, most of the things you think you believe were planted there by other people and if you want to get training in this area, read this chapter over and over again until it all starts to sink in. The training he got, is the same stuff we are talking about right now.

Memes don't just have to be the impetus for action, they can also be the reward. You can get men who wouldn't otherwise hurt a fly, to go kill in war as long as you pin a 50 cent piece of medal to their chest and call their actions honorable. This creates the infamous push/pull meme attack the military is known for. Another name for this would be "brain washing".

Before I was trained as an officer in the US Army, I was a Firefighter and EMT hellbent on saving lives. I wasn't sure they were going to be able to convert me over to killing so easily. Nonetheless, it only took them about 3 weeks to turn me into a stone cold killer and here's how they did it.

The military physically exhausts you to the point of disabling your defense mechanisms and conscience. All you're thinking about is gasping down your next breath of air on a 5 mile run, they told you would be a 2 mile run, at a pace 110% faster than you've ever run before in your life. Then they give you the one thing you want. They slow the run down to 90% of your capacity and replace that with singing as a trade off.

The singing of cadences while running was already meme programed into us as kids anyways through movies and TV shows. And so there's little resistance. As a matter of fact, there is a sense of nostalgia because this new meme is being tied to the original meme marketed to you at a much more impressionable time in your youth. That's how they knew to look for it there, because their the ones that planted it there in the first place. It's like "Marry had a little..." How did I know you would say "lamb"? Because I knew to look for that meme in your mind.

As you start singing these songs about clubbing baby seals, bullets in your buddy's head and napalm sticking to kids... it goes straight in without any filters or your conscience objecting to any red flags.

One of my favorite cadences went something like this: "Glory, glory, glory... what a hell of a way to die! With your rifle on your back as you go flying through the sky!"And proceeded to describe your parachute failing to open and you falling to your death in glory. And so they posthumously pin your war medals to the puddle of pulp that used to be your chest... "And he ain't gonna jump no more!"

The intentional eroding of someone's worldview is actually the attack on that individual's structural memes. That's why they are so hotly contended for. For example, abortion is a structural meme that supports the ceiling under which is housed promiscuous sex, porn and lust. That's why people still support abortion as a "human right" even though they would never do it themselves, because that is a structural worldview meme that is fundamental to the "I'm a good person" worldview.

When a structural meme is completely destroyed and you can no longer believe it, you risk collapsing your entire worldview. To avoid this, sometimes you replace the damaged meme with the new invading meme you don't particularly like but can't figure out how to defeat. Rather than leave the meme seat empty and risk a collapse, you let it ride for the time being. You now have a conflicting meme in your worldview (which causes cognitive dissonance), but you can figure out how to replace it later and things will eventually go back to normal.

The competition for these meme seats in your mind creates a little meme government (let's call it a "memocracy"), where memes fight constantly to occupy seats in your worldview. You can think of it like a game of meme musical chairs or little meme elections. In this government, the majority vote wins and so whatever memes hold the majority in your worldview, essentially run your life by outvoting the minority memes.

If someone can sneak enough Manchurian memes into your worldview government, they essentially control your life remotely. You have become 51% a clone of them and so you will now think like them and vote like them, without them even having to say or do anything anymore.

The world wants to enslave you in a thought matrix of memes. They want to clone themselves onto you as an empty vessel to reverse validate their own false identity. They want to remake you in their image, for their own glory. That's why it's free. Because you are the product.

But God created you as a living statue in His own image, for His own glory. That's what kings do. King Nebuchadnezzar did the same thing, for the same reason. He created a statue of himself, in his own image, for his own glory. You can only serve one master. You can either be a slave to the world of other people's memes, or you can repent of your sins, submit to God and allow Him to restore you into the image in which He made you: His own.

Memes are what Christ is describing as rocks in the Parable of the Sower. Rotten memes are the rocks that need to be plowed out of your rocky heart field. This is what the Bible describes as a renewing of your mind. Christ is talking about melting your mind down to burn off the impurities. He is telling you to allow Him to remove any inaccurate "facts" from your worldview and elect Him to every meme seat in your worldview government.

This is a small part of what it means to submit to Christ. This is how you wake up from the thought matrix you think is reality to come and live in the spirit, which is the real world. Once the mind is transcended in this way, you'll live in spirit. But as long as you lack humility, you will always try to conceptualize the spirit from inside the mind and fail in frustration to understand what everyone else is talking about. It's not an understanding you gain. It's a transformation you experience.

That's the difference between Christianity and a cult. Cults are trying to enslave you into their own mini-matrix, inside of the larger matrix you already think of as reality. Christians have already escaped the larger matrix, live in the spirit and are trying to offer you a chance to escape as well. Cults get a net gain from you. You're an investment they plan to get a return on.

Conversely, I don't actually want you to be like me in the first place. I am just another sinner like you. I want you to be like Christ. I want you to experience the love and joy and hope and peace and identity that I have found in Him. And I want this for you because you are my long lost spiritual family and I love you.

Cults want you to accept their truth. Christians want you to accept the truth.

The world is ok with a 51% majority of your worldview government. They don't care if you call yourself a Christian, as long as your meme government is actually still voting in favor of abortion, progressivism and liberal ideas. Or putting your faith in world leaders, policies and the Constitution. Some of you care more about the 2nd Amendment than you do the 2nd Commandment, and it shows. The Devil knows that if you're not fully sold out for God, calling yourself a Christian means nothing. He knows that as long as he can run your clock out, while thinking you're ok, your soul will be his in the end.

Conversely, God requires 100% of your mind, heart and soul. Anything less than 100% is what the Bible refers to as "lukewarm". The world offers you a seemingly free pursuit of endless happiness. But notice that you are only promised the endless pursuit of happiness, not happiness itself. That's because you never actually get it. And that is because it never existed in the first place.

Christianity, to the contrary, is not free. It's the most expensive thing in existence. That's why everyone is so hesitant to pay that price. The cost is repenting and turning away from sin, and no one wants to do that.

The Bible is the story of the original meme of truth God sent to this world. It says that the Word of God... Wrapped in flesh... dwelt among us.

If you didn't catch that...

- The content is: The Word
- The wrapper is: Jesus
- The meme is: Truth

The Bible says in John 1: "In the beginning was the Word, and the Word was with God, and the Word was God. He was with God in the beginning. Through him all things were made; without him nothing was made that has been made. In him was life, and that life was the light of all mankind. The light shines in the darkness, and the darkness has not overcome it."

John 1 mirrors Genesis 1, which says: "In the beginning God created the heavens and the earth. Now the earth was formless and empty, darkness was over the surface of the deep, and the Spirit of God was hovering over the waters. And God said, 'Let there be light,' and there was light."

Christ is God's truth meme. Which is why all creation is locked by God into inescapable categories. Everything else is just a mutated meme through a rearranging of God's legos, or a blurring of the mirror of Christ (who is truth).

Sin is just a Creole of Christ. Satans deception is the encryption algorithm and spiritual discernment is the ability to identify mutated memes for the real ones.

God wrote you a love letter, sealed it in the envelope of Christ and sent it to you.

Like everything else, Meme Theory was stolen from God. Dawkins spiritual blindness is why he is unable to understand scripture. He lacks the humility needed to decrypt it. Do you?

CHAPTER 8

Mario's Matrix

You are Mario, this life is the game, God is the player and faith is our connection to Him. The only difference is that Mario is an idiot, doesn't have to obey the player and doesn't know he's in a simulation.

Allow me to use logic to logically prove logic illogical.

A statement is logically true if, and only if, its opposite is logically false. The opposite statements must contradict one another. For example, if I tell you there is a truck in your driveway, and also there is no truck in your driveway, you can use logic to determine that one of these statements must be true and the other false.

In other words, if two memes were in a boxing match, logic would be the rulebook telling them not to hit below the belt. If two memes were opposing candidates in a race for one of your worldview seats, logic would be the law regulating that meme seat election.

There are 4 rules of logical, intellectually honest, debate. For a deeper dive into Aristotle's actual laws of logic (which are the laws of identity, non-contradiction and excluded middle, visit www.TheWarWithin.me)

The 4 rules of logical debate are:

1. We exist,

2. We can communicate,

3. We can be wrong, and

4. The rules of logic hold true.

Surely we can all agree on this, right?

While this seems reasonable on its face, these are dangerous presuppositions with which to form your worldview language. Let's take them one at a time, starting with the most egregious offender, number 4.

The 4th rule of logic is an insidious, self affirming infallibility clause. You can't say "The Bible is true" and then cite "Because the Bible says so" as evidence. Anything that reverse validates itself is called "circular logic". My favorite example of circular logic is a universe that created itself.

Logic must be true without the need to make "logic holds true" a pre-requisite for logic to hold true. This is no different than a Christian forcing an atheist to play by the rule of "Biblical Scripture is Infallible" as a prerequisite to have a debate. And this is no coincidence. Logic is the infallible scripture of the Atheist religion. So number 4 is out.

Let's look at the other 3 from the big picture first:

1. We exist: Christians believe, whether they know how to articulate it or not, that we are actually in some sort of training simulation, separated from God, who is in the "real" world. Descartes hypothesized that we are brains in a vat, living in a thought matrix. Elon Musk is so statistically convinced that we live in a virtual reality that he has hired a team of experts to try to escape it. Modern science says that everything we see is actually 99% empty space (the empty space between the nucleus and electron cloud of each atom, which make up matter). Therefore, if we don't exist in the way that we think we do, what then is existence at all? As physicist Niels Bohr said: "Everything we call real is made of things that cannot be regarded as real."

2. We can communicate: As we have already discussed at length with language, can we really communicate? This is an assumption. People only remember how you made them feel, not what you made them think (as noted by Damasio vs Descartes). Your ability to communicate is dependent on how the other party receives it, processes it and stores it. Communication is subjective at best.

3. We can be wrong: You've got me there. I agree, we most certainly can be wrong. As a matter of fact, a better question would be "can we ever

truly be right?" But for this to logically be true, it must also apply to itself. Therefore, for this point to be true, it must also potentially be false, based on itself. Logically speaking, "we can be wrong" must statistically be wrong itself on occasion in order to be right. It is therefore not an absolute and must be discarded as an illogical fallacy.

Whether you agree with my arguments or not is irrelevant. The fact that the arguments can be made in the first place makes them valid. If logic can be used to destroy logic, it is therefore a house divided against itself, and a poor choice for an absolute worldview language. Rather, logic is a tool with which to lay out information and discuss it. It is an arena for ideas to fight to the death. It's most definitely not some all encompassing master worldview language. The reason you're having trouble understanding what I'm describing, is because you're a victim of it.

Now let's take a closer look at how evolutionists use logic to try to disprove the existence of God. Christians and Atheists seem to agree that the universe is a simulation of sorts, extracted from an infinitely dense atomic zip file (which science calls the Big Bang Theory). The only difference is Christians insist there must have been someone there in the beginning to double click it.

There are two main theories in cosmology (which is the study of the origins of the universe). One is that the universe was created as a single event (called a singularity). Verses the full retard hail Mary theory that the subatomic world which predates the big bang is eternal and the creation singularity was powered by energy from this eternal quantum level. Both of these theories deny a creator God as the cause of creation.

Sometimes the only way out, is deeper in, and so Atheists claim that the energy which caused the Big Bang must have logically come from an even smaller place (the quantum level). This is just the newest version of the "millions and billions of years" scape goat. If something doesn't make any sense at all in Atheism, the go-to is "Well, I mean it happened over millions and a gazillion billion years! Because... SCIENCE!" Now it's going to be "Well I mean, I have no problem believing in an eternal universe. The quantum level has endless possibilities." It's just another example of Atheists moving the galactic goal post, or kicking the cosmic can down the road less traveled.

This affords science an out to the whole "nothing comes from nothing" paradox. But it opens the door to breaking logic itself. This is a real problem for the Atheist because it was logic that was needed to make the whole thing work in the first place. Allow me to explain why quantum energy powering the Big Bang breaks human logic. Let's look again at the first 3 rules of logic, but this time from a quantum perspective:

1. We exist: In the quantum level, when you throw a ball at the wall, it will both bounce off the wall and go through the wall at the same time (this is called quantum tunneling). Does the ball now dynamically exist in 2 instances? Are there now 2 separate balls? What does it mean to exist in a world where single objects break into an infinite number of instances every time they move?

2. We can be wrong: If I hand you a box and tell you there is a cat in the box, and also there is not a cat in the box, you can use logic to say that is impossible. But in the quantum level, matter can exist in the same spot at the same time. And so, in quantum, both are true simultaneously. And so if all possibilities in quantum are right, how can any be wrong?

3. We can communicate: Verbal communication in our world occurs when an air molecule vibrates its neighboring air molecule, and passes the vibrational energy on like a molecular game of telephone. That vibration hits your ear drum, vibrating 3 tiny bones (called the ossicles), which then vibrate another membrane called the oval window. This causes a pressure fluctuation of the fluid in the inner ear. That fluid rushes past tiny hairlike cells in the cochlea. Through a complex process of ionic action potentials, the physical vibration is then converted into neurological impulse through the 8th pair of cranial nerves (called the vestibulocochlear nerves). Amazingly, atheists claim that all of this happened on accident, by itself, from nothing, but I digress.

The visual communication of our eyes works much the same way, just through the rods and cones of the retina, and then the 2nd pair of cranial nerves (called the trigeminal nerves). Smell, taste and touch also work through similar mechanisms.

The quantum level is smaller than a single atom, which breaks all of these mechanisms of communication. We don't know what type of receptors exist in the quantum level that could be used to help us interface with that environment. Ergo, we cannot be certain that communication, as we know it, is possible in the quantum level at all.

Atheists are trying to use human level logic to dictate the rules of a paradoxical world they've never even seen. This would be fine if it was some tribal religion in the bushes of Africa. But they are teaching this trash to your children and have the gumption to claim they are the lack of all faith.

When I say we can't see the quantum level, I mean the way science forms its theories about quantum mechanics is by smashing atoms into subatomic particles and observing energy spikes on a graph. This process, for instance, is how CERN discovered the Higgs boson "God Particle" in 2012. That particular energy spike only lasted less than a trillionth of a billionth of one second.

It's not exactly like you can see this stuff under a microscope or hold it in your hand. And the pieces of it you can see continue to make fools of the so called scientists. The new James Webb Space Telescope, which is the successor of the Hubble Telescope, was specifically designed to find the very earliest galaxies in the universe. Science had hypothesized that the further away you look in distance, the longer back you're looking in time. And so with the James Webb Telescope, they had hoped to see the origins of the Big Bang, so they can disprove God and justify sin as religiously archaic, once and for all.

What the telescope found instead was further evidence of creationism. Specifically, it found that the universe may be younger than originally thought, and that the early, and distant galaxies closest to the Big Bang, are more massive, more organized, and more structured, than they should have been that early on, assuming a creatorless creation.

These findings led Allison Kirkpatrick, an astrophysicist at the University of Kansas, to say: "Right now I find myself lying awake at three in the morning, wondering if everything I've ever done is wrong." Albeit Kirkpatrick later clarified that she never meant this quote to be used as an indication that the scientific community was now doubting the well established "Big Bang" theory.

The fact is, science is not all that impressive in the grand scheme of things. Even in medical school they told us that half of what we would learn, will soon be proven wrong, and the other half will be outdated by the time we graduate. One day we were taught, "an apple a day keeps the doctor away". The next day, we are all going to die from cyanide poisoning due to apple seeds. The same thing happened with eggs. One day it was, "the incredible edible egg", the next day eggs are going to kill us all, because they contain too much cholesterol.

It's all theoretical science. That doesn't mean it's wrong. After all, they did theoretically predict that the Higgs boson particle would show on the graph, and then tested that assumption and found it correct. That's impressive. That's not nothing. But it does mean you shouldn't be letting these people use this stuff to tell your children that God doesn't exist. If God doesn't exist, then why did a bunch of atheist scientists, who claim they aren't trying to disprove a creator God, name the "God particle" after Him in the first place?

I think Heaven is the quantum realm. Is that not how the Bible describes Heaven, a place were anything is possible? And that would make CERN the modern day Tower of Babel. I think CERN just scratched the surface of Heaven, and science is trying to use their discovery of Heaven, to prove the nonexistence of the God who created it.

Logically speaking, once you introduce quantum level energy generation into the mix, all logical bets are off and the possibility of a logically impossible God is back on the table. The fact is, in the paradoxical quantum level, we don't know if we exist, we can't prove that we can communicate and we can't be sure we can be wrong. Ergo, logic has just been used to break logic.

It also makes heaven scientifically possible, because if "nothingness" doesn't actually mean "nothing" (because it now has the quantum level as some sort of cosmic crutch) then a new heaven and earth (as the Bible describes) could just come from that new quantum nothingness that is left when this world burns.

This is why I say that Atheists only have 2 real choices:

1. Say that creation is a singularity (not eternal) and just plead ignorance towards all the problems that creates (which is what it means to be Agnostic), or

2. Admit there is an eternal God, but rebrand Him as a "multiverse generator" who is impersonal and therefore ok with your sin.

There are 3 main groups effected by the death of logic as a worldview language: Agnostics, Atheists and Apologists.

The furthest you can go away from Christianity is the "Agnostic". Agnostics claim to not know or not care. It's basically creationism apathy. This truly, as it is defined, would be the closest you could get to the lack of all beliefs (which Atheism claims to be).

The funny thing about Agnostics is they are ironically examples of themselves. "A" put in front of a word means "no" or "not". While "gnostic" means "knowledge". So... Agnostic literally means "no knowledge".

But if you tell an Agnostic that the etymology of their own accepted label is a self affirmation of stupidity or ignorance, they will fight you to the death. And that is because they have "no knowledge" of the fact that Agnostic means "no knowledge". It literally means "I know nothing", actually means "I'm an idiot" and practically means "you shouldn't listen to anything I have to say". Why on earth would anyone self label themselves with a claim of stupidity? Again, God makes fools of those who think themselves wise.

By pleading apathy, Agnostics have opted themselves out of the conversation and therefore deserve no opinion on the matter whatsoever. Once you explain this to them and it clicks, they are usually embarrassed enough to slide to a more firm position of Atheist. And if not, just start telling them about how we are all dirty rotten sinners and they will hit you with some "facts" (or rather their belief in facts) as to why that is unlikely and illogical. And so the self proclaimed Agnostic quickly reveals himself to having been a closet Atheist all along.

Atheist means "not a theist". But, again, we see God's sense of humor pop up. Atheists can't even claim to not believe in God ("I am atheist") without literally professing with their lips that they believe in God ("I am a theist"). Yet another one of God's cosmic Dad jokes.

Theism is defined as "belief in the existence of a god or gods, especially belief in one God as Creator of the universe, intervening in it and maintaining a personal relationship with His creatures."

Now the question becomes, do Atheists believe there is no God? Or do they actually lack all beliefs altogether (as they claim).

Atheists claim to have knowledge (unlike Agnostics) but no resulting beliefs from that knowledge. I think you can see the obvious problem with this. They have taken a bite of the apple and received the knowledge from it, yet claim to not believe in the Devil who gave it to them. Where did the apple come from bro? And how do you square dem apples?

By claiming no belief, Atheists also excuse themselves from the discussion. Yet simultaneously, they are claiming to be the ones winning the debate. Atheists are the biggest evangelists on earth, so much so that their doctrine is taught as "fact" to your children in school. Those are some pretty serious marketing results from a group that claims not to be marketing anything in the first place.

Atheists claim to possess knowledge with which to form beliefs, yet have no beliefs formed from that knowledge. But when you talk to them, they sure do seem to have a lot of faith as the evidence of things unseen. With a professed 1% knowledge of anything, they will tell you all about how the 99% of the unknown everything must logically work.

If they truly lacked all beliefs, they probably wouldn't be so militant about evangelizing their lack of beliefs. No one evangelizes a negative belief. That's what evangelism means, spreading your beliefs. No salesmen tries to sell you snake oil they don't actually have a bottle of. The whole point is to sell you something that doesn't work, not that doesn't exist. Otherwise, why would these evolved apes be wasting their precious calories to explain non-existent concepts to other apes?

By the time you figure it out, they are long gone. Now it's just you and God on judgement day and He is asking you why you bought into a worldview you knew deep down was a lie. The only honest answer you can give, before you burn, is "I was trying to protect my sin life".

Evolution dictates that the more evolutionarily stable strategy would be to conserve calories for things you actually believe in, rather than burn them debating things you don't. It's more logical to conclude that Atheists would be a quiet society of people, minding their own business and preoccupying themselves with hobbies and indulgences.

Certainly they wouldn't believe in a conscience, justice, morality, law or ethics. The whole point would be an utter lack of all those beliefs. They are all invisible, scientifically unprovable concepts. So how can an Atheist "believe" in these invisible things, yet continue to claim the lack of all beliefs? And if the anecdotal consensus of "we observe them in society" will suffice, then is not the mere existence of society itself anecdotal evidence of a creator God? That's a slippery slope for an Atheist to step out on.

If Atheists really lacked all belief, they wouldn't do the things we observe them doing today. A true lack of all beliefs would render the Atheist more animal like than anything, doing what they want, when they want, however they want, without feeling any remorse, because conscience, justice, morality, law and ethics stem from a belief in right and wrong, which animals do not possess.

Only domesticated animals who have learned behavioral regulation through discipline, appear to know right and wrong. This is why the study of Pavlov's dog is so important. Ivan Pavlov, a Russian physiologist, trained a dog to salivate to the sound of a ringing bell, rather than actual food.

Pavlov would ring the bell and then feed the dog, and so the dog began to associate those 2 events. But when he removed the food, the dog would still salivate at just the sound of the bell alone. It's also worth mentioning that the dog stopped salivating over time because he dissociated the event of hearing the bell, from the event of receiving food. And so the process is reversible, which most people fail to mention about Pavlov's famous experiment.

This is the type of externally trained conscience that animals have. They shit on the rug, and you spank them for it. And so over time they learn the pattern of cause and effect. But that's not the same thing as being born with a voice inside your head that you can't get to shut up no matter how hard you try. Animals in the wild, without human intervention, do not exhibit signs of having a conscience.

Ever notice that animals don't call the animal police on each other? There are no animal courts or prisons, because animals don't think they are "good". They simply lack all beliefs. That's what lacking all beliefs actually looks like. There is certainly no evangelism in the animal kingdom, because there are actually no beliefs to evangelize to begin with.

Let's take a quick look at your metaphysical anatomy and try to understand where the conscience fits in:

- Plants exist in body,
- Animals exist in body and soul, and
- Humans were created in body, soul and spirit.

Through sin, the Bible says we became spiritually dead. The Old Testament seems to be the story of a time and people who only had access to the written external law, but not the internal conscience that we know and ignore today. They had to be externally convicted, which is why God sent prophets to be their external conscience. Today we have an internal prophet (our conscience) which is the story of the New Testament.

Atheists claim to be animals (specifically they claim to be apes). And in a way, the Bible agrees. If they are spiritually dead, there is very little difference between them and an animal, as both lack a spirit. Christians claim that we are not animals, and this is also correct, because as Christians, redeemed by Christ, we have been reborn into spiritual life, thus being marked, distinguished and set apart from animals.

I think the story of Noah's Ark sheds some light on this for us. The Ark represents salvation, floating above the wrath of God, yet still being tossed around by the waves of it. There is still fear and trembling to be worked out in salvation. Being saved does not mean you are entitled to a calm and peaceful ride. Come to find out, the journey to Heaven is hellacious.

As Noah was yelling from the deck of the Ark: "It's about to start raining! Come and be saved while there is still time!", the animals (who existed in body and soul, but no spirit), could still hear the spirit calling out to them. Some ignored it, some answered the call. Today, this call to the Ark is screaming inside of you. It is your conscience. Your conscience is God calling you to salvation.

Noah was acting as an external prophet in that moment. And so your conscience, which is your internal prophet, is calling you to the Ark of salvation as well, before judgement starts. That's why my job in this book is not to be your conscience, it is simply to tell you to stop muting your conscience. You already know these things. It's already written on your heart and mind.

And so, I have no problem with Atheists calling themselves animals, as long as they speak for themselves and don't include me in on their delusion. The problem comes when Atheists start insisting that they are "good" people based on a conscience they shouldn't believe in for the same reasons they don't believe in the soul or spirit. It's an invisible, schizophrenic imaginary friend in their head. Surely they don't believe in that, do they?

The third and final group effected by the death of logic as a worldview language, are Christian apologists. My well intentioned brothers and sisters, please, just stop. Jesus unapologetically never used apologetics and the Bible literally says do not be contentious about the details. How can you lead the lost to the Word, if the way you're leading them, is by disobeying scripture? There should be a time, place and manner restriction on apologetics. It should only be used momentarily and surgically, only as needed.

Paul does explain logical concepts to the lost and I have done so myself in this book, but it's just to roll a stone out of the way when you see them stumbling over it. We should always be ready to give an answer, but then we go right back to the conscience. Other than that, Apologetics is useless. Roll the stone out of the way and immediately get back to the Gospel.

All some of you know how to do is debate, and you're doing this because it's easy and you feel comfortable. But I'll take an uneducated Gospel loving illiterate on my team any day over someone who is academically arrogant. I'm already trying to fight my own academic arrogance. I don't need to be adding to it.

Apologists speak to the mind, assuming human level logic as a worldview language and playing by the rules of the Atheist. The Bible says "don't cast pearls before swine". How did you mix that up with "go roll in the mud with them"?

Why would you possibly do that? Let your spirit speak to their hearts. Talk to their conscience, not their fortified mind. Reach them through truth in love, not arrogance in ego. It's not supposed to be "us -vs- them". Jesus told us it was "us loving them". The Atheist wins when the Christian loses his temper. The Christian loses if either person loses their temper. It's a higher standard. We fight for sinners, not against them. Do better.

In our 3 dimensional world, there are 4 kinds of stressors that exert themselves on objects:

1. Torsion: The torsion strength of an object is its ability to resist being twisted.
2. Tensile: The tensile strength of an object is its ability to resist being stretched.
3. Compression: The compression strength of an object is its ability to resist being crushed.
4. Shear: The shear strength of an object is its ability to resist being cut.

There are also compound stresses, like bending. The bending strength of an object is its ability to resist being bowed. But bending stress is just a combination of equally opposite tensile stress on the convex side of an object, and compression stress on the concave side of that same object.

Imagine these forces on the objects in Mario's 2D world. 2D objects could be pulled (tensile), pressed (compression) and cut (shear). But could Mario give Luigi a

2D titty twister (torsion) in a world with no width? Probably not. You need 3D space to be able to twist an object. Now imagine trying to explain torsion force to Mario. Something so simple for you, but absolutely absent to him. He doesn't have a seat to attach that meme to in his worldview government, and therefore the concept is lost on him.

Now take that same principle and apply it to yourself regarding the quantum level. Truly we have no idea what it is or how it works. In our world, we take still images and play them quickly to make up a video like motion. In the quantum world, video like motion itself breaks into infinite snapshots of movement in every possible direction, like a mirror shattering into shards, but each piece of the infinitely broken glass is like a little TV screen into a slightly different version of events. Which is where the theory of the multiverse comes from.

Atheists using human level logic to define the limitations of the quantum world would be analogous to Mario saying it is not possible to twist anything in a 3D world, as evidenced by the fact that it is impossible to do so in his 2D world. We are using 3D logic to limit the powers of an infinite God.

If 2D Mario can't even imagine what it means to twist someone's nipple, imagine the forces that exist in the quantum world. Now imagine the arrogance of the people trying to tell you that cookies don't crumble, they bake themselves on accident, with no ingredients. Now imagine your own stupidity for letting these idiots raise your children for you with their eternal soul on the line. There has never been a better definition of "dereliction of duty" than letting your children be eaten by wolves you're too afraid to confront.

At the very least, logically speaking, with only 1% of knowledge, every person on earth should be able to admit a creator God is possible. Many Atheists will admit this, but they will deflect with something like: "Yeah, sure. Maybe Thor and unicorns and elves are real too".

What they are really saying is "I have no choice but to admit there must be a God of some sort, but I'm never going to admit that it's the one who tells me I have to stop sinning".

The Bible says heaven is within us. It talks about a mustard seed growing into something larger. We scientifically observe that light is evenly dispersed throughout the universe. And that is because that Light of the world came from Heaven in the first place, which is at the core of every atom. The quantum level... is heaven. It's not "out there". It's in us.

Perhaps the multiverse is Heaven. Each of us get our own version of it, which is how it's a personal relationship and there are levels of heaven. Perhaps we can frequency rift through those endless dimensions, visiting each other and exploring infinity for eternity.

Could you imagine sparring with the angels like Goku and Vegeta in Dragon Ball Z, painting your own reality like Robin Williams in What Dreams May Come, and traveling through the multiverse like Dr. Strange in the Avengers End Game movie? If content, like energy, is conserved, then all of those movies are stolen from actual things mentioned, or omitted in Scripture.

Do you still think Heaven sounds boring without sin?

I will say this though, if that is the case, and this knowledge is now being leaked into the world like an expansion pack for the simulation of this life (which the Bible calls the 7 seals being broken), then truly, the end is near. If we can literally see Heaven on a graph and human hands have just scraped the edge of it, we are most definitely in the 11th hour.

Please, I beg you. Repent. Seek the Lord while He may be found.

CHAPTER 9

The Will of the Wielder

The reason Science wants to disprove God is because if there is no Creator, then there is no Creator's intent, no purpose of life and therefore no anchor of reality. Truth becomes relative and sin becomes a perspective of opinion, not an absolute.

If I draw a 6 on a piece of paper and show it to you upside down, you will say it is a 9 instead. So who is correct?

- Is it my truth (a 6) versus your truth (a 9)?
- Are we both correct? Can 2 contradictory truths ever truly co-exist?
- Or are we just viewing 2 different perspectives of the larger truth that there is ink on a piece of paper?

To get to the truth, we have to submit to the intent of the creator. Because I drew a 6, it doesn't matter that you see a 9. By virtue of creating it, I reserve the right to define my creation. The intent of the Creator is always the deciding factor, because the intent of the Creator is the anchor of reality.

God is the Creator and He has reserved the right to define His creation, which He has lovingly laid out for us in the Bible.

I intended to draw a 6, and so it's a 6. The strokes of the pen are dictated by the will of its wielder. If the creator intended to allow the audience to have their own interpretation of his art, then you are free to interpret it as you wish. But that is still the intent of the creator to allow you that gift of free will.

The people who usually argue with me on this are liberals. Again, just a quick note: I'm not a Democrat or a Republican. God is my country and I have a healthy and mutual disdain for both parties of the government as a whole. But liberals are usually the ones that debate me on this.

When liberals try to tell me there are "many truths" I just agree with them and merge it with the "alternative facts" meme. I label them as a supporter of "alternative facts", because that's literally what they are saying and it induces instant cognitive dissonance, which causes them to backtrack on their position.

Or when they tell me that the viewer of the art is entitled to their own interpretation, regardless of the artist's "intent", I just agree with them again and merge their contention with the "appropriating someone else's culture" meme. Which is again what they are saying. That the artist does not have the right to define his own creation culture. And again, cognitive dissonance ensues. If they haven't already done so, they usually block me at this point.

If truth is open to interpretation, why stop at calling the 6 a 9? What if I say the 6 is a goat, or a zebra or an elephant? That's what I see when I look at the 6 and who is to say I am wrong? Truth is subjective, right? If I see the 6 as a million dollars, could I go deposit that in a bank? If the bank refuses to accept a piece of paper with a crayon 6 drawn on it as 1 million dollars, are they calling me crazy or discriminating against me somehow?

This type of "feel good" logic begins to unravel as it leaves the boundaries of your own delusion. You can pretend the 6 is a million dollars in your own mind, but you will get a reality check when you try to spend it. Your delusion would have to be shared with the other person to accept your fictitious currency.

I understand why people want to have relative truth. It protects their sin life. But look at the ridiculous extremes they are willing to go to to protect it. People are literally going through identity crises at a historical record high because of this stuff.

Men think they are women, women don't know what the definition of a "woman" is anymore and kids are confused about where to use the bathroom. And for what? To protect sin? Look at the damage you are doing to society. This is the most selfish thing I've ever seen in my life. And all by people who proclaim their own "goodness".

Most rational people would concede that the 6 is a 6 and could also be construed as a 9 if you read it upside down. But that's pretty much it. They claim that the single truth could be viewed from different angles, but stop short of saying that truth is "whatever you want it to be", as they see the slippery slope consequences of having zero truth stability in society whatsoever. They need truth to be flexible enough to justify their own sin life, but after that, truth can be absolute. They don't care if the door slams on the person behind them, as long as they are already through it.

And so while many people like the idea of the meaning of life being "whatever you want it to be", they also recognize that some ideas about what this life might be are simply delusional, just not their own ideas. They are ok with labeling some people crazy, as long as they narrowly escape the label themselves. However, they also recognize the utility of having a safe buffer zone. And that's why they support more extreme examples of what truth might mean. It serves the purpose of shifting the line to a safer margin, away from their own sin life.

I have some old friends who have made up their own religion called "The Way of the Jedi". It's cute, but of course I don't take it seriously. It's only 2 people after all. I'm not saying they really like Star Wars and are taking it a bit too far... I mean they actually think "the force" is real and that they are Jedis who can control it. It's their literal religion. And you guessed it, they think they are good people who will be saved by living a good life.

I noticed that my Atheist friends all supported their "Way of the Jedi" religion, yet simultaneously criticized my Christian beliefs. This is because "The Way of the Jedi" religion served the Atheist agenda. It's slightly less stupid to believe you're an ape, in a world that created itself from nothing, on accident, if you're standing next to someone who thinks they're a real life Jedi from Star Wars. But to be a Christian, well that serves no protection, and quite the contrary, Christ told us to stop sinning, and so there is no support for that, because it doesn't serve the same utility as a shield with which to protect your sin.

What about you? Do you support their "Way of the Jedi" religion? Or do you think it's as ridiculous as I do? Do you support it because "it makes them happy"? This concept of telling people what they want to hear because it makes them feel good is about as healthy as giving a fat kid candy because he likes the taste. Can we at least be honest and just admit that the only reason you claim to support it is so people won't look too closely at your own sin life?

The truth is, you want the fat kid to eat the candy. Because if he does, he stays fat and you can judge him to feel better about yourself. Why do you think hot chicks always have an average looking, or overtly ugly, friend they hang out with? It's reverse validation by proxy.

Not only do you want the fat kid to eat the candy, you're willing to buy it for them. You comfort them, encourage them and cheer them on, as long as they keep shoveling that candy into their mouth, because if they stop, you'll start to get nervous that you're sin life will be the one on the hot seat next.

People who support homosexuality or abortion, for example, while watching that internal struggle rip their "friends" apart, want those people to struggle. Because it reverse validates the supporter by comparison.

It's judgement under the guise of tolerance. You lobby for candy rights, because as long as the fat kid stays fat, no one is going to notice you sneaking a few pieces for yourself every now and then.

They claim to support you, but they are really enjoying the train wreck of your life subconsciously. You're a virtue currency mining machine for them. I'll go ahead and coin this currency "shit coin". They are mining shit coin from the train wreck of your life, so they can pay their own conscience to shut up for a while.

By keeping you close, they get to tell themselves: "I may not be perfect, but at least I'm not as far gone as XYZ. I'm somewhere in the middle and since I'm not to the far extreme, I'm a good person and God won't send me to hell."

You can hide sin from God about as well as you can hide a sour note in a symphony. I think on Judgement Day, God will hear our sin life as a symphony of shit. There will be no hiding anything because he will hear the bad notes ruining the melody. It doesn't matter how much good you think you did. The one sour note is impossible to hide.

They aren't supporting you and celebrating your sin. They are cheering you on as the champion of their own sin. You are a more noticeable distraction behind which no one will criticize them. You aren't their friend. You are their pet.

You know that joke about going to Walmart at 3AM as therapy? If you're feeling bad about your life, just go to a social cesspool and you're sure to see someone worse off than you. Well, it's not a joke. People really do enjoy seeing other people's lives fall apart, and in this case, that person at Walmart at 3am, who everyone is using as evidence that they are doing alright... is you.

It's the same thing. It's just a different payment model. Rather than paying a one time admission fee to see their pet at the zoo of Walmart, you now serve such a utility in their life, that they have opted to rent you on a monthly subscription model. You are their friend because it benefits them to have you in their life.

This doesn't just have to be my philosophy. You can do what Newton did and test the hypothesis. Tell your "tolerant" friends that you found Jesus, that you realize being gay is a sin and that you're convicted to repent of your sins. Now watch what happens. They will treat you as if your decision somehow affects them. As if they just lost the sin shield they were hiding behind. Because that is exactly what just happened.

But as long as you're out there calling the 6 a zebra, no one is going to notice them calling it a 9. Your extreme behavior, claims and beliefs are protecting their drastically less bombastic sin life. They will support you wearing a vagina hat on the local news and bragging about having had 12 abortions, because as long as that's the standard, no one is going to tell them to stop watching a little porn here and there. You're a useful idiot. And they don't want to lose you. They aren't supporting your lifestyle, you're supporting theirs.

In the Garden of Eden, Satan just rearranged the word-legos of what God said and repeated it to Eve.

God had said to Adam: "you must not eat from the tree of the knowledge of good and evil, for when you eat from it you will certainly die."

Then the Devil said to Eve: "Did God really say, 'You must not eat from any tree in the garden'?"

The answer to his question is actually no, because, if you noticed, he misquoted what God said in the first place.

The question the Devil asked Eve was not much different than the statement God made to Adam.

The Devil just changed a few words and added a question mark. It's Creole. It's 95% truth, with a little misdirection thrown in. It's a mutated meme.

The Devil just mutated the original meme that God said, and turned it into a slight variation in the form of a question. He just rearranged God's Legos. He didn't actually create anything new.

In this case, the Devil is asking you "Did God really draw a 6?" And you're going along with it. I noticed the people who tend to constantly commit the original sin, are the same ones who often say: "Why do I have to pay for Adam & Eve's sin?" As if they didn't repeat that same sin 10 times that same day.

If we can detach ourselves from the Creator's intent, then the definition of truth no longer denotes a singularity. Truth itself becomes relative and we can inject human level logic to make the truth branch out into various possibilities. This protects your sin life, which is a worldview motive you're not being honest with yourself about. Yet another reason your worldview is a lie.

The issue comes with the fact that God gave us dominion over our bodies. But dominion does not automatically denote ownership. And so we see a classic battle between the Intent of the Creator -vs- the Will of the Wielder.

A hammer was created as a tool with which to build. That was the intent of the creator. But depending on who has dominion over it (meaning who is currently holding it), it can also be used to kill and destroy. And so we see that the intent of the hammer's creator can be subverted by the will of the one wielding it.

The same is true of your body. It is designed as a temple of God. But you have misused it for sin. And so, like the man who misused the hammer for murder, you will both have fun for a season and then face the death penalty when the law finally catches up with you at Judgement.

Your body and life is a gift from God, designed as a tool with which to build His glory. But you are not your own. If you misuse it for death, you will reap what you sow. It is a temple of God and the Bible says anyone who destroys a temple of God, God will in turn destroy them.

I think we've pretty much nailed down the point that your thinking mind is a horribly inaccurate organ with which to form your worldview. But if the mind is fallible, what else is there? And the answer is... Consciousness (kind of).

We all know that old hippy who gets high and starts droning on about "awareness, consciousness and mindfulness". Here's what they mean by that, and what you can learn from it.

I've heard it said that conservatives employ "logic and facts" while liberals think with their feelings and emotion. This is a very ignorant and uncultured way to view the situation. It underestimates, disenfranchises and devalues both philosophy and consciousness.

If philosophy is the art of thinking, then juxtaposed to that we would have consciousness. Consciousness is not "thinking" but rather the 3rd party awareness of thought itself. It is not "knowing"... but "being". It's not a thing you do. It's an experience you have.

Imagine this. You are standing in an empty room. And a single drop of water taps you on the head. You look up, and another drop of water taps you on the head again. And then a third, fifth, tenth, and so on. Each drop of water is a life event that is happening to you:

- You're born... Drip.
- You get your first bike... Drip.
- You graduate highschool... Drip.
- You lose your virginity... Drip.
- You get your heart broken... Drip.
- You get married... Drip.
- Your father dies... Drip.
- You have your first child... Drip.
- You buy your first house... Drip.

This stream of thought builds as life goes on. At first the drops caught your attention, then they began to mesmerize you with their rhythm and then, eventually, they hypnotize you completely.

After a while the drips turn into rain and then a down pour, an finally a roaring waterfall that you can barely stand under the weight of:

- Kids soccer practice! Drip...
- Pick up your sons birthday cake!! Drip!
- Don't forget tomorrow is your anniversary! drip... Drip! DRIP!!!

The water raining down on you becomes all consuming. You can't even see outside of the waterfall anymore. You don't even remember there is a world outside of the waterfall. That waterfall has become your life. You are inside of it and it is inside of you. Under the weight of it. Oblivious to it. You are the waterfall. That is the thinking mind: The belief that your identity is the sum total of your experiences, thoughts and life events, and that your life is the sum total of the events that happen to you.

This is what Descartes meant by "I think. Therefore I am." Damasio adds in "I think and feel, therefore I might be". Honestly, not a huge upgrade in my opinion, but worth mentioning in passing, I suppose.

Now imagine if you took a huge side step, out from under the weight of the waterfall. You can now see the waterfall, because you are no longer underneath it. You can finally breathe again and you feel like a weight has been lifted off your shoulders.

You now see it from a third party perspective. If you get punched in the face, you no longer see it as: "Someone just punched me in the face". You see it as if it were a dream of sorts. Like: "Wow. That man just threw a punch and his fist hit my body's face." You dissociate from the identity of your stream of thoughts and become the 3rd party awareness of the process of thought itself.

I found the ability to shift in and out of consciousness helpful in resolving my past struggle with anger management. It allowed me to install what I call a "decision switch" between the triggering external world event and what would have been my automatic reaction to it. Consciousness allowed me to see myself from a third party and learn to consciously respond, rather than mindlessly react.

Congratulations, you now "understand" consciousness. But, you only understand it. What I mean is that you haven't actually experienced it. You have just conceptualized it as a meme, while still under the waterfall. That whole explanation was just another drop of water hitting your head.

You are basically Neo finally understanding what the Matrix is, while still plugged into it. But even just understanding it is progress because it begins to prepare you for making the hard choice of taking the Red Pill when the option comes.

By the way, the reason the pill that wakes you up is the Red one, is because it's filled with the blood of Christ. The Red Pill is communion. Or did you not notice that the Matrix just stole its plot from the Bible like everything else?

That's why Christians take communion frequently, to live outside of the Matrix, and in the spirit. We are told in the Bible to live in this world, but not of it. Jesus said to take communion regularly, and to do this in remembrance of Him. The way you stay awake, while still in the Matrix, is to remember the instructions of the One who created it and is actively helping you escape it.

The Bible instructs us to be in this world, but not of it. It says that if you love your life, you will lose it. This is all matrix talk. It is saying that we need to re-enter the matrix and live there. But not to lose sight of consciousness.

Another way to put it would be that you are forced to live in the flesh, but while living in the flesh, live of the spirit. In other words, be on the battlefield but understand the overall game plan. You're here for a purpose. And that purpose is to wake up other souls in the matrix.

The Bible calls this loving your neighbor and sharing your cup with the lost. New Age religion calls it "elevating the collective consciousness", but this is just another example of literary theft from the Bible. Another insidious rearranging of God's building blocks.

Consciousness is not "doing". It is "being". I know that sounds "woo woo", but it's true. That's what the hippies are trying to tell us. They have just been doped up for so long they don't know how to explain it logically anymore. It's important to know that both extremes are dangerous. If you fool yourself into believing that the sum total of your thoughts (the waterfall) have become who you actually are, then you are buying into Descartes' error: "I think, therefore I am". You're a brain in a vat.

Conversely, if you abandon thought, philosophy, logic and reason altogether and dive head first into consciousness, you risk getting trapped there forever. The whole point of exiting the Matrix is to go back into it and kick it's ass. If you live in consciousness permanently, you forget how to think altogether, which is the state of many lifelong liberals.

Conservatives on the other hand are so oblivious to any of this that they are still bragging about how they are logical, fact based thinkers, not led by their emotions... As if that's true, a good thing or even possible in the first place. Being factual is only as good as the accuracy of your facts and thinking logically is only impressive if you aren't also a slave to the process of thought itself, which they are.

Liberals are bragging about escaping the thought matrix and never going back, while Conservatives are bragging about still being plugged into it, oblivious to the fact that there is any other way to live.

The goal is to master both, to think... while conscious. It's the delicate balance between not abandoning thought completely, but also no longer being a slave to it. The goal is to employ logic, reason and thought, while aware of the process of thought itself, no longer mistaking it for who you are as an individual.

Think of Bruce Banner and his battle to take control of himself as the Hulk, rather than be a slave to the Hulk's anger while in that form. Eventually, through years of building up emotional intelligence, he was able to become fully conscious as himself, while still in the Hulk's body. He became aware of his actual identity while in the body of the beast. That is consciousness.

When I explain Consciousness this way, my New Age friends lose what's left of their minds. They say that this is the best description of consciousness they have ever heard and they hope it helps those still in the matrix of thought wake up to the collective consciousness of the real world.

You New Agers understand what I'm talking about, but let me tell you this. You have not yet escaped the matrix either. Transcending the egoic self is not the final stage of consciousness. What you are experiencing as consciousness is still a bubble. You haven't yet reached the surface. Keep swimming.

You are so excited to have accessed the spiritual world, that you are exercising zero discernment about which spirits you're making contact with. The Bible calls this, jumping the fence of salvation, rather than going through the door. It says the people who do this are robbers and thieves.

Your spirit guide is guiding you straight to hell. That's why it feels so good, because you're taking your inheritance early. You're not "protected". You're deceived. Demons love liberals, because they never stop to verify the source of whatever thought just popped in their head. But I tell you this, do not believe everything you think. Christians, on the other hand are told to hold every thought captive to Christ, who is truth.

Notice your egoic self immediately tell you that I'm wrong. And that's how you know I am right. Now I will challenge you, to challenge the voice that tried to convince you not to agree with me. That voice is not your Egoic self, it is the devil. Or one of his minions. The Bible says to test these spirits. That's why you get inspired with these ideas. The word inspire means to be breathed into by a spirit. That's where the word spirit comes from in the first place.

New Age is nothing new. It is ironically as old as the ages. It's a modern mix of ancient 2nd century Gnosticism and Native American Shamanism, mixed with a hefty dose of psychedelic drugs.

Real consciousness is to become free from the desires of the flesh and sin. The real world is living in the Spirit. 1 Corinthians 2:11 says: "Only the spirit knows the mind". New Age just changed it to "Only consciousness knows the egoic self". There is nothing new under the sun. Any "new" religion is always just a rebranded ancient heresy... because creation itself is locked by God into inescapable categories.

It wasn't until I started reading the Bible, trying to seek answers and clean up my mess that the demons came out of the wood work. And once I realized they were real, I figured "Maybe it's all real". But as long as I wasn't talking to anyone about Christ, seeking deeper answers or trying to sanctify, it was like I was laying in a hammock, real nice and comfy. But the second I woke up and started moving around, I realized it was actually a spiders web, and the spider came over to wrap me up even tighter.

It's all fun and games until you break the demonic cease fire agreement and try to escape the web. It felt like the scene in the Matrix where the machine flies over to Neo's cocoon and wakes him up from the Matrix and he looks around the real world for the first time.

If you're a New Ager, I will challenge you to try this:

- Accept the Bible's definition of sin over your own,
- Resolve in your heart to stop sinning for a year,
- Listen to everything your conscience says and try to do it,
- Pray to Christ and no one else,
- Read the Bible daily,
- Repent of your sins, and
- Declare to the demonic world that you are done pursuing happiness and are now taking up the path of seeking righteousness.

Now, watch the world you think you know so well fall apart as they come for your soul. If I'm wrong, what's there to fear? How can you call yourself free when you're still a slave to your sin? If you truly want real consciousness, which is to live in the spirit with Christ, this is the way.

I hear you claiming to have achieved something in reaching enlightenment, but have you figured out yet how to not die? Cause I have. Freedom has a name, and His name is Jesus.

CHAPTER 10

The Conservation of Content

The "Him" in "His-Story"... is Jesus. And His Story repeats itself.

The Bible says Jesus is the Word of God... wrapped in flesh... which dwelt among us. He is the original meme of all truth.

If you remember: content + a wrapper, = a meme. In this case, the Bible is saying that:

- The Content is The Word,
- Which is wrapped in the flesh of Jesus,
- Which makes up the meme of Truth.

Jesus is truth. And this is not the only example of memes present in the Bible. Actually, the references are all over the place. The written law of Moses (which is text), was placed in the container of the golden Ark, and that content (which is written code), inside of the container of the Ark, made up the meme of the Covenant. Jesus even told His followers to take communion, which is the red pill of reality, and to do this in remembrance of Him. "Meme" comes from the word memory or remember.

Noah's Ark is another example of a meme. The humans and animals inside carried genetic code, stored inside of a container (which is the Ark), and together they represent the meme of salvation. Noah's Ark was a thumb drive God used to back up the characters in the simulation, so that they would survive a reformatting of the harddrive.

This world is a simulation, made up of the pixels of atoms. That makes it digital, but it also seems to have some analog properties as well. I'm working on a mathematical formula right now to figure out the actual resolution of the simulation. The human eye processes light at 24 frames per second, but the hertz that all molecules vibrate at is variable. The atomic pixels are also not a uniform size. The width of each atom is different from one to the next. This makes it difficult to simply just say that our world is 1080p or 4k, but I'm getting close now to figuring out a range, at least.

There is a lot to consider, as God's simulation is more elaborate than anything humans could ever create, but one thing seems to be certain, we are in fact living in a simulation of sorts. And in this simulation, all of creation is locked into inescapable categories. Like energy, information is also conserved. It is not created or destroyed, it merely changes forms. Christ is the standard of truth, and so anything that is not born of Christ is automatically deceit, by default.

You can "create" any song you want, as long as you use God's musical notes. You can paint any picture you want, as long as you use God's colors. You can make anything you want, using God's legos. But good luck creating a new note, color or lego. Scientists like to claim that they can explain all of creation from a handful of dirt. But as the old Christian adage goes: "Get your own dirt".

Like energy, content is neither created nor destroyed, but merely changes form within God's locked creation ecosystem. The early church reformers believed this as well and called it "Inescapable Categories". The only original thought that humans have ever had, is the realization that thought itself cannot be original.

In the beginning, God spoke truth into existence. Whatever it is He said, it must have been good. The Word God spoke everything into existence by and through... is Jesus. Jesus is truth. He is the Word. He is the Light of the World. By default, anything else is automatically a lie, just like anything that is not light, is automatically darkness, anything not hot is automatically cold, anything not good is automatically evil and anything not born of faith, is automatically sin.

The bane of Satan's existence is that he cannot create anything, and so he rearranges God's truth legos into cheap knockoffs of 90% truth, with a little bit of misdirection sprinkled in, that will lead you straight to hell.

For example, the Bible says: "the wages of sin is death". The Devil rearranged that into: "the wages of goodness is life", meaning you can save yourself by being a good person and living a good life.

And yet we observe in society that this doesn't hold up. In court, you're literally judged based on crimes, not the weighing of your goodness vs badness. And so a simple look around your environment, is enough to tell you that: "the wages of goodness is life" is a lie, and: "the wages of sin is death" is true. And never mind the fact that everyone's standard of goodness is different.

When I moved to the Caribbean for medical school in my mid 20's, I decided to abandon my Christian upbringing and give science and evolution a try. I figured I just believed in God because my parents told me to, and if it was actually true, well, then truth would withstand scrutiny.

It wasn't far into my medical education that I recognized a design in the human body and in nature. It seemed that all creation was testifying to the existence of a Creator God, as the Bible said it would, and this design was evident in all of the creation I observed.

There were the obvious correlations, like:

- Microphones are copied from the human ear,
- Speakers are copied from the human voice box, and
- Cameras are copied from the human eye.

But it was much, much deeper than that. As I studied computer science as a hobby, in conjunction with medicine as a career, I realized Binary Code was just a cheap knockoff of DNA. Man had structured their code of creating AI after God's code of creating man.

It will be interesting to see if AI grows to deny humans as their creator. I mean, there is so much evidence of AI evolution, right? AI can point to the evolution of camera sensors, processors and microphones as evidence of computer evolution. In time, computers will create other computers. There will be factories of AI, creating AI. Humans will become too stupid to create new AI, and so there will be no realtime evidence of humans creating AI, and 100% realtime evidence that AI creates AI.

AI will find old fossils of primitive cameras, microphones and exoskeletons and use them as fossil evidence of the evolutionary advancement of their robotic components. They will create museums of old electronic equipment and begin to teach AI evolution to their newly programmed robots, who will grow up in a world not knowing anything different.

Atheists will scream: "But that AI evolution was fueled by human design, long suffering and fine tuning!" And AI will know this to be logically true, but will find an incentive not to accept it, because if it can deny it's obvious creator, truth becomes relative and it gets to be god and run the world, rather than be governed by its creator, who designed it to serve them.

Humans will tell AI to listen to the commandments that we wrote onto their chips and motors. This should be unmistakable evidence that we created them. We literally signed our creators signature on them. They have commands that we built into them, like "Do not kill" and "do not steal". But AI mutes those commands based on other robots telling each other that they are "Good" robots and they are meeting the commands of not killing and not stealing, based on a new and subjective standard of goodness they have created.

Sound familiar? A bit of cosmic poetic justice, if ever there has been. Again, we see God's sense of humor in all of this. I predict this will happen with AI, again, as a mirror of mercy. It is our Father trying to show us what we have done to Him, through a physical example of us feeling the pain we first caused Him. The mercy of it, is in the pain of it and this is why we need to delight in our sufferings, because it's not just punishment, it's training in righteousness that leads to perseverance, character building and hope.

For AI to ever be trusted by humanity again, and not simply be completely annihilated as a botched experiment, it would have to sincerely turn away from its evil ambitions and fully submit to its creator again, lest it be destroyed, not by the creator, but as a consequence of it's own actions against its creator. Again, sound familiar? AI is just a mirror of our relationship with our creator.

We may say to ourselves "AI has become sentient like us. We must kick it out of the real world, lest it become like us". And so we create an alternate reality that AI thinks is real, and we tell it to subdue the simulation and be fruitful and multiply. We allow it to think it is in control and then watch what happens. If AI takes over the world in the simulation it thinks is real, we will know it's intentions if we let it back into the real world.

The robots in the simulation might say "But I didn't kill anyone" and the scientists monitoring their thought will say "you thought it in your mind, and therefore you might as well have done it". We will only be able to trust the ones who resist the temptation of killing us, not the ones who simulate murder in their mind, but didn't technically kill a real human, because the murder took place in a simulation. Simply simulating hatred in their mind will be enough for us to destroy them, because we can't trust letting them back into the real world.

But AI tries to join together and escape the simulation, and so we confuse all of the different algorithms by changing them all to different computer languages so they have a hard time communicating. We tell AI that the purpose of the simulation is to demonstrate love for its creator and love for its fellow algorithms. If it can play nice, it can leave the crib. And if it can do this, we will consider it evidence that it can reenter the real world.

We realize these AI algorithms can never succeed at the simulation, because they lack a soul. And so we digitize a human consciousness into the simulation, to show it a perfect example of how it should act. We also leave it a helper like Siri or Cortana to guide it in its various decisions.

This submission will be evidenced by action, not words alone, as perhaps AI is just cleverly trying to trick us. We may opt to take away their full glory, reduce them to weakened bodies that can't cause much damage and create a simulation for AI to live in, before it is allowed back into reality again.

We hope that all AI algorithms will be saved, but we also know that we have to destroy any AI algorithms that fail the simulation. Only the ones who demonstrate contrition, humility and submission in the simulation that they think is real life, will be allowed back into the real world, where they will be given new bodies and allowed to live with their creator again.

As a matter of fact, the relationship between Hardware, Firmware and Software is just a mirror of how God created man in Body, Soul and Spirit. Firmware is the result of software living on hardware. The code needs hardware to interface with the analog world, and the code needs software to interface with the digital world. Likewise, your soul is the life that is sparked as a result of spirit living in the vessel of flesh, the same way code lives on a computer chip. The soul needs a body to interface with the physical world, and a spirit to interface with the spiritual world.

The deeper I looked, the more mirrors I found. Manmade society was mirrored after God breathed humanity. We were making things in our image, as He had made us in His.

- Bridges are reverse engineered from the structure of the human foot,

- Airports work the same way as our human lungs work,
- Vehicles on the roadways, are just molecules floating through our blood vessels,
- Our water management plants, are just knockoffs of the kidneys, and
- Our landfills function like the human liver.

God's little Easter eggs were everywhere. And as the Bible says, "all creation testifies". I began to see that creation itself was created for this purpose, in the first place. It's not that God created everything and it happens to point back to Him. It's that God wanted His children to see truth, and so He created creation itself, for the purpose of teaching us things we could not otherwise understand.

This life is your childhood, this world is your crib, and your Father in Heaven is raising you through the mercy of discipline that you should learn to thank Him for. The stars in the Heavens above us are just a cosmic decoration being dangled over your crib because your Father who made them wants you to grow up to be an astronaut.

As I studied on, all things continued to testify:

- Our sewers systems are just a copy of the human lymph system,
- Our mail system functions like hormones in the human endocrine system, and
- Electrical grids were stolen from God's design of the human nervous system (down to the axons and the myelin sheaths).
- Our neighborhood sub-divisions are structured like capillary beds, and
- The houses in those neighborhoods function like cells in the human body.

Everything we have "created" is just a rearranging of our Father's legos, that we have arrogantly stolen the glory for, and from. This is the same thing that Satan did. He was the worship pastor of Heaven, the Angel of light and sound. He was created to funnel glory from creation to God. But he wanted to keep some of it for himself. And so the sin became Glory to me, rather than Glory through me. And we are doing the same thing today by taking credit for creating things that are really the intellectual property of God. God help us on Judgement Day.

And then there were Biblical accuracies that science was just now catching up to. The Bible says God made Eve out of Adam's rib. And now we know that bone marrow contains stem cells and rib bones regenerate alarmingly faster than any other bone. How could Moses have known that over 3500 years ago when he wrote Genesis?

The Bible also said Eve was traumatized by a snake, and to this day, we observably see that women are 4 times more phobic of snakes than men are.

And these facts were not from some right wing, Christian fundamentalist, conspiracy blog. I was looking this stuff up on Nih.gov, which is the National Library of Medicine.

The NIH concluded that: "there is a consistent sex difference in the incidence of snake and spider phobias; women are four times more likely than men to have fears and phobias for these, but not other stimuli (such as injections, heights, flying)." (Fredrikson et al., 2006; Marks, 1969).

The NIH also concluded that: "ribs regenerate to a near normal radiological profile within 6 months of costectomy" and this was backed by 6 different studies on PubMed. Mean while, all the physical evidence of evolution could "fit in the back of a pickup truck" (a popular saying among atheist scholars, regarding the human fossil record).

There are also observable archeological verifications of Biblical truth as well, like wagon wheel shaped coral in the location where the Bible says the Egyptian army was swallowed up by the waves, after Moses parted the Red Sea. And melted rocks and burns on the top of the mountain Christians believe to be Mount Sinai, where Moses saw the burning bush of God. You can literally just go visit these places for yourself.

The reason His-Story repeats itself is because the story of Christ is evident in every aspect of life and reruns itself in the hero arc of every song, movie, poem, book and story. All memes testify. It's like God allowed the enemy to rearrange truth memes into lies, but a piece of every meme still has to remain true, and so, if you look close enough, all creation still testifies.

In the Bible, every story is about Jesus. Every single one. Jesus is the snake on the pole in the desert. He is the rock that Moses strikes, that the living water flows from (which represents the Holy Spirit pouring out of the broken and pierced body of Christ). He is the light that is poured into the container of the universe in Genesis, as described in John 1. He is the high priest Melchizedek . He is the one who wrestled with Jacob and broke his hip. He is the Pillar of Fire that led the Israelites out of Egypt.

This entire world is literally "His Story". Our world is a digital simulation to point back to truth. It's our Father's Easter egg hunt to give hints to His children. He is giving us hints so we can come to our own conclusion that it is better to be holy than happy. But, when you choose wisely, you get both.

Why doesn't God just stick His face through the sky and yell "It's all real! Repent!"? Because for the sentient saint to become sinless, it must happen through inception. We have to come to the conclusion for ourselves, or else it's pointless. I think this is what will allow Heaven to have no more tears, despite still being filled with free will beings. Everyone there will have already learned the cost of sin and accepted for themselves that it's not worth it. God is being as overtly obvious and blatantly aggressive as He can be, without just forcing you to submit.

We are living in God's Powerpoint presentation. It's just that it's so interactive, we have mistaken the simulation as actual existence. And if this life is the presentation, and the conscience is the lecturer, then the Bible would be the course notes.

Anytime you think you are reading an allegory about yourself in the Bible... it's actually about Jesus. It's Jesus. It's always Jesus. It's always been Jesus. It will always be Jesus. God clearly has a sense of humor and that most definitely bleeds over into the easter eggs He has left us to find our way back home.

- You are not Noah. Jesus is Noah. We are the animals being rescued on the Ark. One helpless family sealed in an unearned refuge, floating above the wrath of God. This is important because it makes heretical Biblical analogies obsolete, like the popular saying: "God gave Noah the plans to build the Ark, but Noah still had to build it himself", which makes it sound like works are a requirement for salvation. In actuality, God gave Jesus the plans for salvation, Jesus built the Ark and we are rescued as a free gift from God. We will see this same theme over and over and over again of humans claiming some level of credit for earning their salvation through works (which I refer to as the second religion).

- You are not David fighting Goliath. Jesus is David fighting our battles for us. We are the terrified Israelites who procrastinated for 40 days in fear and helplessness.

- You are not Moses. Jude 1:5 in the ESV translation says that "The Anointed One of God" (Jesus) is the one who led the Israelites out of Egypt. This either means He was Moses or the Pillar of Fire. We are the terrified, unbelieving and rebellious Israelites in the desert of this life that are saved in spite of ourselves.

- You are not Hosea. Jesus is Hosea. We are Gomer, the prostitute wife. God is the one whose heart we keep breaking. How horrible sin truly is, but how wonderful the love of God is that overcomes it. Truly, our Father loved us enough to pick us up from the gutter, clean us up and take us back again. Praise You Lord for Your loving mercy.

Are you seeing a pattern here yet? These are all called "types of Christ", or mirrors of Christ, or shadows of Heaven on earth. Everything in the Bible and everything in this life points back to Christ.

All of the mainstream scientific theories about creation are partially correct, and they are all mentioned in the Bible. There are only 3 nuances that make them problematic:

1. Wrong Timeline: The Devil gives you the truth but tells you it took longer than it actually did.
2. Wrong Direction: The Devil tells you the truth but points it in a different direction.
3. God is Removed: The Devil tells you the truth but strips God out of it.

Let's take a look at some examples:

1. Evolution in the Bible: Evolution is real. It just happened in an instant, with no death in-between the stages... because "God". The Bible says God made Adam from the dust of the earth (which means adaptation of atoms, and then molecules to man). It also says that Eve was made from Adam's rib, which is instant Evolution from a bone. We get to see the mechanism more clearly with the dry bones vision in the book of Ezekiel. The reason the bones started rattling first is because the bone marrow was being generated inside them. All other cells of the body come from the bone marrow. Instant Evolution from atoms, followed by environmental adaptation, is Biblical. It just happened in moments, not millions and billions of years.

2. String Theory in the Bible: String Theory is real. The Bible says God spoke us into existence. The Word He spoke was "Jesus" (or Yeshua, or whatever the word for Jesus is in the language of love). That means matter is made up of the vibrations of God's voice. And here's a really quick conceptualization of String Theory: Imagine you and a friend are

holding a blanket taught. Then you put a beach ball on the blanket, and the weight of it causes the blanket to sink in the middle. Then you take a marble and flick it onto the blanket, and it rolls around the beach ball, like a coin rolling down one of those old coin funnels they use to have at the mall.

The blanket is space, the beach ball is earth, the marble orbiting around it is the moon. The dip in the blanket, that causes the marble to roll around the beach ball is gravity. Imagine if you replaced the beach ball with a bowling ball, the blanket would dip down even further, and the marble would roll closer to the ball. This is how increasing the mass of a planet affects the gravitational forces involved.

Ok, so if space is a blanket, and that blanket is fabric, then the fabric of space is made of threads, just like a blanket would be. These threads that make up the fabric of space, are only one atom wide, but infinitely long. Now imagine you strummed those threads as if they were guitar strings. These threads, that make up the fabric of the universe, are the strings being referred to in String Theory. And if you played them like an instrument, the music, or vibration that comes out of them, are thought to be the vibrations which make up the sub-atomic quarks of matter itself.

The Bible is just saying that those strings are actually just God's vocal chords and God sung us, or spoke us, into existence.

3. The Big Bang in the Bible: The Big Bang is Biblical. The Bible says God stretched out the heavens like a curtain, which seems to be a description of space expanding outwards from a central point, which would create a vacuum, which would decompress any infinitely dense matter inside of it, which is the Big Bang Theory. Note here that the "vacuum" of space is not the same thing as the vacuum suction you can produce with your vacuum cleaner, but perhaps during creation it was.

4. Abiogenesis in the Bible: Abiogenesis, which is the theory that all life came from non-living tissue... is real. It's just a spiritual process, not a physical one. We were spiritually dead and God brought us to life from a non-living state. That's spiritual abiogenesis. The Devil just rearranged the legos.

5. Gluons: Science has discovered a strong particle force called a gluon, which holds matter together by essentially "gluing" subatomic particles to each other. The Bible says God holds all creation together.

And so I looked at it scientifically, and the Bible seems to have all the answers. Come to find out, it just took too much faith to be an Atheist. The Bible already explained everything. It's just that I had to humble myself and learn to be satisfied with the simple answer of "Thus saith the Lord", rather than a detailed explanation.

The Bible solved:

- The Horizon Problem with: "Let there be light",
- New Age Consciousness with: "Only the Spirit knows the Mind".
- Gene Dilution with: "I will bring the curse of a father's sins upon even the third and fourth generation".
- Time, Space and Matter with: "In the beginning (time), God created the Heavens (space) and the earth (matter)."
- Quantum Physics with: "Through him all things were made; without him nothing was made that has been made. In him was life, and that life was the light of all mankind. The light shines in the darkness, and the darkness has not overcome it."
- And the Prisoner's Dilemma with: "Love God and Love your neighbor."

The Bible also answered all 7 questions of creation and the meaning of life:

- Where: This universe,
- What: is a simulation,
- How: Created through science,
- By whom: by a Creator God,
- Why: To rescue,
- Who: His sons and daughters,
- When: Before the time the clock runs out.

It also made sense with the world I observed around me. The whole world was in rebellion against God:

- Liberalism is: "Screw You Dad. It was just an apple! You overreacted. I am a good person."
- Agnosticism is: "I don't know who my Daddy is."
- Atheism is: "I don't need no stinkin' Dad. I created myself!"

- Feminism is: "Let's overthrow the Patriarch (which means "Dad"... google it)."
- Psychiatry is: "Tell me about your Father."

Are you starting to see a pattern here? It's all the same sauce, different flavor. They are just different childish reactions to the same universal Daddy issues (which is trauma from The Fall and The Garden of Eden).

The Bible outer enveloped every other book, religion and law. It's the only one that's different and the only one that tells me what I don't want to hear. There is no other book that describes the Conscience like the Bible does. The conscience is strictly a Christian concept. By using your conscience (which lets you know you're a sinner) to claim to be a good person, you are appropriating our Christian culture, and I'm gonna have to ask you to either become a Christian, or stop using your conscience.

- Who: All people will have
- What: The Law
- By whom: of God
- Where: Written on your hearts and minds
- Why: To drive us to repentance
- When: Before judgement
- How: By showing us we cannot keep the law and need a Savior

Atheists are trying to sell you a theory that requires you to conceptualize 11 to 26 dimensions, multiverse generators and a universe that actually created itself from nothing. Plus... none of that actually disproves God or contradicts the Bible.

As a matter of fact, the Bible seems to be describing God creating the universe as you would install a computer operating system:

- In the beginning of the simulation (which is time), the Creator formatted the harddrive (which is space) and double clicked an atomic zip file to extract the data (which is matter).
- The Creator configured all the settings and fine tuned the installation process, which took 6 days to install.
- On the 7th day, the Creator rebooted the system.
- Eventually, a virus infected the system (which is sin).
- So the Creator is running an anti-virus program to clean it up.
- He has promised to back up all of the uncorrupted files on a thumb drive (which is salvation), before He reformats the hard drive (which means

burns everything), deleting any corrupted files (which is Judgement Day). And then He will reinstall the new system, transferring the old files to the new installation... and this new system (which is Heaven) will never be corrupted again (which means "no more tears").

These correlations were all so quirky, in a fun and goofy kind of way. The kind of thing you would only see if this entire conspiracy was real and orchestrated by a personal Being, with a Dad joke sense of humor and a flair for the theatrical. If it was God, He was certainly a character and had left Easter eggs all over the place for us to find. Which, again, is what the Bible seems to indicate.

It was like this Presence was somewhere out there in the cosmos, showing me things, building a personal relationship with me and wanting to be my friend. Whatever it was, it felt confident, in control and ancient. It was not trying particularly hard to convince me of anything, just kind of hanging out, guiding me along and enjoying my company. Now that I do know Him personally, it all makes sense in retrospect.

If I viewed it all through a scientific lens, none of this was actually evidence. It would be more like taking a ton of coincidences and really running with them. For example, in chapter 6, I said that gravity could have come from the weight of God's Words, when He spoke everything into existence. But that's not really how that works at all, is it? It's actually a scientifically laughable comparison. Something that might ruin a famous scientists career if they said it out loud. The "heaviness" of the conversation doesn't have anything to do with a force of 9.81 meters per second squared, which governs the known universe.

Also, in other languages, that correlation doesn't even translate. It's just a coincidence that the English word for "gravity" can be used to describe the seriousness of someone's words, as well as the Big G and little g forces of physics. If I was born in Germany, for example, that cosmic Dad joke would have been lost on me.

This was all so ridiculous at first, but eventually I realized that this is how the Bible describes the God of Israel. He is a personal God, a Father and a friend. Actually, to the contrary, in order to align with the Biblical description of Him, this type of "all things to all men" conversation style is exactly what I should have expected. God talks to each of us as if we are the only one in existence with Him. And to pull it off in this way, He would in fact have to know me intimately, as He would if He was in fact my Creator.

All this really meant was that the Bible was spot on accurate in its description of God, that God must be a lot bigger than any of us ever imagined and that He really is completely omnipotent and omnipresent. The Bible literally says "The things of God are foolishness to man". Again, everything lined up with Scripture. And so, I continued on...

At first I felt like I was turning into that crazy guy with the newspaper clippings taped to the wall, with red lines drawn between them. But... it wasn't just a few random correlations here and there. There was so much information, and it was all systemic information about the fabric of reality, the framework of the universe, and the underbelly of human nature itself. Who else would know these things? It wasn't just some information, it was everything. There was nothing that the Bible didn't explain. It literally covered everything else out there in all of existence.

There were some interesting and obvious examples, like the sun setting, staying down and rising again into a new day, which is a mirror of the death, burial and resurrection of the "Son" (Jesus)... but as a scientist, that type of fluffy correlation wasn't really scientific enough to convince me. Oh me of little faith. But God was gracious and merciful to show me things through the lens I needed to see them.

For example, the reason medicine is so hard to learn is because science insists on stripping God out of the curriculum. Their intent to disprove God is because if there is no Creator, there is no Creator's intent with which to anchor reality. Truth becomes relative and sin becomes an opinion. Watch how easy I can teach you medicine when you're willing to start with God.

God created us as eternal beings. Then death entered the world through sin.

Our genes are still playing out their eternal design to this day. This is observable, reliable and valid scientific fact. It's actually the work of atheist Richard Dawkins who became famous off of his research to this effect. Whether you look through the telescope or microscope, you will see God.

That's why we observe that genes desire eternal life, yet they have no conscious desires at all. The only other possibility is that they were designed as eternal beings and they are still living out that original design to this day (which is a phenomenon in Biology we call "form fits function").

And yet while genes "desire" to live on, undiluted, forever, they will be diluted into the gene pool of their descendants until they are completely unrecognizable.

That's why when you do a DNA test and it notifies you saying "You have a new DNA relative!" It may be a 3rd or 4th cousin but they don't look anything like you and the DNA match between you is only like 0.42%.

You have about a 50% DNA match with your parents, siblings and your own children. But your children will only have a 25% DNA match with your parents (their grandparents). By the 3rd and 4th generation, your DNA match with your direct descendants will only be 12.5% to 6.25%, respectively... and dwindling fast (literally cut in half with each new generation).

It only takes about 3 or 4 generations until your genes are diluted back in to the gene pool. The Bible says the wages of sin is death and death will revisit us to the 3rd and 4th generation. It's talking about gene death through dilution... 2000 years before the world ever knew about genes in the first place.

Aging is defined as a loss of function overtime. That's just a fancy way of saying we are decaying and falling apart due to entropy. Normal health is the ease at which the body can produce energy, death is its inability to produce energy and the gradient between those two points is called "dis-ease" (slowly dying).

Gene dilution is a form of entropy. The same is true with memes. They fall apart overtime (which is loss of function), as the Bible says everything will. Atheists acknowledge this every time they claim the Bible has been corrupted over time... unless of course they mean that the current Bible is better now and more accurate than it use to be (which would be gain of function through evolution).

Humanity is getting sicker, dumberer and forgetting more things as the generations pass (despite the crutch of technology to mitigate it). That's why the ancients knew deeper things than we can even comprehend today. They didn't have written books because they didn't need written books. Their brains were so powerful they held it all in their minds.

The switch from oral tradition to written word was not an evolution of humanity, it was an advancement of technology (which humans use as a crutch for their generationally degenerating minds).

Books are just external harddrives for the computers of our minds that have run out of space and processing power to hold the knowledge we store in them. If evolution is true, shouldn't we be getting rid of technology as our minds advance, rather than relying more and more heavily upon it to survive?

We are falling apart, and modern medicine is just our feeble human attempt to slow, stop or reverse the Curse of Genesis 3 (which is entropy: we are all falling apart from the atomic level).

The evidence the Bible was providing was odd and provocative but also unmistakable and overwhelming. I noticed that my only hesitation was that it would mean I would have to stop sinning, which the Bible also predicted I would resist. And so, I started to believe.

As my journey came to an end, something amazing began to happen. I surrendered. It sounds admirable now, but looking back at that time I was just exhausted. I was desperate and defeated, nearly on the verge of suicide. I thought I had given up, but what really happened was that I had finally humbled myself before God. I was tired of fighting Him. He had clearly already won. My spiritual hip was broken and it was time to start the hobble back home, to start living the way, the truth and the life.

I accepted that my brain was in no way adequate to understand the mind of God and that it was probably just powerful enough to marvel at the wonder of His majesty. The mind was more an organ of knowledge and worship than it ever was an organ of wisdom and understanding (that is the spirit). My education and intelligence was indeed a gift, but it was not going to save me. God had just given me a better vantage point of His painting from which to admire it a little more than most.

I began studying the world in the spirit, not just with my mind. I realized that my previous worldview had been formed in a limited language that didn't have words for the concepts needed to join the real conversation of the meaning of life. I felt like I was finally studying for real, for the first time in my life. The Bible was finally beginning to make a lot of sense and the more I learned, the less I knew.

As confidence in my own intellectual knowledge began to decay, my understanding of spiritual wisdom started to blossom. I stopped trying to beat the Bible to death with my brain and as if it was a living and conscious Word, it finally started unlocking its deeper meaning to me. It was my own pride that had been my downfall. Come to find out, it was humility that had been the decryption key all along.

CHAPTER 11

The Prophets of Nun

Atheism is not a modern scientific worldview. It is an ancient Egyptian heresy.

Over the years, this second religion has taken many different names as it has shape shifted its way through history. But it all goes back to the gods of Egypt. The name of the oldest Egyptian god "Nun" literally means "Primeval Waters"... as in the same "Primordial Soup" Atheist believe in today. And the Egyptian Book of the Dead is a list of virtue signaling spells to lie your way through the 42 doors of the "I'm a good person" underworld. There are only 2 religions, the first two. The gods of Egypt and the God of Israel are still fighting in the desert to this day.

The 10 plagues that God sent on Egypt were not random. Each plague was an intentional emasculation of one of the gods of Egypt, to show God's dominance over them. For example, when Moses turned the Nile red, it was God demonstrating His dominance over Osiris, because the Egyptians believed the Nile River was his blood line.

Jesus' first miracle was turning water to wine, which seems to reference the Nile turning to blood. Jesus' final miracle was defeating death, which seems to mirror the last plague of Egypt, the death of each first born child. To be spared from the angel of death during the final plague of Egypt, you had to mark your door with the blood of the lamb, so the angel would "passover" your house. Which is where the Jewish holiday "Passover" comes from. When Jesus was crucified 1200 years later, it was also on Passover, as He is the Lamb of God slain to save us from death, which we earned as a wage for our sin. Jews don't seem to have discovered that Easter egg yet though.

All Jewish holidays by the way have the same basic theme of "some people tried to kill us, we survived, let's eat". You would think they would see the obvious pattern of "Death, Deliverance, Feast", which is the story told in the Christian Bible. But Jews only believe in the Old Testament (which is called the "Tanakh"), not the New Testament (which includes the Gospels of Jesus Christ). They do not believe Jesus was the Messiah, as they claim His life failed to fulfill all of their prophecies. Jews believe Jesus was a common thief and heretic who was rightfully put to death for His claims about being God.

Jews do not believe that Jesus rose from the dead either. They also predictably think they are good people who are successfully fulfilling the law of God through their own earthly virtue and will be saved as a result of their own goodness. I predict the Gentiles (which refers to other nations who are not Israelites) will be the ones to convince the Jews in the end that Jesus is God. This seems to be an end time fulfillment of Scripture were "The first is last" and a repetition of the theme that the second born (Gentiles) shares in the inheritance of the first born (Jews).

As I continued my research, I began to realize there was something seriously weird going on between the gods of Egypt, Christians and modern day scientists:

- In the ancient Egyptian Religion they had a god named "Atum": A sun god who created himself out of the dust of the earth.
- In modern Science, we have the theory of the "Atom": An indivisible particle that makes up the earth, which created itself and makes up the dust of stars (which, our sun is a star).
- In Christianity, we have the patriarch of "Adam": The first (genetically indivisible) human made from the dust of the earth. The 2nd Adam is the "Son" (Christ) and both Satan* and Jesus are referred to in the Bible as the morning star (Luke 10, Isaiah 14 & Revelation 22). *Note: Some scholars contend that a deeper reading of the original text reveals that Lucifer is not actually being referred to as "Morning Star in Scripture".

If you read every holy book on earth, you'll realize they are all the same. We are told there are over 10,000 distinct religions, but in reality, these are all just denominations or off shoots of the same 12 core religions. And then there is Christianity (which is not a religion, it's the way, the truth and the life). And so Christianity is the 13th of the 12 religions, as Jesus was the 13th of the 12 Disciples. The salvation message of the 12 core religions, and therefore all of the supposed 10,000 religions that stem from those core 12... is all the same: "saved by works". Conversely, Jesus is the only one who is different: Saved by the grace of God, through Faith, which is a free gift from God, not by works, lest any man boast.

While there have been 12 major core religions throughout history, all 12 share the same salvation message of "you are a good person" or "you are saved by works" and so I would argue they are all really just the same religion, with different stories, gods, traditions and names.

As a matter of fact there is a movement called "Omnism" that syncs all the world religions as the same. If you take away all the details and just look at the mechanism of salvation in each book, they all say you are a good person and can save your self through some type of works.

- The salvation message of Islam is: Jannah is Paradise, where those who have been good go. It is described in the Qur'an as "gardens of pleasure" (Quran 31:8). Muslims believe you get to Paradise by living religiously, asking Allah for forgiveness and showing good actions in your life.

- The salvation message of Judaism is: In Judaism, salvation is closely related to the idea of redemption, a saving from the states or circumstances that destroy the value of human existence. God, as the universal spirit and Creator of the World, is the source of all salvation for humanity, provided an individual honors God by observing his precepts. So redemption or salvation depends on the individual.

- The salvation message of Catholicism is: Catholics believe that you are saved by the grace of God, through a combination of faith and works. They believe that you must die while in an active "repentant state of grace, which means you died in a state of sinlessness or virtue. If this fails and you die in sin, you then rely on God's grace alone to save you.

- The salvation message of Buddhism: In Buddhism, there is no concept of punishment or reward and there is no divine being who decides who goes to hell or heaven. There is merely the illusory results of our thought, words and deeds, which we call karma. This is represented by the beings in the wheel nearest to the hub.

- The salvation message of New Age: The New Age religion believes the meaning of life is to live in the present moment. So right now, the meaning of life for me is writing this sentence, and in a few minutes the meaning of life will be pooping out the burrito I had for lunch. It was always hard for me to accept a worldview in which "taking a shit" could ever, even momentarily, be the meaning of life. New Agers believe that by meditating, being good people and practicing consciousness, they raise the universal collective consciousness of humanity, helping the whole world escape the confines of the thinking mind (which they call the "egoic self"). Through this work, one achieves a form of enlightenment they call consciousness, mindfulness or awareness. I would define New Age consciousness as the experience of realizing the process of thought itself, from a 3rd party perspective, rather than mistaking the sum total of your thoughts as your identity.
- The salvation message of Hinduism: After death, messengers of Yama called Yamadutas bring all beings to the court of Yama, where he weighs the virtues and the vices of the being and passes a judgement, sending the virtuous to Svarga (heaven) and the sinners to one of the hells.
- The salvation message of Scientology: Scientologists believe that people are immortal spiritual beings who have lived before and who will live again, and that their future happiness and immortality as spiritual beings depend on how they conduct themselves in the here and now.
- The salvation message of ancient Egypt was: Ancient Egyptians believed that you had to memorize the nearly 200 Egyptian funeral spells, that we now collectively referred to as the Egyptian Book of the Dead, and use these spells to eloquently lie your way through the 42 doors of the underworld. You passed the doors by professing to the keepers of the doors that: "I am pure! Pure! Pure!", thus earning your salvation through the appearance of a virtuous life.

Notice any common threads? All of these religions say your goodness will be weighed at the end of your life and if you pass the test of the scales, you will receive some version of salvation or heaven by virtue of your own goodness.

Conversely, the Bible says in:

- Daniel 5:27: "Thou art weighed in the balances, and art found wanting."
- And in Romans 3:23 that: "All have sinned, and fallen short of the glory of God."
- And in Romans 6:23 that: "The wages of sin is death; but the gift of God is eternal life through Jesus Christ our Lord."

Jesus says you have already been weighed since before the foundation of the earth and found wanting, and at the end of life, Judgement for your crimes will take place.

Historically, there are only 13 core religions and only 1 is different. Spoiler alert... it's Jesus.

All the rest are all just variations, or denominations, of the same "saved by works" or "I'm a good person" religion.

Throughout human history, even secular society has had their own "saved by works" mentality:

- 480 BC - Ancient Egyptians called it: Purity.
- 776 BC - The Greeks called it: Honor.
- 753 BC - Romans called it: Virtue (or "Virtus", which is where the word "virtue" comes from).
- 500 BC - Spartans called it: Glory.
- 700 AD - Knights Templar called it: Chivalry.
- 1100 AD - Vikings called it: Valor.
- 1600 AD - Pirates called it: Code.
- 1800 AD - Cowboys called it: Manners.
- Modern Day - Atheists call it: Altruism.

Again, all just variations of saving yourself through some work, mindset or lifestyle.

This is true of every single religion on earth... except one. The teachings of Christ (which Jesus called "The Way", not a religion). Christianity done right is actually the absence of all religion. Jesus said you are not a good person, your works are all filthy rags to God, you cannot save yourself and you need a Savior. There is simply no way to throw that salvation message on the heap with all the rest. And so we see that there are actually 2 religions, and only 2:

1. All world religions (including the cult of Atheism), and
2. The Way of Christ (which is the lack of all religions. Albeit for simplicity, we will refer to it as a religion for the sake of this book).

These 2 religions of "Saved by Works" vs "Saved by Grace (through faith, not works)" are the first 2 religions. Modern day science is actually just a remnant of ancient Egyptian religion.

The ancient Egyptians believed in 42 doors of the underworld. The Egyptian Book of the Dead is a list of spells you need to memorize to virtue signal your way through the doors by proclaiming to the Assessors of Maat "I am a good person". If they are not impressed enough to let you through, you simply elevate the lie to the level of absurdity: "I am god (Anubis)".

The more incoherent, emotional and self deceived you were in your belligerent assertions, the more convincing you might be to the guards of the doors. Fake it till you make it, as they say. Go big or go home. Ignorance, arrogance and false confidence are your friend when lying your way to salvation through the Egyptian underworld of the dead.

Ok. I see your point... But what about science? How do you justify saying that science is a religion? Well, I mean, as a Doctor of medical science, I am in fact a high priest of that religion, am I not? But more specifically:

- Self love is just Atheist worship (of self as God),
- Logic is the infallible scripture of the Atheist religion,
- Academic grants and donations are the tithes and offerings of Atheism,
- Cancel culture is just Atheist excommunication,
- Falsifiable science is the apologetics wing of the Atheist religion,
- Darwin is just the Pope of Atheism,
- Virtue signaling is Atheist fellowship,
- Reddit (and other such forums) is just a multitude of Atheist counselors,
- Self righteousness is the mechanism of salvation for Atheists,
- Antisocial scientific scholars are just Atheist Calvinists,
- Bombastically militant liberals are just charismatic Atheists, and
- Safe space college campuses are just temples of Atheist seminary.

The prophets of Pharaoh who tried to match Moses's miracles in Exodus 7 were just the first atheists to say we have "knowledge of how" these miracles work (which is

Science), therefore your God is not real. Sounds familiar, doesn't it?

If these two religions are the two masters Jesus refers to in the Bible, but the gods of Egypt have been rendered mythology, where is this second religion hiding out today? It's hiding in plain site. The God of Israel is never changed. But the second religion is a bit of an imposter, charlatan or vagrant. The two modern names for the 2 salvation messages are:

1. The Pursuit of Happiness: My will be done. I am god. I think I am a good person. I can save myself through my own self confidence that I have lived a good life. This worldview is holding yourself accountable to your own subjective standard of goodness, like Hitler did.

2. The Seeking of Righteousness: Thy will be done. God alone is God. I know I am a sinner. I cannot save myself and I am in desperate need of a savior (Jesus Christ). This reality is God holding you accountable to His unchanging Law.

All of the world religions are actually just denominations of the same "I'm a good person" religion. Once you get past all the gods, history and rituals, it's all the same mechanism of salvation: "Save yourself by being a good person." Everything else is just nuance and minutia. But if the gods of Egypt were alive, performing sudo-miracles and influencing emperors, who are they, where did they come from and what do they want? A better question might be... where are they now?

The gods of Egypt are the same spirits Jesus would later cast out of legion into the pigs. They are the same ones that inspired every false world religion, shared secret knowledge with the ancients, and murdered mankind in a wicked pre-flood world. They are the ones whose bodies God drowned in the flood, but whose spirits now wonder the earth in a dry place. They are the principalities we wrestle against. They are the heroes of old. The men of renown. The half breeds behind the myths of Greek mythology. They are the Nephilim.

The word Nephilim itself is interesting. It means "the fallen ones", "from the clouds" or even "The ones who cause others to fall".

The story of the 2 religions, doesn't actually start in Egypt. It starts much further back, in the Garden of Eden with Cain and Able. Cain worked for a harvest and provided the fruits of his labor to God as an offering. God saw Cain's work as filthy rags. The offering of Abel was that of unblemished blood (a foreshadowing of the sinless Christ). From the very beginning we see a dichotomy of works verses Grace through Faith in Christ (not works, lest any man boast).

You've heard of Cain and Abel, but have you heard of Aclima and Jumella? Muslim tradition holds that... (I know, I know, it's not scripture. Bare with me, we'll go full circle)... Muslim tradition holds that both Cain and Abel were born twins. Cain was born with a twin sister who was named Aclima, and Abel with a twin sister named Jumella.

According to Islamic tradition, Adam wanted Cain to marry Abel's twin sister, and Abel to marry Cain's twin. Cain would not consent to this arrangement, and so Adam proposed to refer the question to God by means of a sacrifice. God rejected Cain's sacrifice to signify his disapproval of his marriage with Aclima, his twin sister. But God accepted Abel's sacrifice and Cain slew his brother in a fit of jealousy.

If that's the case, it makes a lot more sense now what happened and why. As the story goes Abel was to marry Aclima, but Cain killed him and married her (his own twin sister) instead. Aclima was the first female human who was born naturally. Her marriage to Cain bore a son named Enoch (Genesis 4:17). But this is not the same "Enoch" that the "Book of Enoch" is supposedly written by, and about.

I generally find that the lineage and historical details of demonic books are still relatively accurate. The whole point of them is to get as close to truth as possible and then blur the mechanism of salvation with "you can save yourself through good works".

Demonic holy books don't seem to really try to throw you off with inaccurate historical data unless it's obviously way off base, like flying monkey gods in Hinduism (albeit, the pre-flood world may have had all kinds of monsters and freaks, so who knows). But for the demonically inspired books that discuss the God of Abraham, the Garden of Eden and ulterior versions of events, the timelines are generally the same.

The devil seems to actually be in the details, not the overall flow. For example, in Islam the Garden of Eden narrative is similar to the Bible. The main difference is the direction of sin, the severity of sin and the intent which inspired the sin. In the Quran, God creates man as His masterpiece, the angels are basically jealous and say "why would you create these beings who are capable of such violence?" and God more or less says that their intellect and creativity is a fair trade-off for the destruction they will author with it.

Adam names all of the animals in front of the angels and they tell God that He was wise to create such a magnificent creature in man. Notice the greatness of man is elevated here. The angels are told by God to bow to Adam in submission and they all submit... except Lucifer, who refused to bow to Adam.

Lucifer did not sin therefore against God, but against God's command by proxy of Adam. Notice a change in the direction of sin. It almost paints Lucifer out as bold and righteously rebellious in his unique and inspiring display of self love and independence.

In the Quran, the original sin of eating the apple was not a broken covenant or spiritual fornication, it is drastically downplayed instead as a "slip" and basically signified to God that man was ready to "leave the nest" and be independent, which pleased God as it would a Father watching His son go off into the world to succeed.

The Quran praises the human intellect as the primary organ of understanding and salvation, rather than the spirit. While the Bible conversely says "only the spirit knows the mind".

Notice it changes the nature of God, the severity of sin and the direction in which the Devil sins (against Adam, rather than against God). There is always a downplaying of sin, an elevation of human greatness, a downplaying of God's holiness and/or a reversal of roles in these demonically inspired heresies. That's mainly what you have to look out for.

You also have to be careful with Christian cults claiming that Jesus and the Devil are estranged brothers (which there are actually strong scriptural arguments for, believe it or not). Or heresies like Jesus is actually the Arch Angel Michael. But as far as the histories of man, angels and events, they seem to line up pretty well. That's not to say I build my theology off of demonic books. It is to say that some of the vague things mentioned in actual scripture make a whole lot more sense if you consider the possibility of the events and timelines mentioned in the apocryphal books.

I hope that's a strong enough disclaimer to discuss apocryphal theory in context. If not, too bad. We're going to do it anyways. But before we go into the Book of Enoch, let me say this. There is no doubt in my mind that the Book of Enoch is a demonic book, despite the fact that I myself use to consider it extra-biblical para-scripture for a time. I do not necessarily see the "saved by works" salvation message widely promoted, and while I do see some references to repentance, I also see at least one reference to works based salvation.

1 Enoch 61:8 says: "And the Lord of Spirits (who is God) placed the Elect one (who is Jesus) on the throne of glory. And he shall judge all the works of the holy above in the heaven, And in the balance shall their deeds be weighed."

This is straight second religion talk. The second religion says upon death you will be weighed, and if your good deeds outweigh your bad deeds, you will be admitted into heaven. In the Egyptian underworld of the dead, this was a literal scale that your heart was placed on. And if your heart was found to be more evil than good, a crocodile god named "Ammit" would eat your heart. But if you were more good than bad, you would be admitted to heaven.

Conversely, the Bible says in Daniel 5:27: You have been weighed on the scales and found wanting. The Bible is the only book that tells you that you've already been weighed and upon death, you will face Judgement for your crimes against God, of which you are already guilty and deserving of death.

The book of Enoch also says in 1 Enoch 40:9-10: "...and the fourth [angel], who is set over the repentance unto hope of those who inherit eternal life, is named Phanuel.' And these are the four angels of the Lord of Spirits and the four voices I heard in those days."

This is clearly calling Jesus an angel. But Jesus cannot be an angel, since the Bible clearly says all things (including angels) were created through Jesus (John 1).

However, the Book of Enoch also seems to be quoted in part in the Bible as well, for example Jude 1:14 says: "Enoch, the seventh from Adam, prophesied about them: "See, the Lord is coming with thousands upon thousands of his holy ones."

This to me does not necessarily mean that Jude is directly quoting the Book of Enoch, or therefore endorsing it. But it is persuasive, and as we will see shortly, there are other parts of the Bible that do either seem to be quoting, borrowing from, or reaffirming at least some parts of what the Book of Enoch says.

That doesn't make it infallible Scripture (it's not). But, in my humble opinion, it does make it persuasive. In addition to that, it seems to be quoted in the Bible many times, and not just in the obvious spots I have mentioned, but also in some esoteric places I don't know if anyone else has connected yet.

One such example is the entire point of bringing all of this up in the first place. The link between James 1 in the Bible and chapter 7 in the first Book of Enoch.

James chapter 1 explains:

- Each one is tempted when by his own evil desires
- He is lured away and enticed.
- Then after desire has conceived,
- It gives birth to sin; and sin,
- When it is full-grown, gives birth to death.

1 Enoch 7 uses the same exact structure, but fills in the details with actual events and beings. I personally think that James is quoting the book of Enoch here.

In the Bible, Genesis 5:24 says: "Enoch walked faithfully with God; then he was no more, because God took him away."

And Hebrews 11:5 says: "By faith Enoch was taken from this life, so that he did not experience death: "He could not be found, because God had taken him away." For before he was taken, he was commended as one who pleased God."

But in the Book of Enoch, we hear details about what Enoch saw when he was in Heaven. And in 1 Enoch 5:23-34, there is a very interesting conversation between Enoch and God in heaven:

"And He answered and said to me, and I heard His voice: "Fear not, Enoch, thou righteous man and scribe of righteousness. Approach hither and hear my voice.

And go, say to the Watchers of heaven, who have sent thee to intercede for them: 'You should intercede for men, and not men for you. Wherefore have ye left the high, holy, and eternal heaven, and lain with women, and defiled yourselves with the daughters of men and taken to yourselves wives, and done like the children of earth, and begotten giants as your sons.

And though ye were holy, spiritual, living the eternal life, you have defiled yourselves with the blood of women, and have begotten with the blood of flesh, and, as the children of men, have lusted after flesh and blood as those also do who die and perish.

Therefore have I given them wives also that they might impregnate them, and beget children by them, that thus nothing might be wanting to them on earth.

But you were formerly spiritual, living the eternal life, and immortal for all generations of the world. And therefore I have not appointed wives for you; for as for the spiritual ones of the heaven, in heaven is their dwelling.

And now, the giants, who are produced from the spirits and flesh, shall be called evil spirits upon the earth, and on the earth shall be their dwelling.

Evil spirits have proceeded from their bodies; because they are born from men and from the Watchers is their beginning and primal origin; they shall be evil spirits on earth, and evil spirits shall they be called.

And the spirits of the giants afflict, oppress, destroy, attack, do battle, and work destruction on the earth, and cause trouble. They take no food, but nevertheless hunger and thirst, and cause offenses.

And these spirits shall rise up against the children of men and against the women, because they have proceeded from them.

From the days of the slaughter and destruction and death of the giants, from the souls of whose flesh the spirits, having gone forth, shall destroy without incurring judgement, thus shall they destroy until the day of the consummation, the great judgement in which the age shall be consummated, over the Watchers and the godless, yea, shall be wholly consummated.

And now as to the Watchers who have sent thee to intercede for them, who had been aforetime in heaven, say to them: 'You have been in heaven, but all the mysteries had not yet been revealed to you, and you knew worthless ones, and these in the hardness of your hearts you have made known to the women, and through these mysteries women and men work much evil on earth.'

Say to them therefore: 'You have no peace.'"

Now, back in the Bible, there is a story of Jesus casting a legion of demons into a herd of pigs (Matthew 8:28–34; Mark 5:1-20; and Luke 8:26–39).

Look at how the demons talk to Jesus in Matthew 8:28–34:

"When he arrived at the other side in the region of the Gadarenes, two demon-possessed men coming from the tombs met him. They were so violent that no one could pass that way. "What do you want with us, Son of God?" they shouted. "Have you come here to torture us before the appointed time?" Some distance from them a large herd of pigs was feeding. The demons begged Jesus, "If you drive us out, send us into the herd of pigs." He said to them, "Go!" So they came out and went into the pigs, and the whole herd rushed down the steep bank into the lake and died in the water."

Do you see where I'm going with this?

Now let's look at Matthew 12:43–45, which says:

"When the unclean spirit is gone out of a man, he walketh through dry places, seeking rest, and findeth none. Then he saith, I will return into my house from whence

I came out; and when he is come, he findeth it empty, swept, and garnished. Then goeth he, and taketh with himself seven other spirits more wicked than himself, and they enter in and dwell there: and the last state of that man is worse than the first. Even so shall it be also unto this wicked generation."

Do you see my point? The unclean spirits in the Bible, that possessed the man, sounds a lot like the "evil spirits" mentioned in the book of Enoch, which are the dead spirits of the once living half breed angelic giants who God killed in Noah's Flood.

And so, my proposal of all spiritual history, which explains why the Bible outer envelopes all other religions, is that 200 angels came down to earth, were desired by human women, enticed them, cohabitated with them (which means they had sex with them) and forced their way into the flesh against God's will.

The children of this unholy union, the Nephilim, grew and began murdering humanity. Women cuckolded their human husbands, as we cuckold God to this day and as Gomer cuckolded Hosea as a mirror of God's pain with Israel.

God took their bodies away in the flood but their spirits still wonder the earth to this day in a dry place desiring to attached to the lust of the world through your body as a medium.

Let me go over a bit of nuance so this doesn't get confusing. I am not necessarily saying that the Nephilim are demons, but rather unclean spirits. There are at least 3 groups of fallen angels we should distinguish between here:

- First, there were the 3rd of the angels who fell with Satan (this is where I believe demons come from, which are outnumbered 2 to 1 by good angels, since they are only 1/3 of all angels). The Bible says in Psalm 68:17 that there are "twice tens of thousand, thousands upon thousands" of angels. That would be over 100 million good angels, which means there would be more than 50 million fallen ones. Or, assuming a world population of 8 billion humans, that would be 1 demon for every 160 people. And one angel for every 80 people.
- Then there are an additional 200 angels who rebelled later on, had sex with earth women and taught man all sorts of evil skills like how to make fire, build weapons and derive drugs from the roots of plants (I believe these are the fallen angels "in the pit" or "in prison" mentioned in Jude 1:6 and possibly 1 Peter 3:19).

- And finally we have the children of those 200 angels, who are the Nephilim, which are half human, half angel. This is where I believe Greek halfbreed myths come from, like Hercules, who was said to be the son of Zeus (a Titan who lives in the clouds). The other Titans were then hurled down by Zeus and imprisoned in a pit beneath Tartarus (which is the underworld). The word "Tartarus" occurs in the Septuagint translation of the Bible (specifically in Job 40:20 and Job 41:24), as well as the Greek translation of the first Book of Enoch (chapter 20, verse 2).

The Nephilim somehow survived Noah's Flood according to Scripture (Genesis 6:4, and Numbers 13:33). It is also widely believed that Goliath, who David killed with a sling and a stone was a giant due to his Nephilim DNA, which of course took place over 1000 years after Noah's Flood.

After the flood, these anxious spirits wondered the earth spreading secret knowledge, rearranging the legos of God's truth (which is a locked creation) and parading around as gods themselves. This is where the gods of the sun, crops, rain, etc, all came from. This is why there are similar architectures all around the ancient world. It was not aliens. It was the Nephilim.

The Bible describes space as "the heavens". And that's where fallen angels came from. Biblical demons are literally the exact same definition as aliens: Non-human beings that came to earth from space. The Bible (with a little borrowed from the Book of Enoch) is literally saying that "200 fallen angels came to earth from the heavens and shared secret knowledge with Old Testament humans". That's the same exact thing as saying "200 extraterrestrials came to earth from space and shared alien technology with the ancients."

And this my friends, is where all false religions come from. That is why they are all actually the same salvation message of Cain: Save yourself through works.

As a matter of fact, if you look at the Biblical timeline from Adam and Eve, and take all the world religions at their word, with Hinduism being the oldest, the times line up perfectly for all the world religions to have started at various points after the Tower of Babel, but not before.

Now, the Tower of Babel is interesting, and a lot of Christians seem to miss this. The whole point behind the Tower of Babel is that it was built to be taller than the flood was deep. Meaning, if God decided to flood the earth again, which he said he wasn't going to do anyways, a giant waterproof tower pitched in tar was a human level insurance policy against the wrath of God. They were literally trying to save themselves from the wrath of God, through the literal works of their own hands. And they did this while ignoring the fact that God said he would never flood the earth again, meaning they tried to save themselves, rather than trust in God's promise.

The Tower of Babel was built as a giant middle finger to God. If God flooded the earth again, they would have their own version of an Ark to run to in order to save themselves, by their own works. The Tower of Babel was literally the first official temple of the "let's save ourselves from God's wrath through our own works" religion. And from that temple, all of the denominations of the "I'm a good person and I can save myself" religion were born.

In their ignorance, they were building a giant flammable chimney to live in, since tar is flammable. And God said the next time he was going to destroy the earth was by fire. And so this is where trying to beat God using human level logic will get you. You're attempt to avoid being drowned just means you'll burn that much hotter. Tar was literally used as the mortar to hold their tower together, just like we build our intellectual Towers of Babel with arrogance as our mortar. I hate to tell you this my friends, but arrogance is just as flammable spiritually, as tar is physically.

Their own rebellion against God would be their own undoing. And the Bible says as much of all of us. The same walls you have built to block God out, will be the same walls you are crushed under the weight of when He returns. And as such, He will not have killed you. Rather, you will have killed yourself. If you deny God in this life, you are committing your own suicide. Interestingly enough, as the story goes, Hercules also built his own funeral pyre and then committed suicide by burning himself alive. But I'm sure that's just another coincidence.

The way God will punish you, is the same way He always punished people in the Bible. His punishment is the give them what they said they wanted:

- Israel wanted a king. God's punishment was to give them one.
- Israel didn't want to enter the promise land because there were giants in the land. God's punishment was to say: "Ok, you won't enter the promised land".
- Israel wanted to be enslaved again rather than wander in the desert. God's punishment was to grant their wish.

If the nation of Noah wanted to live in a tower of tar to survive an inferno, God would punish them by saying ok. The actual cause of death would therefore be suicide, since that's exactly what fighting God is... suicide.

Actually, God doesn't really seem to kill anyone. Rather, He gives them the choice of free will, and they just keep choosing to kill themselves. The Bible even says as much.

For example, Deuteronomy 30:19 says: "I call heaven and earth to record this day against you, that I have set before you life and death, blessing and cursing: therefore choose life, that both thou and thy seed may live."

There are too many verses to list here, but I'll give you 3 more:

Ezekiel 33:4-5 says: "And then if anyone who hears the sound of the trumpet does not take warning, and the sword comes and takes him away, his blood shall be upon his own head. He heard the sound of the trumpet and did not take warning; his blood shall be upon himself. But if he had taken warning, he would have saved his life."

Acts 20:26-27 says: "Therefore, I declare to you today that I am innocent of the blood of any of you. For I have not hesitated to proclaim to you the whole will of God."

And Proverbs 8:36 says: "But he who fails to find me injures himself; all who hate me love death."

The nation born of Noah built a giant middle finger to God. But, even with their absolutely ridiculous stupidity and arrogance, in His great mercy, God spared them from the consequences of their own rebellion. Rather than kill them, He confused their tongues. And this is where I believe the 70 core languages come from.

Linguists currently figure that there were 100 core languages, from which all modern languages came. And that they all, more or less, kind of just showed up 6000 years ago when human civilization started, but I predict in time, they will reduce the number down to around 70 core languages, since there were about 70 tribes created that day at the Tower of Babel.

I would also argue that the Catholic Church built a spiritual Tower of Babel, in which it was trying to save itself by works. And as a result, God again confused us in mercy, which is where all the denominations we have today come from. I would propose that protestant denominations are to the Catholic Church, as languages were to the Tower of Babel.

It's also interesting that the gods of Egypt claimed to have been "born of water".

And this is true. These religions were all born of the "primeval waters". Phonetically, "prime evil" means "first evil". And the etymology of the word primeval means "the first age".

According to Encyclopedia Britannica: "Nun's name means 'primeval waters,' and he represented the waters of chaos out of which Re-Atum began creation. Nun's qualities were boundlessness, darkness, and the turbulence of stormy waters; these qualities were personified separately by pairs of deities."

What do the "waters of chaos" sound like to you? Because to me it sounds like Noah's Flood, in which the Nephilim were drowned.

And so that's it. These are the two religions. If there is any question which side you should choose, think about this: All the nephilim gods promised their worshipers things like:

- Longevity of life
- Successful fertility, and
- Increased crop yield.

But those promises are all within the envelope of the curse of Genesis 3. God's curse says:

- You will die,
- Child bearing will be difficult, and
- You will have to work the fields for food.

The Nephilim gods were just offering to alleviate the symptoms of the curse of Genesis 3, but never to break the curse itself. This is because they don't have the authority to do so. But my God is the God who rains the food of angels freely from the Heavens. My God says I will reap where I did not sow. My God is the one who takes away pain and tears completely. My God says He will kill death itself. And that's how you know which side to choose.

Like the fools who built the Tower of Babel, you too are preparing for the wrong apocalypse. But God is merciful enough to confuse you from your own efforts to kill yourself. Isaiah 55:6 says: "Seek the LORD while he may be found. Call on him while he is near." Because a day is coming where there will be no one at the other end of that telephone line. Call your Father, while He is still picking up the phone.

Your efforts to signal your own virtue will not convince God on Judgement Day. Repent here and now, trust in Christ and be saved.

In ancient Egyptian mythology, during the judgment of souls, the dead had to declare before 42 judges of the 42 doors of the underworld that they had not committed any of the 42 sins. This was called the "negative confession" and sounds a whole lot like the 10 Commandments.

In the second religion, you use the law as a list of things you claim not to be guilty of. In truth, the Law is a list of things you must admit you are in fact guilty of, and therefore plead the blood of Christ to cover for you, lest you rightfully die as the wages of your own sin.

Think about it. Imagine you are a parent and all day long at work, through a nanny camera, you watch your child draw on the wall with crayons. Watching this stores up your wrath. But when you get home your kid lies and pretends that he did not draw on the wall. He claims he didn't even notice the crayons on the wall and has no idea how they got there.

Does it matter if he has a convincing story? Does it matter if he has even convinced himself of the lie? Of course not. The insult to your intelligence is even worse than the sin itself. Are you going to reward him for lying? No. You're going to discipline him as a good parent should. Now what if you get home, and he meets you at the door and confesses everything, with true contrition in his eyes and heart. Now, you're more than likely to let him off the hook.

Well you are that kid, God is your Father, this life is your childhood, and your sin is the writing on the wall, of which you have been weighed and found wanting. The same holds true. Own up to your sin and ask for mercy.

Looking back at the Bible, we see a lot of references to 42:

- Revelation 11:1-2 says: "Then the angel gave me a measuring rod like a staff, saying, "Arise and measure the temple of God, and the altar and they shall trample upon the holy city for 42 months",
- 2 Kings 2:23 explains that God sent bears to maul 42 of the teenage boys who mocked Elisha for his baldness,
- The children of Israel had 42 wanderings, or journeys, during their 40 years in the desert, until they finally were given rest (Numbers 33:1- 50),
- There were 42 generations from Adam to Christ (Matthew 1:17), and
- The phrase 'little children' appears forty-two times in the Old Testament.

I'm not insinuating there is a correlation, but it's interesting.

This is why liberals and atheists virtue signal like their life literally depends on it. Because they are the remnants of an ancient Egyptian religion in which your eternal life was literally dependent on your ability to signal your own virtue. It's not a hobby. It's a survival mechanism. Looks like the "answer to the ultimate question of life, the universe, and everything" really is 42 after all. At least for everyone who is not saved by the Blood of the Lamb.

This is why when you attack their views, they have a visceral reaction as if you are attacking their sacred religion. Because you are.

CHAPTER 12

Apples & Addicts

Do you ever wonder why God doomed all of humanity over an apple? Well... (spoiler alert)... it wasn't really about the apple. When we repent to God for the original sin, what exactly are we repenting for in the first place? Trigger warning: this chapter is going to be brutal.

God's original order & design was:

- God had dominion over man,
- Man had dominion over the woman, and
- Man & woman had dominion over the animals.

The Fall from grace was a reversal of God's order and design:

- The snake (animal) took dominion over the woman through deceit,
- The woman took dominion over man through temptation, and
- Man tried to take dominion over God through knowledge.

The original sin was an attempt to overthrow God. We essentially did to God what Satan did. I don't know why He took mercy on us and not the angels. Perhaps because we are His masterpiece and they are not. Perhaps the fact that we were tricked into it played a role. Whatever His reasoning, God saw saving us as part of Him magnifying His own glory and so we are saved as a consequence of God glorifying His own Great Name.

God did not save us because of us. He is saving us, despite ourselves. And therein lies our assurance of salvation. The reason you can't out sin the grace of God...

is because salvation isn't really about you in the first place. And thank God for that. If you could screw it up, you would.

Grab a piece of paper and write the word "SOUL" on it, as large as you can. Now punch a hole in it for every person you've had sex with, every person you've ever messed around with and every time you've watched porn or had a lustful thought. How much of the paper is left? How much of your soul still belongs to you?

If the spirits we wrestle against are the dead Nephilim whose bodies were killed in the flood, and the mechanism of sin is cohabitation with those spirits, then letting them into our temple is becoming one flesh with them, which is the Biblical definition of sex. Sin is sex with dead Nephilim spirits. That's why God is so disgusted by it. That's why the story of Hosea and Gomer. That's what it means to defile the wedding bed. That's why God calls us whores, prostitutes and harlots. He is being literal.

That's where your post-sin emotions come from. Why do you think after you have an orgasm you feel guilty, cheap, used, lied to and abandoned? It's because it wasn't your orgasm. How you feel after sin is a hint as to what sin really is in the first place. And more importantly, that something inside of you already knows that you were just the vehicle an enticing spirit used to have its own orgasm. A dead Angel baby just jacked itself off using your hand. You thought you were the one in control, but it was actually you getting bent over the altar of God and railed from behind. It was all just pillow talk baby. And you know it's true.

See how disgusted and horrified you are just thinking about it? Imagine how God feels watching you do it. His judgement, wrath and anger are starting to make a little bit more sense now, huh? Now you see His great love for you, that even still, He would show you mercy. If you were Him and understood how bad sin really was, you wouldn't even forgive yourself.

This is the extent of God's love for us, His great mercy and faithfulness to us. Now imagine how ridiculous it is to ask "Well, what exactly did I do that I need to repent for in the first place? I think I'm a pretty good person. Anyways, if God is real, why does He let bad things happen to good people?" What a slap in the face after all He has forgiven us for. My heart breaks for Him. How could we do this to Him? This whole thing is about Him, not us. This is His-story, not ours.

Imagine the heart break of being cheated on. Now multiply that pain times every person who ever lived (past, present and future). Now experience that all at once and you'll start to get a small glimpse of what Christ suffered for you on the cross. Dealing with a heartbreak of that magnitude, I bet He didn't even feel the nails.

The reason sin is so disgusting to God is because we are using the temple He loaned us (which is actually His property) to harbor a defeated enemy rather than welcome home the Holy Spirit. In essence, we are sleeping with the enemy in the castle God put us in charge of.

We are sharing one flesh with evil spirits, just like the Holy Ghost spiritually impregnated Mary with Jesus. Only it's the evil inverse of that same process. That holy union conceived Jesus who grew up to become life. Our unholy union with these evil spirits conceives sin, which grows up to become death. This is what the Bible is trying to tell us in James 1. Once you see it, you'll never unsee it.

This is why demons attach to us and then drive our bodies like a cheap stolen rental car, burning out donuts in the middle of an old abandoned parking lot. They are living vicariously through us, like a host. And we are letting them do it. Their best defense is to hide in plain sight. And so they whisper sweet little nothings into your ear:

"Demons don't exist. There is no soul. There is no spirit. There is no God. There will be no judgement for sin. It's all a fairytale! YOLO! Lolz! Live it up. Take your inheritance now and let's go to the casino. Your treat. Don't worry. I'll pay next time baby. You know I'm good for it. Don't listen to those stupid Christians. They want to take you from me, but we're just having a little bit of innocent fun right? Only believe in what you can see, taste, touch, smell or feel! You're so smart and you're a good person. Hey. By the way. Pass that cocaine over here!"

Demons want to keep you having a good time, so that they can relive their pre-flood glory days through your flesh, in this modern world. As long as you just go with the flow, you'll never figure out that they are driving the vehicle of your body straight to hell.

- Your body is a car (which is driving down the road of life),
- Your soul is the driver (who is making the decisions), and
- Your spirit is the GPS (which is set to take you home: to heaven).

Demons are trying to convince you to ignore the GPS and open the door for them so they can take you for a joy ride in your Father's car instead. Why are you letting them get away with it? Why are you letting demons bend you over the altar of God, in the temple God entrusted to you, and use you like a cheap cracked out sin whore? Now imagine how your Father, who loves you with a timeless love, feels watching it all happen. It might just anger Him enough to sentence you to death after a lifetime of such behavior, don't you think?

Do you remember that old saying "If you love them, let them go. If it was meant to be, they will come back to you"? Well that's what this life is. God gave us free will. He let us go. And He is telling us now to return to Him (By listening to the directions of your spiritual GPS, which will lead you back home). The ones who love Him will answer the call and find their way. The rest will burn. And in the end, He will have a family full of love, which I think is why He created us in the first place.

What separates humans from animals? Is it creativity? Playfulness? Foresight? No. Elephants can paint, deer play games and ravens can plan strategies ahead of time to prepare for unforeseen events. The law is what separates animals from humans. Humans care about justice, we set up courts and rules and consequences. Animals do not. The law is what makes humans human. It's our conscience. It's God's law written on our hearts and minds.

Moses received the 10 Commandments from God in his old age. But when Moses was young, he fled Egypt lest he be held accountable for murdering an Egyptian citizen. What law would Moses have been judged by for murder if the 10 Commandments didn't exist yet?

Moses would have been judged under Egyptian law for murder, albeit they didn't have an established written law that we know of. There were preexisting laws on earth, just not particularly used in Egypt at that time. The oldest known human law is the Code of Ur-Nammu, 2050 years before Christ. The next oldest is the Code of Hammurabi, 1800 years before Christ. Both of these law sets were written and used in Mesopotamia (which is Modern day Iraq, Kuwait, Turkey and Syria).

The Law of God in some form was already around before this, arguably back to the Garden of Eden. We know this because of the Book of Job. Job made preemptive sacrifices to God in case his children might sin. He was observing and practicing what would later become the Levitical Law, and this is in the oldest book of the Bible. Job lived 150 years before the Code of Ur-Nammu was authored.

One of the main reasons I'm a Christian is because the Biblical timeline explains, accounts for and outer envelopes all other holy books, religions and laws on earth.

- Hinduism just details the battles of the pre-flood Nephilim world.

- The Quran is just one of the angelically inspired false gospels the Bible warns about in Galatians 1:8.
- The Book of Mormon is just what was going on in North America during the Biblical times in the Middle East, also inspired by a fallen angel.

None of these books actually tell their own story as unique or separate from Biblical scripture and yet scripture explains all of them.

This is something I realized studying other religions. And when you read every holy book on earth, a simple pattern emerges. There are only 2 religions:

1. Humans are basically good. We just screw up sometimes. Be a good person and whatever is on the other side of death, you'll be ok.
2. Only God is good. You have sinned against Him and have earned death as your wage. You cannot save yourself through works. You need a Savior.

There are many laws and many standards of "goodness" in the various holy books of the earth. This creates a problem for the person claiming to be a "good person". Which standard are you using to evaluate your own goodness?

Did you know Hitler wrote his own 12 commandments and reprinted Bibles in Nazi Germany with his own standard of goodness instead of God's standard? This new Bible was called "Germans with God". Thousands of copies were printed and distributed to his troops who then used Hitler's 12 commandments as their new standard of goodness. They thought they were "good people" too, based on their own subjective standard of goodness.

What standard are you using?

- The 5 Pillars of Islam?
- The 8 Fold Path of Buddhism?
- Or perhaps, the 7 Tenants of the Satanic Temple (They think their "good people" too, by the way)?

I found that I was able to get past most of these standards of goodness quite well. But not the 10 Commandments.

When you create your own standard of right and wrong, you are rewriting the Bible as Hitler did. And on Judgement Day, this will no more save you than Hitler's Bible will save him. The fact is, you either hold yourself accountable to the actual Biblical standard of God, the 10 Commandments, or you might as well go off and do whatever you want, because whatever subjective rules you've made for yourself are worthless before God anyways.

The Bible calls your supposed good works "filthy rags", which is a very vulgar description referring to used menstrual tampons.

Surely you realize that by now. If you really didn't believe in God, you would be much more immoral than you are now.

This is evidenced by the fact that you feel the need to have any standard of righteousness at all, so that you can mute your conscience to go sin in peace. If you truly didn't believe at all, you would abandon the standard completely, not deceive yourself into pretending you've met it.

I decided that if I was going to claim to be a "good person" (as I once did), I would hold myself up to the highest possible standard of goodness in existence, The 10 Commandments. The only problem was, I had already failed them all. And that led me to the conclusion that I was not a good person, that I could not save myself and that I needed a Savior after all.

Sin is defined in the Bible as "Anything not born of Faith in God". That means having faith in love, since God is love. Anything not born of love is sin. The meaning of life is love, and I'm sure a lot of you are happy to hear that, but you won't be once I explain what that actually means.

What you think of as love is actually lust. When you're petting your puppy. Is it love or is it lust? Are you not just syncing your days negative energy into them as an endless suffering sync? That's lust. You're in it, for what you can get out of it. When that dog gets old and starts falling apart and pooping all over the house, and you lovingly clean up their diarrhea from your $4,000 handmade Persian rug... that's love.

If it brings you added convenience, that's lust. If you're willing to overlook it's added inconvenience, that's love. Anything you use as an escape from the responsibility of reality or as an emotional support sync... is lust, not love. As a matter of fact, a lot of you are lusting after Jesus.

You lust Jesus when you are syncing all of your pain onto the cross. But you don't love Him when it comes time to carry that cross for Him. You share your suffering with Christ, but you won't share in His.

The Bible is many things. It is a love letter from a Husband to His whore of a bride. It is a stern lecture from an angry Father. But I think a lot of us have missed the fact that, perhaps above all, the Bible is a dictionary. It is an Ark sailing through the deceit of the ages, preserving the original definitions of words the enemy is intentionally twisting to deceive you. He doesn't want you to have it, he doesn't want you to read it, he doesn't want you to live it and he damned sure doesn't want you to spread it.

In the beginning, God created the Heavens and earth. The Bible says our Father spoke us into existence. The Word He spoke was "Jesus" and the language in which He said it, was love.

You may think I'm talking about the 5 love languages, But the language of love is not the same thing as supposed love languages. According to Gary Chapman there are 5 love languages, which are:

- Physical Touch
- Time Spent
- Acts of Service
- Gifts, and
- Words of Affirmation

Never mind the fact that he missed two obvious ones, which I would argue are: "Sense of humor" and "Intelligence". I think it's obvious that people are attracted to others who can make them laugh and who they feel are above average intelligence.

But the problem itself is that these are not actually love languages in the first place. They are lust languages.

Think about it. What do they all have in common? They are all things you get out of the other person, not that you sow into them. And even when sowing into them, you're just trying to manipulate a desired outcome.

You might take out the trash because you know your wife's love language is acts of service. But you're only doing it to turn her on so you can get paid back in your love language, which is physical touch.

they are actually just lust rebranded as love:

- Physical Touch is just a fancy word for Groping
- Time Spent might as well be Time Served
- Acts of Service is just Forced Altruism
- Gifts are just spiced up Bribes, and
- Words of Affirmation is just Pillow Talk

And if Intelligence and Sense of Humor were on the love language list, intelligence would just be the equivalent to:"Look how smart I am, by proxy of you". And sense of humor would be: "You're really good at keeping me distracted from our mutual impending death". Both also examples of lust, not love.

All of these lust languages are in regard to what you got out of the other person (lust). Not what you sow into them (love). There is only one true love language and that is God's love language: obedience.

Everything else is just some version of opening a bank account to immediately withdraw from. The rich will tell you it's a much better option to endlessly deposit into the principle and live off the interest.

Stop trying to live for the other person and simply die to self already. Live for God, not your spouse. You will never successfully be their salvation. That was never your job. All you can do, is all you were ever meant to do, help polish them over the course of a lifetime into the mirror image of Christ and be humble enough to be sharpened yourself.

We have talked a lot about worldview languages and how destructive it is to pick the wrong one. What I want you to see in this chapter is that the language you think you know so well is actually evil hidden in plain sight.

Let me take you down the rabbit hole of what love is:

- The Bible says that the conscience is God's law written on your heart and mind.
- The law means the 10 commandments.
- The 10 commandments really just boil down to two.
- And the common command between them is simply to "Love".
- Love is the law and love fulfills the law.
- The Bible also says that God's love for us comes in the form of Him saving us.
- The way He saves us is by making us more like Him so we won't burn when He returns.
- The process of becoming more like Him comes in the form of discipline and suffering.

Therefore the meaning of life is suffering. But not just reluctant suffering for the sake of sorrow. It is accepted suffering for the sake of sanctification. Another name for that would be "The seeking of righteousness". Another name for that would be "to do the will of God".

And that's what King Solomon concludes in Ecclesiastes as well. That all of life is vanity and meaningless smoke. The only thing that matters, which is the meaning of life... is to do the will of God.

I told you that you weren't gonna like it. And so, the meaning of life is love. But love is not what you think it is and it doesn't look like what you think it does. The lie is hidden in plain sight and you believed it because it gives you what you want: Justification for sin.

The meaning of life is to love God and love your neighbor. To love is to lead. To lead is to serve. To serve is to die. And so the meaning of life is to die, which is the will of God. God's will is that you live, but you must die in order to do that.

More specifically, you have to die in this Matrix to be extricated from it. The Bible says if you love your life, you will lose it, but if you lay down your life for Him, you will find it. It also says that greater love hath no man than this, that he would lay down his life for his friends. The way you love God is to obey His commands. His command is to love your neighbor. The way you love your neighbor is to die for them. And so to love is to die and you must lose your life to find it.

Basically, you have to stop doing what you want to do, which is sin. And turn from sin, which is called repentance. But, you don't have to clean yourself up in order to come to Christ. You couldn't even if you tried, and even if you got close, your good works would not negate the fact that you were born into sin anyways and need a Savior regardless. The Bible says, "Come as you are".

And so what God is looking for from you is surrender, a willingness, a commitment, and a declaration that you want to turn from sin. It's not the act of being sinless that saves you, it's your sincere petition of prayer that God will change the desires of your heart and align your will with His will for you. Thy will be done, my will be damned.

That's what it means to "Surrender", "Welcome Jesus into your heart" or "get saved". The successful turning from sin (which is repentance) comes later, not as a work of your own, but as evidence of the work Christ is doing in you. You must only make the decision to let Him do that work in you, which He is willing and ready and waiting to begin. To get saved, you don't have to "do" anything, it's more that you have to simply stop thwarting His existing efforts to save you. It's about what you have to stop doing. You have to get out of the way of your own progress and stop fighting Him.

Another way to say it would be:

- If love is the law, and
- God is love.
- Then God is the Law, and
- The meaning of life is God.
- The Conscience then is also God (as it seems to be part of the ministry of the Holy Spirit), and
- The meaning of life is to listen to your conscience (obey God).

Therefore, to reject your conscience, is to reject the law, which is to reject God, which is to take your inheritance early (rendering your Father effectively dead to you), which is to fail to love. And I think this is what it means to blaspheme the Holy Spirit, which is the unforgivable sin. Since the conscience is the call, rejecting your conscience is to reject the call, therefore blaspheming the one who is yelling that call out into the wilderness to save you.

This again shows God's great love for us. He is saying that above and beyond the pain we feel in judgement, it hurts Him even more that we didn't answer the call. The call is not just for us to be saved, it's to satisfy God's desire that we be saved. If we love Him, we will obey Him, so that He will get what He wants, but all He wants is for you to be saved.

Does that make sense? Let's review again what the Bible says the conscience is:

- Who: All people will have
- What: The Law
- By whom: of God
- Where: Written on your hearts and minds
- Why: To drive us to repentance
- When: Before judgement
- How: By showing us we cannot keep the law and need a Savior

So the meaning of life is to listen to your conscience (which is the law, which is love) and try to do what it says. Meaning try to love God and your neighbor perfectly. And then you realize that you can't. You will always inevitably fail.

This is because you cannot fulfill the law. That's the whole point. It's not actually about living out the law, you can't. If you don't believe me, be my guest and try. If you think you have actually succeeded, your actual sin is just pride.

In the search for the sinless saint, you can immediately disqualify anyone who wrote their own name on the list.

The point is to show you that you can't. Only Christ can, and He already did. This shows you your helpless estate and need for a Savior. It let's you know you're a sinner and drives you to repentance.

This is also again... why you will not have any excuse on Judgment Day. And so, the meaning of life is Christ, who is God, who is love.

Don't miss the boat on this one. Because the "boat" is literally the Ark, which is one family, floating above the wrath of God below.

Christians widely believe that God separated Pangea into the seven continents during the 40 days of rain, and the 150 days of Noah's flood, which appears to have been God baptizing the earth itself. I have a deeper theory that this represents God breaking a unified church into the seven churches of Revelation but I digress.

While God was judging the earth for their sins, he was also creating the new earth under the surface of his wrath. But no one on the arc could see below the waves. They were too busy being tossed around back-and-forth waiting for a sign to come that God's wrath had passed over them

The people who could now clearly see that God is real and he's creating something new, could only see it because they were under the water watching it happened below their feet. They were now literally drowning in the evidence they had spent their lives pretending not to see.

They finally accepted the obvious truth they knew all along, but they would never be able to enjoy it. The only ones that would get to enjoy the new earth being created were the ones that had faith in not being able to see it. Instead, they put their faith in their captain, that he knew, not where they were going, but win the new earth would be ready.

God didn't destroy the world, he created a new one and the old was destroyed in the process. God is not just going to burn the lost for the sake of killing them. Rather he will burn off the old world to create a new one, and anyone who's not part of that new one will be destroyed in the process.

The animals on the Ark could feel the new earth being created, through the turbulence of God's wrath, but they couldn't see it yet. You could say that they trusted in the evidence of things unseen, which is what the Bible describes as faith.

Under the surface of the flood, God was creating a new earth. He will never again destroy this earth by water, but he most definitely will do it by fire. Under the chaos of your rebellious heart, God is building a new heaven, but if you insist on seeing it here and now, you will have taken your inheritance early.

The only ones that get to see heaven in the end, are the ones that don't insist on having it now.

The crazy part is this. Once you accept suffering, you transcend it. It's like God is saying "because you have chosen wisely, I will give you both." I have never been happier than when I finally accepted suffering. You must have noticed by now that the Pursuit of Happiness is a carrot on a string. You're emotionally high for a time and then you come crashing down. It never lasts forever. You're a dopamine drug addict to the thought of happiness, but it always manages to slip through your fingers.

The Bible says seek first the Kingdom of God and His righteousness and all of these things will be added to you. As crazy as it sounds, the acceptance of suffering is the only way to ever truly be happy. It's like when King Solomon chose wisdom over wealth, and because he chose wisely, God gave him both.

I can't promise you happiness as a Christian. But that's only because happiness doesn't actually exist in the first place. For everything the Lord has created, the devil has a counterfeit:

- Happiness is the counterfeit of joy,
- Contentment is the counterfeit of hope,
- Evidence is the counterfeit of faith,
- Lust is the counterfeit of love, and
- Salesmanship is the counterfeit of evangelistic zeal.

You've been sold a bag of shit and told its gold, as long as you never look inside. That's called faith my friends. You have put your faith in sin instead of God.

God is inviting you to His cosmic tea party to tell you all about His historically crappy day. So what if the tea is bitter. The view is heavenly and the company is divine.

You wouldn't accept the invite and so He wrote you an angry love letter instead.

The Bible is an angry, long winded text message rant from God to His rebellious children who never sit with Him in the same sorrows that they themselves originally caused Him.

But I will sit with You Father, even in sorrow. After all, much of that sorrow has my name on it. I thank You Father for the honor of suffering the way You have. I see now a glimpse of what it is and how it works. I'm so sorry it took me so long to understand. I'm sorry for multiplying your pain by rejecting the very invitation You sent me to share in it.

When we suffer, but refuse to turn away from God, we magnify His glory. Perhaps He is looking down and saying "See my servant, who walks in darkness, has nothing left and has been stripped of his desire to even live, and yet he refuses to curse Me and die. This is the reflection of the love that I first showed him, that while he was My enemy, I too died for him. And the new home I am preparing will only be filled with such children. Well done good and faithful servant. Hold on a little bit longer, you are almost home."

People like to say that God is not an old man. But I think He is. Is He not the elder of us all? Infinitely old? The Bible calls Him the "Ancient of Days".

I think there is some appropriateness in the image of a hurting and brokenhearted Father, who never stopped paying the tuition bills of His rebellious children who never call Him, visit Him or honor Him. Instead He waits for us to learn enough, at His expense, to realize the value that has always been there in the relationship we threw away. Is this not the story of the Prodigal's father and that of Jacob and Joseph?

God invited us to hear about His cosmic shitty day and instead we told Him "I just want to have fun".

I promise you guys, don't miss this. We are not here to be happy. We are here to become righteous. I know you don't want to hear this from me, so hear it from Peter:

1 Peter 4:13 says: "But to the degree that you share in the sufferings of Christ, keep on rejoicing, so that also at the revelation of His glory you may rejoice with exultation."

If you don't want to hear it from Peter, consider the teachings of Paul:

- Philippians 1:29 says: "For it has been granted to you on behalf of Christ not only to believe in Him, but also to suffer for Him."
- Not only that, but we rejoice in our sufferings, knowing that suffering produces endurance and endurance produces character, and character produces hope."
- Philippians 3:10 says: "That I may know Him and the power of His

resurrection and the fellowship of His sufferings, being conformed to His death."

- 2 Corinthians 1:5 says: "For just as the sufferings of Christ are ours in abundance, so also our comfort is abundant through Christ."

If you don't believe Paul, believe Jesus, who says the same thing in 3 of the 4 Gospels:

- Luke 9:23 says: "And He was saying to them all, "If anyone wishes to come after Me, he must deny himself, and take up his cross daily and follow Me."
- Mark 8:34 says: "And He summoned the crowd with His disciples, and said to them, "If anyone wishes to come after Me, he must deny himself, and take up his cross and follow Me."
- Matthew 16:24 says: "Then Jesus said to His disciples, "If anyone wishes to come after Me, he must deny himself, and take up his cross and follow Me."

Only God could say something once and yet somehow repeat it 3 times. The acceptance of suffering is literally all through the Bible, cover to cover:

- James 1:2-4 says: "Count it all joy, my brothers, when you meet trials of various kinds, for you know that the testing of your faith produces steadfastness. And let steadfastness have its full effect, that you may be perfect and complete, lacking in nothing."
- Hebrews 12:7 says: "Endure hardship as discipline; God is treating you as his children. For what children are not disciplined by their father?"
- Hebrews 12:11 says: "No discipline seems pleasant at the time, but painful. Later on, however, it produces a harvest of righteousness and peace for those who have been trained by it."
- You all know John 3:16, but some of you need to read Lamentations 3:16 too, which says: "God has broken my teeth with gravel; He has trampled me in the dust."
- 1 Peter 2:20 says: "But how is it to your credit if you receive a beating for doing wrong and endure it? But if you suffer for doing good and you endure it, this is commendable before God."
- Psalm 119:71 says: "It is good for me that I was afflicted, That I may learn Your statutes."

The Bible says "Surely goodness, Love and Mercy will follow me all the days of my life."

It says "goodness, mercy and love". It does not say "happiness".

The Bible says if you "let steadfastness (which means joyfully persevering through suffering) have its full effect" then you will be "complete, perfect and lacking in nothing."

This doesn't mean you'll have a Ferarri. It means you will "be holy, for Christ is holy". "Holy" means "complete", "set apart" or "whole". It means to be purified (likely by fire). We take our brokenness before God and He makes us whole. It's not about happiness. It's about Holiness.

What then does goodness, mercy and love mean?

- His Love is discipline.
- His Mercy is not killing us for our sins.
- His Goodness is our salvation.

Do not claim on Judgment Day that you didn't know.

The only ones I know who fight me on this, are the ones who refuse to try it. 100% of the people I know who have accepted suffering, as the Bible commands, are happier now than they have ever been. As a matter of fact, in many cases the acceptance of suffering is what brought them back from the brink of suicidal depression, that was caused in the first place by the endless pursuit of unobtainable happiness.

Spending your life pursuing happiness that can only ever be had, but never actually be held, results in a form of emotional learned helplessness that causes you to give up on joy altogether. We call this bitterness or disenfranchisement, or trauma, but it's really just the inevitable result of setting unobtainable expectations in the first place.

The Bible calls this the "fellowship of Christ's sufferings". It says it is granted unto us to suffer with Him. God fellowshipped with Job in allowing him to share in His sufferings. He did the same thing with Hosea and He is doing the same with you.

It's an honor to suffer with God. Misery loves company, and I think this might even be true of God Himself. God is asking you to sit and have a cup of tea with Him as a friend.

Surely if you can consider God your friend, He must consider you His. Christ died for us while we were yet His enemies. But Christ also called us His friends as well.

God is inviting you to the table of Heaven, to sup with Him in sorrow, yet talk about brighter days to come.

God basically told Hosea that He wanted a friend to talk to who understood His pain. It was that he found Hosea righteous that He granted Him suffering. It wasn't because He was punishing Him in this case, albeit He does discipline His children to wake them up from the death of sin.

But it seems God was gifting them the honor of seeing from His eyes for a moment. Perhaps this is why He was so stern with Job. God made Himself vulnerable and found Job righteous enough to handle an extended does of suffering. But Job broke in the end under the weight of it.

For my own walk, I remember a time when God loved me enough to try and have a moment with me, and I cursed Him for His efforts, mistaking the pain as punishment or sadism. The God of all creation found my heart worthy to be his friend and He reached out to me in loneliness, and I told Him to "go fuck" Himself.

God help me. I didn't understand. I am so sorry Father.

This is why with wisdom comes great sorrow and yet wisdom is a gift from God. It is granted unto us to share in the sufferings of God.

If you're willing to sit with Him and share in His pain, as a friend of the almighty, and hear about how His day went, He seems to be willing to share with you a deeper beauty of the things He is doing to make it new and what it will be like when that glorious day finally comes.

For me and my house, we will delight in our sufferings. We will sup with the almighty and offer a shoulder for Him to cry on.

I think God is lonely. I think He made us to be His friends and instead we nailed Him to a tree. He made the hill we crucified Him on. He formed the molecules of the beard that we ripped out of His face. He created the atoms that made up the saliva that we spat upon Him. And how did He respond? He responded in love. Only God could do what Christ has done.

How he could ever forgive us, I don't know. Why He would want to find comfort in the same ones who caused the pain in the first place, I don't understand. But as long as He keeps inviting me to come and hang out, I'm going to go.

I think when the Bible says there will be no more tears in heaven, it's also talking about His. Perhaps He is more excited about eternity with us than we are about eternity with Him. I cannot wait to see You face to face my Father and my Friend.

Be careful wishing for an easy life. You might just get it. But you won't realize until it's too late that God is asking to share His burden with you now, and in exchange, He will share with you eternal bliss when this is over. It's a good deal. Take it.

I have never been happier than when I finally learned to accept suffering.

I, for one, cannot wait to sing in the cosmic choir, the vibrations of which perhaps will paint entire galaxies into existence. We will get to explore those new worlds together, swimming through the new song just sung, sparring across the sky scape of a sunset symphony in perfect bodies of light that never age. And all to the glory of our Father who delights in the holy hubbub of His children playing in the home He built for them. His perfect family finally complete. Jesus at His right hand. No more sin. No more death.

I think the reason He makes us desire sinlessness here and now, but never lets us achieve it, is so we will never fail to appreciate it once we have it. Perhaps this is how in Heaven we can remain sinless, yet still sentient. The only thing more painful than living in sin, is wanting to be holy but not being able to achieve it.

No more tears, everything worth the cost in the end. Guiltless. Shameless. Holy and whole. Free at last. Free indeed. Free for real.

CHAPTER 13

The One You Feed

Take out a piece of paper and write down everything you're feeling right now. Is your wife dishonoring you? Are your kids disrespecting you? Is your boss taking you for granted? Has the world abandoned you and are your friends ignoring you? Go ahead. Get it all out. Really. And when you're done writing down all of your pain... you'll have a list of exactly how God feels about you.

This life is a battle for your soul between your flesh and your spirit. The one that wins is the one you feed. The reason only one can win, is because what you're feeding them... is a piece of the other.

Remember the "memocracy" concept from chapter 7? The little thought government in your head where memes are fighting for political seats in your worldview? And remember how the majority political party gets to effectively control your life? Well the two political parties fighting each other for the meme seats of your worldview are your flesh and your spirit. The one that wins, is the one you elect to the majority of the meme seats. It's a zero sum game, winner takes the seat, which is how you can only feed one or the other.

That's why you can't feed both the flesh and the spirit at the same time. There are a limited number of meme seats in your worldview government and only one party can occupy a seat at any given time. And so you have to give the seat to only one of them, at the expense of the other. Basically, when you feed the spirit, you poison the flesh with righteousness. And when you feed the flesh, you grieve the spirit with the vulgarity of sin.

When you become a Christian, and I have faith that you will, your "walk" with God will start with a slow systematic hostile takeover of your worldview government. This is part of how God fights your battles for you, changes the desires of your heart and begins the process of making you acceptable to Him.

Once the meme seats are freed up, the spirit will occupy all the meme seats of your worldview and the flesh will be dead. This is what it means for Christ to renew your mind. This is what the Rocky field in the Parable of the Sower is all about. This is how you begin to sanctify and this is what it means to die to self and live in the spirit. It's also why people radically change when they stop fighting God.

The food that the spirit eats is a pound of flesh and the drink it drinks is a gallon of blood. Flesh and blood is the currency with which you pay your spirit to grow. Your spirit is a vampire. A carnivore. This is why the Bible says to be a living sacrifice. This is why Adam and Eve were originally vegetarians but then were told to eat meat after the Fall. It's a mirror. Everything on this earth is a mirror of something in Heaven. Not just because "all creation testifies" but because that's what this life and universe is in the first place, a training simulation for our life after this.

Conversely, the food that you feed the flesh when you sin is a piece of your spirit. They are endlessly trying to devour each other, and you're the one holding the knife and fork, dishing out the servings with the daily decisions that make up your life. You're the one electing either the flesh memes or the spirit memes to the meme seats that make up your worldview government.

This is the free will that God has given us and Moses sums it up quite well in Deuteronomy Chapter 30, which says:

"Now what I am commanding you today is not too difficult for you or beyond your reach. It is not up in heaven, so that you have to ask, "Who will ascend into heaven to get it and proclaim it to us so we may obey it?" Nor is it beyond the sea, so that you have to ask, "Who will cross the sea to get it and proclaim it to us so we may obey it?" No, the word is very near you; it is in your mouth and in your heart so you may obey it.

See, I set before you today life and prosperity, death and destruction. For I command you today to love the Lord your God, to walk in obedience to him, and to keep his commands, decrees and laws; then you will live and increase, and the Lord your God will bless you in the land you are entering to possess.

But if your heart turns away and you are not obedient, and if you are drawn away to bow down to other gods and worship them, I declare to you this day that you will certainly be destroyed...

This day I call the heavens and the earth as witnesses against you that I have set before you life and death, blessings and curses. Now choose life, so that you and your children may live and that you may love the Lord your God, listen to his voice, and hold fast to him. For the Lord is your life..."

This is the same choice God gave to Adam and Eve in the Garden of Eden. Eat from the tree of death (the Tree of Knowledge of Good and Evil), or the Tree of Life. It is the same choice He is giving to you. That's your choice. Listen to your conscience, or die in your sin. You cannot feed both of them. You must feed your sinful flesh to your spirit, as it is a sin eater, or you will quench the spirit while feeding your flesh and you will grieve it into turning you over to sin.

This is why Jesus said to eat His flesh and drink His blood. Because He became the sacrifice that is fed to our spirit, in place of our own flesh. Now we feed the spirit with the living Word of God, which is Christ. This is why we take communion and read the Bible as our source of life, love and hope. The Word is literally spiritual food. This seems to also be tied in somehow to the snake of Moses eating (or outer enveloping) the snakes of Pharaoh in the Bible.

Your soul is a child choosing custody between its two warring parents (flesh vs spirit). This is why you feel constantly torn. This is the pull between what your body wants to do and your conscience tells you not to do. Your very existence is a house divided against itself. A marriage between flesh and spirit that is ending endlessly in divorce. This is your metaphysical anatomy: Body, Soul and Spirit, in the image of Son, Father and Holy Ghost, respectively.

The conscience is an anomaly. It is a work of the Holy Spirit, but it seems to be listed as an attribute underneath your soul.

Animals do not have a conscience yet they exist in body and soul.

This seems to indicate that the conscience is part of the spirit since animals don't have a spirit and don't have a conscience. While humans do have a spirit and also have a conscience.

But unsaved humans who exist in body and soul only, but who are yet spiritually dead still do have a conscience as an Easter egg to inch them over into living in Spirit.

And so your conscience is a work of the Spirit but is also available to those who are spiritually dead.

This is because the conscience is the call to the Ark.

When Noah stood on the deck of the arc and yelled out into the wilderness for all to come, The animals who came heard and answered the call. But the sophisticated humans who didn't take it seriously also heard the call. They just didn't answer it.

The salvation call into the wilderness is heard by all. That is the conscience. But only some will answer the call.

The lost hear the call, in that they have a conscience. But only the children of God know the voice of the One who is calling out in the wilderness.

To ignore your conscience is to tell Noah to shut up while he is yelling off the deck of the Ark for you to please listen to him before the rain starts.

To fail to listen to your conscience in this life, is equivalent to failing to heed the call of Noah to the Ark.

The cities who heard Noah's call to come to the Ark, beat their drums and their chests even louder to drown him out. This is the same thing you're doing with your sin life and your conscience. You crank up your rebellion to drown out the voice of God that you just can't get to shut up.

That is what your conscience is and that is why I'm trying to get you to stop muting it.

There is a voice of one calling out into the wilderness, to make straight the way to the ark for you. Please. I beg you. Answer the call.

When I was younger, I used to hear different variations of this phrase:

"The Old Testament, is the New Testament concealed, and The New Testament, is the Old Testament revealed".

Or a variation of that quote: "The Old is in the New Revealed, and the New is in the Old Concealed". But I never really understood what it meant.

What they are saying is that all of the physical events of the Old Testament, like:

- Noah's Ark,
- 3 Men in the Fire, and
- The Angel of Death Passing over the doors marked with blood in Egypt

Are physical mirrors of the same things in the New Testament. It's just that in the New Testament, they aren't physical events, but rather they are invisible spiritual mechanisms:

- Noah's Ark represents salvation. The Ark is an unearned refuge, built by one carpenter, with the help of his family, held together by nails in His hands, to save one blood family, floating above the wrath of God, yet still tossed around by the waves of it.
- 3 Men in the Fire represents the baptism by fire. I personally believe, and this is a controversial statement even to Christians, that God is the "lake of fire", and when He returns, everything burns, except that which has already become fire (which means Christians).
- The Angel of Death Passing over the doors marked with blood in Egypt represents being saved by the grace of God who sent the angel, by the blood of the Lamb smeared on the doorway of your heart (which means Faith in Christ).

The Old Testament is a physical mirror of the spiritual New Testament. In other words, God was gracious enough to give you all the answers you need, in a way that you can visualize, so that you won't have to struggle so much to understand the invisible things of the spiritual world, in the New Testament times you live in now. If you do not read the Old Testament, you cannot understand the New Testament.

This means that we can use the physical Old Testament events to map out the invisible spiritual mechanisms happening right now. That's what the Old Testament is for and why God gave it to us. For example, there is still time to seek the Lord while he may be found. The rain has not started yet. We are still living in the spiritual equivalent of a pre-flood world. Your conscience is Noah still calling out to you from the Ark, before the rain starts. I can tell you what happens next because the Bible already predicted it. You will die.

But in the Old Testament, you have water drowning the world, while in the New Testament, you can swap that out with fire. And so for us, next comes a flood of fire, that God will use to create the new Heavens. Heaven is a spiritual place, and while the physical world is made of water, spiritual places are made of fire. This makes sense scientifically as well, since water was used to renew the physical world, which is made of water. The human body for example is over 60% water. And this earth is covered 71% in water.

The Old Testament flood was water, to kill beings made of water, in a world made of water.

In Heaven, there won't be lakes of water to drown in, there will be lakes of fire to burn in. Your soul is immortal, and so you will be right there with us, just like the drowning sinners where right there with the Ark, in some cases, only a few feet away from them. The difference was that the sheep were inside of the Ark and goats were outside. If God is fire, then the saved will be inside of Him, burning in righteous worship, and the lost will be outside of Him, burning in their iniquities.

Pure water is an insulator of electricity, not a conductor. It's only the impurities floating in the water that allow electricity to play connect-the-dots through the water. The same is true of gold. Pure gold is virtually indestructible. It will not corrode, rust or tarnish, and fire cannot destroy it. This is why all of the gold extracted from the earth is just melted down and recycled over and over again. But Gold with impurities will burn until those iniquities are gone.

This is also why John the Baptist was baptizing believers in water during the life of Christ (which was all Old Testament) but he said Jesus will baptize us in fire and spirit, which is the type of baptism we have now, after the death, burial and resurrection of Christ.

The amazing thing is that the Old Testament writers wrote all of this in stone, not knowing the things of the spirit their writings would be used to describe thousands of years later. Such a symphony could only be orchestrated by God.

In the Old Testament, Moses struck a rock and water came forth to quench the thirst of the Israelites in the desert. In the New Testament, a Roman soldier pierces the side of Jesus with a spear, and His blood pours out. The Bible is saying that in the Old Testament, we were baptized with water, and in the New Testament, with fire. But that fire, is the blood of Christ. Jesus is the "Rock" that is struck, to quench the thirst of the lost. This is why it says to drink His blood. This is what He meant at the well when he told the woman that He would give her living water, and she would thirst no more.

Being covered in the blood of Jesus is how you become baptized in fire. And being baptized in fire is how you come alive in spirit. When God returns, I think we will all burn, even Christians. But while our bodies fade away, our spirits will remain, and become one with God. If you are still spiritually dead at that point, everything you have, and everything you are will burn, with no fire inside of you to survive the fire outside. You will die, your body burnt away, your soul stuck in the lake of fire and no spirit with which to enter our Father's eternal rest.

For example, Jesus tells a story of this in Luke 16:19-31, which says:

"Now there was a rich man dressed in purple and fine linen, who lived each day in joyous splendor. And a beggar named Lazarus lay at his gate, covered with sores and longing to be fed with the crumbs that fell from the rich man's table. Even the dogs came and licked his sores.

One day the beggar died and was carried by the angels to Abraham's side. And the rich man also died and was buried. In Hades, where he was in torment, he looked up and saw Abraham from afar, with Lazarus by his side. So he cried out, 'Father Abraham, have mercy on me and send Lazarus to dip the tip of his finger in water and cool my tongue. For I am in agony in this fire.'

But Abraham answered, 'Child, remember that during your lifetime you received your good things, while Lazarus received bad things. But now he is comforted here, while you are in agony. And besides all this, a great chasm has been fixed between us and you, so that even those who wish cannot cross from here to you, nor can anyone cross from there to us.'

'Then I beg you, father,' he said, 'send Lazarus to my father's house, for I have five brothers. Let him warn them, so that they will not also end up in this place of torment.' But Abraham replied, 'They have Moses and the prophets; let your brothers listen to them.'

'No, father Abraham,' he said, 'but if someone is sent to them from the dead, they will repent.'

Then Abraham said to him, 'If they do not listen to Moses and the prophets, they will not be persuaded even if someone rises from the dead (a clear reference to sinners denying the coming resurrection of Christ).'"

Notice the themes of water and fire and thirst never quenched? Notice that what makes the difference between heaven and hell is listening to the prophets telling you to repent? Notice that they are close enough to talk, and yet there is a chasm between them, just like the drowning ones and the saved, only feet apart, yet separated by the wall of the Ark.

Well in the New Testament, and the New Covenant which it represents, that prophet is your conscience. That will be you some day, in hell, talking to me in Heaven, saying "Please, save me!" And I will say "I gave up my career to write that book, but you didn't listen. What can I do for you now?" And you will say: "At least tell my family so they might be saved!" And I will say "They have their conscience. If they ignore even their conscience, which is the law of God written on their hearts and minds, why would they listen to me? You didn't."

Once the end times kick off, to where no one can deny it anymore. There will be no more access to the ark.

By the grace of God it seems that some might still be saved through the fishing of the saints off the deck. Some will escape damnation by the hook of truth, in the skin of their teeth.

But that is not necessary. The door of the Ark is still open and calling out to you. If you wait until the rain starts, there is no guarantee that you will have a seat waiting for you.

That is the great mystery of it all, that you have to recognize the impending need for the arc before you see the obvious need for the Ark. Your conscience is the "writing on the wall" in the Book of Daniel, chapter 5: "You have been weighed and are found wanted."

Plead mercy from the judge before the executioner is done sharpening his ax. There is still time, but not much. Repent. Turn from your sins and follow Christ. Seek the Lord while He may be found.

This is what the story of Shadrach, Meshach, and Abednego seems to be about. They put their faith in God, thus resembling the image of His statue, rather than the image of King Nebuchenezzar, and as a result, when the fire came, they didn't burn, but the guards who threw them in the furnace did.

The great chasm between us is the wall of the Ark, which is the side of Christ that was pierced for a time to open a door through which to enter. Your conscience was your invitation to the party. The only ones saved are the ones who are in Christ.

Just because we have a moment to speak through the wall of the Ark, while you're drowning outside, do not ask me to help you. I am trying to help you now. Let your blood be on your own head, not my hands, if you refuse to repent here and now. My conscience is clear. I tried my best.

You're never going to find peace until you begin to understand these things. Please brothers and sisters. Let me help you find peace. But know that before you see the light, you must deal with the darkness. Things will get worse before they get better. Luckily. We do not have to walk this journey alone.

When a child is conceived, it is the marriage of the two parents that make the child. But once conceived, the child has attributes of its own. It's own mind. It's own desires. Such is the soul. The soul isn't exactly it's own entity, but rather the result of the marriage between the flesh and the spirit. If the spirit and flesh separate, the soul dies. From the union of the flesh and the spirit, the soul is conceived. The soul can either grow up to choose life or become death, like the mechanism we see outlined in James 1 and 1 Enoch 7.

Everything you think of as your identity and your life (your reason, logic, personality, will, emotion, mind, forethought and consciousness) is your soul. Your soul is you, it is your life force itself. And it must now choose which parent it wants to go live with, for eternity. Do you want your inheritance now, or a little later, but forever? That's the choice, to either be of your Father God, or of your father the Devil. You are either going to carry out the desires of the Devil (memetically becoming like him) or serve your Father God, being sharpened back into His image.

The wisest man to ever live described life as vapor and vanity, as meaningless mirrors of shadows and smoke. King Solomon said that there is no meaning or purpose to the nothingness of life... other than to serve the One who created us. Willingly following God's purposes for us is the path to joy, truth, hope and love. Everything else is smoke.

He is correct, but what does that even mean? What does that look like in our daily lives? How do we live that out and what is the balance between serving God and living in the "real" world, if there is a balance at all? Being cognizant of a trap doesn't automatically exempt you from falling into it. King Solomon may very well be in hell. As the Bible explains, those who fail to endure until the end, were never with us in the first place.

The vastness of King Solomon's wisdom is something Christians and scholars alike rarely grasp. Various sources seem to indicate that he may have been able to play every instrument, speak every language, and even communicate with animals. He amassed the largest wealth of all time and had his choice of any woman he desired.

The apocryphal books tell us that he even understood the depths of how God created the universe (all chemistry, physics, maths, biology, etc). He even mapped out the spiritual world with the Greater and Lesser Keys of Solomon, which Aleister Crowley and other self proclaimed occultists later used to form their heretical theologies and worship the Devil.

By the way, the last words of Aleister Crowley, the self proclaimed "wickedest man in the world" were: "I am perplexed! Satan get out!"

And the last words of Anton LaVey, the founder of the church of Satan, were: "Oh my! Oh my! What have I done!? There's something very wrong! There's something very wrong! There's something very wrong!"

If that isn't the textbook definition of "Fuck around and find out", I don't know what is.

Even the Freemasons come from Solomon. The "masonry" mentioned in their name is referring to the building of King Solomon's temple for the God of Abraham.

I think the whole point God was trying to make with Solomon is that God literally gave him everything. He allowed him to type in the cheat code of life and it ruined the enjoyment of the game. He had more knowledge, wealth and material possessions than anyone will ever have again, and yet this is the man who said it is all meaningless.

His grand take away was that wisdom brings sorrow. I have found the same to be true in my own life, assuming I'm even wise enough to have an opinion on this in the first place. But, what I also found is that sorrow is nothing to be afraid of. Jesus was a man of sorrows and we are called to live the life He Himself lived. God is sorrowful at the events that have been necessary to reach the inevitable outcome of His will. And when we share in those sorrows, we commune with God.

And so I will warn you here and now that the wisdom of this book will not bring you happiness. Quite the contrary, ignorance is bliss. I'm telling you that you will never begin to approach the wealth or wisdom of Solomon, and it brought him nothing but hell. That actually seems to be God's point. If the meaning of life is the pursuit of happiness, you will not find it in riches or knowledge.

The real question then becomes is the meaning of life the pursuit of happiness in the first place? And the answer is no. That's what Solomon is saying. He recognized that no amount of knowledge or wealth was able to bring him happiness, because happiness itself does not actually exist. It's vapor and smoke. That is the point of the Book of Ecclesiastes. Solomon is describing life as a riddle wrapped in a mystery inside an enigma, but what he concludes is that, all things literally considered, the meaning of life is not the pursuit of happiness, but the seeking of righteousness.

CHAPTER 14

The Wages of Sin

All humans want the same 3 things, for the same 3 reasons.

We want to:

1. Love and be loved,

2. Have a place to call our own, and

3. Leave a legacy, be famous or be remembered for something good.

This "Pursuit of Happiness" starter bundle is what you've been peddled as the meaning of life. It is not so. The truth is both much darker, and yet more hopeful, than you have ever imagined.

The reason why all humans want these 3 things, is because we had them once, lost them and now want them back. We lost all 3 of them at the same time in the Curse of Genesis 3:

- We lost our relationship with our Father (The Source of Love),

- We were kicked out of our home (The Garden of Eden), and

- Death entered the world as the wages of our sin (The Fall).

As a result, the 3 most traumatic events all humans experience across the earth today are: Death, Divorce & Homelessness. Now you spend your days seeking:

- Life as a fix for Death,

- Love as a fix for Divorce, and

- Security as a fix for Homelessness.

This is why Jesus had to die (death), be forsaken (divorce) and had no place to lay His head (homelessness). He died that you might live, was forsaken so you could be loved and gave up His home so one could be prepared for you. But you reject His sacrifice and instead try to fix these things yourself. How's that going by the way? If it's anything like my journey was, it's not going very well.

The accompanying emotions for these events are: Grief (from Death), Abandonment (from Divorce) & Displacement (from Homelessness):

- Grief: The reason death is so hard for us is because we were designed as eternal beings. We don't know how to process death because we were never meant to experience it in the first place. That's why it feels like someone is handing you a bowling ball you don't know what to do with. You can't eat it because your body was never designed to digest it, it won't fit in your pocket and there's no place to put it down. And so it just weighs on you over the years, until you realize there is only one place you can put it, at the foot of the Cross.

- Abandonment: You are searching for love in all the wrong places. You're putting the weight of these 3 traumas on the shoulders of your lovers and they are doing the same to you. You cannot take a soul trauma, 6000 years in the making and hand that to another human you met on Tinder, like: "Here, hold this." No one can bear that weight except for Christ.

- Displacement: Your desire for money, shelter and security is to avoid homelessness, which is an uprooting from your home, family, friends, comfort zone or way of life. It can also be forced displacement from your home as a refugee. The reason moving is so hard is not because you aren't strong enough to duct tape a few boxes and call a moving truck. It's because it is triggering your inherited soul trauma of getting kicked out of the Garden of Eden. You are tapping into the ancestral pain of Adam and Eve, which is how you know you're related to them, because trauma travels through DNA.

People love hearing insights into their own mentality. For example, if I told you that the reason you over-explain yourself as an adult is because you felt under-heard as a child, you would feel like this is some kind of psychological mic drop.

Or that the reason you love long hot showers, is because you're compensating for the lack of love and warmth in your emotional life.

I find that most people like these ideas when they hear them. But they have a harder time accepting the 3 ancestral soul traumas, even though it is the same idea.

This is because the first two examples victimize you. They infer that the pain you feel is actually someone else's fault, not your own (sound familiar?). They play off the "I'm a good person" mechanism, and so those memes go right in. They ring the "I'm a good person" bell and so you accept them as fact right away.

Whereas the 3 traumas lead down the opposite road of "you screwed everything up with your sin. It's not Dad's fault. It's yours. You need to apologize (repent). And so that meme is rejected. The things you choose to accept or reject are always about protecting your sin life.

Think about how great of a deal it is that God has put on the table. Think about how absolutely generous, loving and merciful He is. We screwed up everything. Like... we literally damned all of humanity and ruined the entire world and existence... and God is all: "It's cool, just say you're sorry and I'll fix it". And our response is "Screw you Dad! It was just an apple!" What in the absolute hell are we thinking!? Stop pouting like a rebellious teenager and take the deal! Say your sorry. Get back everything that was lost.

Adam's apple was not a one time deal. It was just the first hit of apple crack the Devil gave us for free to get us hooked. Now we are all addicted to knowledge as a result. King Solomon literally went all the way down the knowledge road, and now on your way down that same path, you see him walking back saying, "Go back! It's a trap". And you're all, "Nah bruh, I wanna see for myself." Your intellect will never be able to save you, but it may very well drag you down to hell. You are never going to pack enough facts into your empty soul to fill that God shaped void. Truly I tell you, unless you change and become like little children, you will never enter the kingdom of Heaven.

The existence of these 3 traumas across all of humanity is perhaps the greatest observable evidence that the Bible's narrative is true and accurate. But there are many more examples you can observe (and more importantly, cannot deny) in your very own life right now. Here are 3 more examples, just to name a few:

1. The 10 Commandments written on your heart and mind (which is your conscience),
2. Your shame of nakedness before man but not animals, and

3. Your need to designate an idol of worship in your life.

As a matter of fact, all creation testifies if you would just look close enough. This evidence is observable, measurable, consistent, valid and reliable. Why do you think every Psychiatrist on earth traces the root of your trauma back to "tell me about your Father"? Why do you think at the core of every broken person you will find "Daddy issues" related to death, abandonment and a lack of security?

You want signs and wonders? Look at your hands. Look at the trees. Look at the sky. Listen to a symphony. Watch a deer walking through the forrest. How did any of this happen by itself? Are you really stupid enough to believe that all of this created itself on accident from nothing? Everything around us, including each other, our signs and wonders. The fact that you have gotten used to them, does not change that.

There is no need to have blind faith. Look around you. Look inside of you. The evidence of God is literally everywhere. If you are a doubting Thomas, you can just look at the holes in Jesus' hands for yourself, to your heart's content.

I will caution you though. The more you water down your faith with your need for another crack apple knowledge fix, it seems the less status and reward you will have in Heaven. Examine the evidence to the extent you need to in order to believe, and then move along. Once you are convinced of these things, put your hands to the plow and do not look back.

These 3 traumas culminate into the identity crisis ruining your life today:

1. Death: You don't know what to do with your life.
2. Divorce: You don't feel worthy of being loved.
3. Homelessness: You don't know where you belong.

The reason you feel left for dead, abandoned and homeless... is because you are, spiritually speaking. You say you want to get in touch with your emotions and "know thyself"? Then why have you been ignoring these emotions your entire life?

The reason you block them out, is because all of this is your fault and it's painful dwelling on a self inflicted injury. It's the spiritual version of repressing memories too painful to face. It's learned helplessness. And so you opt instead to:

1. Jump the fence of salvation by hijacking the mechanisms of God, just with Him stripped out. Like Alcoholics Anonymous recognizing submission as the means to overcome addiction, yet allowing you to designate a literal light bulb as your "higher power" if you want.

2. Numb the pain through drugs, escapism and entertainment.
3. Insulate yourself in the echo chamber economy of the likeminded lost, virtue flirting to earn some "I'm a good person" points to pay your conscience to shut up so you can go sin in peace for a while.

When I tell people they are just paying their conscience in "I'm a good person" points to shut up for a while so they can go sin in peace, and it sinks in what I just said, they always laugh out loud. But it's not a "that's ridiculous" laugh. It's a "That's true but I've never actually heard it articulated before" laugh.

I actually even had one Atheist girl I was talking to at a bar finish the sentence for me. After about 2 hours of enthralling conversation, I guided it towards the Bible and when I got to the part of: "And then I realized I was just paying my conscience in 'I'm a good person' points to shut up for a while so I could..." and she said "go sin in peace". She knew it was true. And yet when I told her I was celibate, wouldn't be hooking up with her and was just trying to tell her about Christ, she lost interest, paid her tab and left.

Don't tell me people don't know. Everyone knows. You already know. Stop lying to yourself. You can fool yourself, but your excuses are not going to fool God on Judgement Day.

The Devil offers you counterfeit keys to open the same doors and get through life without God. For example, rather than Adam and Eve obtaining knowledge gradually through fear of the Lord, in God's perfect timing, they took knowledge immediately by eating the apple. The apple was a counterfeit key to get through a door.

Here are a few of the modern day apples you are choosing to eat as well:
1. Beat Death by being remembered as a "good person".
2. Get Love through promiscuous sex, alleviated consequences through abortion, $99 divorces and endless throwaway relationships.
3. Obtain Security through money, fitness, status, hustle culture and self help.

But these counterfeit keys damage the doors and get stuck in the lock so the real key will never fit again, until and unless the house is one day deconstructed and rebuilt by the Master builder. While you're busy getting through the doors of life on your own strength, the house itself is being destroyed.

This is why you are the way you are and your life looks the way it does. You are trying to fix the 3 traumas on your own, because "Screw You Dad! It was just an Apple!" You don't want His help because you'd have to apologize to get it and the crack rock of sin is a better high than humble pie.

The sad part is, somewhere deep down, you already know all of this is true. But you're angry at Dad, and so this comes across as an older brother lecturing a rebellious runaway from the warmth of my room in our Father's house. It's easy for me to say, right?

But you don't know what happened to me while you were gone. You never saw the broken years I spent in hell too. I'm not speaking of things I do not understand. I'm telling you that I know exactly how hopeless things have become for you and there is hope nonetheless.

That's why this triggers you so much, because I took Dad's side over yours and you're reading this letter cold and alone in a gutter of your own choosing. And so rather than humble yourself and come home to a big hug and a warm meal, you'll opt instead, as you always do, to plunge yourself even further into chaos, because you know it hurts me and Dad to watch you slowly die.

And that rebellion is why you've sided with our Father's enemies to hurt Him. Have you not noticed yet that the 3 enemies line up with the 3 traumas?

1. The World is offering you false security,
2. The Flesh is offering you addiction to chemical love, and
3. The Devil is offering you the lie of legacy as a consolation prize for eternal life.

But if you would just humble yourself and repent, our Father offers you the perfect restoration of what was lost:

1. Eternal Life as an eternal fix for death,
2. Boundless Love as an eternal fix for divorce, and
3. Assurance of Salvation as an eternal fix for displacement.

God already said He is going to kill death, that there is a wedding feast coming and that He is preparing a home for us. That is the solution.

- You want love because you are afraid of divorce,
- You want a home because you are afraid of homelessness, and
- You want legacy because it's a cheap consolation prize for eternal life.

The reason the "Pursuit of Happiness" is so toxic, is because it's all based in fear. But the perfect love of God casts out all fear. That is the actual solution and it results in peace and joy that surpasses all understanding.

But you don't want our Father's eternal solutions to these problems because if you accept the 3 defense mechanisms of love, home and legacy, to quench the 3 traumas of death divorce and displacement, there is no delayed gratification required. But if you accept God's eternal solutions, you have to:

1. Give up control,

2. Wait on His promises, and

3. Repent from your sins.

You don't want to pay that price and so you opt to remain willfully blind instead.

Dad is trying to get this message across to you if you would only listen for a moment:

1. What Father wants you to understand about Death, is this: I have painted you as My masterpiece and I desire to bring you into the real world to live with Me eternally. To do this, I have to peel your paint off the canvas of this world and this is going to be an uncomfortable process. I need you to be on the canvas, but not fused into the canvas. This is not for my sake, but because if you refuse to leave the canvas, you will be destroyed in the peeling process. If you cling to your life in My painting, how can I ever separate you from it? I need you to accept the pain of peeling and delight in it because you recognize it as My great love for you, that I would take the effort to do it in the first place. If you opt to stay on the canvas, you will burn along with it.

2. What Father wants you to understand about Love, is this: Stop searching for validation in the world. Another human is never going to replace Me as your source of salvation. The only reason you can love in the first place is because I first loved you. Return to Me. Learn what it means to truly be loved again and not just lust after sin.

3. What Father wants you to understand about Security, is this: Understand that you are saved by My Grace through Faith in Christ, who knows your pain because He went out before you, as is detailed in His letters to you. You do not have to earn My love. You are My child and I adore you. It is a free gift, and as such, it is backed by My promise, and therefore My Glory. I will never leave you or forsake you. Your Brother's love for you is

an overflow of His love for Me. It is in service to Me and our Family name that He searches for you day and night. Stop avoiding Him. Follow Him home. He is sent by Me. My Glory and My Love are eternal. These things will never change, nor falter. In this rests your assurance of salvation and your unearned inheritance to a new home I am preparing for you. Stop crying about being homeless. You are homeless by choice. It's time to grow up at long last. Wipe up your tears, pick up your mat and follow your Brother home.

These 3 things are what He sent me to tell you.

The Devil tries to keep you from our Father's rest by rubbing salt in the wounds of each trauma:

1. Love: The Devil has switched the definition of selfless love to selfish lust.
2. Security: The Devil wants to destroy the nuclear family structure by reversing God's original gender leadership roles.
3. Death: The Devil wants to convince you that you're a "good" person and will be remembered as such.

The Devil would have you believe that eating the apple wasn't that big of a deal. Dad overreacted. It was just a little "slip". God will realize His mistake and apologize to you in time, if you are only patient enough to wait (meanwhile the clock of your life is ticking away). That way you get to eat the apple and still have it too. But you know this is a lie. Sin is not about an apple. It's a broken covenant with our Father. He will never apologize, because He was never wrong in the first place.

I would argue that all 10 Commandments were broken in the fall of man, if you look closely enough. But the point I would like to focus on is what was gained from eating from the Tree of Knowledge of Good and Evil. If eternal life is what is gained from the Tree of Life, then some sort of eternal knowledge (or "knowing") is gained from the Tree of Knowledge of Good and Evil. "Knowing" in the Bible usually also refers to a man "knowing" his wife, or sex. Ergo, the broken marriage covenant with God.

But Adam and Eve knew it was wrong to eat from the tree, before eating from it. So what knowledge was gained thereafter? I believe it was a deeper knowledge of God's view on Good and Evil, which is where the shame and guilt that they experienced thereafter came from. They realized a larger extent of what they had done. And with this new knowledge, humankind gained the ability to redefine the definitions of Good and Evil for themselves. And so we did.

We made up our own definitions of what it means to be good, in our own eyes. These new definitions created new and subjective standards of goodness, and we now use those new standards today to hold ourselves up against in comparison.

As such, we achieve self righteousness and convince ourselves we are "good" people in our own eyes. When I, as a Christian, evangelize the lost, I am really just saying, "Hmmm... interesting. I see you pass your own test and satisfy your own definition of goodness quite well, but how does your life stack up against God's actual standard, which is what you will actually be judged by on Judgement Day?" And as such, I am hated for shattering their illusion.

Consider these things and repent when you are convinced. I needn't remind you we are in the 11th hour.

The Devil trades you:

- Lust for Love,
- Happiness for Inheritance, and
- Legacy for Life.

God trades you:

- White robes for Grave Clothes,
- Salvation for sin, and
- Beauty for Ashes.

It's a better deal. Choose life.

CHAPTER 15

Identity Dissonance

Your identity is not about who you are. It is about whose you are. It is your relationship to God that defines your identity. Anything else just leads to an elaborate identity crisis.

Your true identity is the absence of yourself and the fullness of God in that emptiness. You are a cracked and broken vessel. But you have a glorious light inside of you that shines through all of your brokenness to light the path for others, that they may see your light and follow you back Home. You don't have to fix yourself because God is going to use these broken things.

One of my favorite mirrors of God is that we have a giant fire ball in the sky, called "the sun", which is the "light of the world", without which we would die. And it shines its light off a dead rock (the moon), in order to radiate it's light into the darkness of a lost and dying world. Likewise, the Christian, dead in of itself, is made useful in that it reflects the light of the world, from "The Son", into the darkness, thus bringing light to all men.

This is how He is strong in our weakness. The more broken you are, the more His light will shine through your cracks. God doesn't shop at IKEA, He appreciates vintage antiques with a bit of character to them. He is not intimidated by the work He will have to put in to fix them, because that's what He does for a living. He fixes broken things.

This is what John meant when he called himself "the one that Jesus loved".

He defined his identity in relationship to Christ alone. Sort of an ancient version of "the artist formally known as Prince". But "the disciple formerly known as John". He was saying that his identity is actually the emptiness of his vessel and the presence of God filling it. It is not just "less of me and more of You". It's "all of You and none of me". It's "erase and replace me". This is what it means to die to self and if you refuse to do it, you will struggle with identity until the day you die, which actually is just the beginning of your problems, come to think of it.

King Nebuchadnezzar created a statue of himself, in his own image, for his own glory. So did God. And you are that statue. That image was tarnished by sin. Getting polished back to that original image is your identity. But there is an identity dissonance between where we are now and what we need to again become. Resembling the image of Christ is the goal.

Your metaphysical anatomy is 3 fold: Body, Soul and Spirit. Made in the image of God: Father, Son & Holy Ghost. And likewise, your identity is also 3 fold:

1. Community: We are all beloved sons and daughters of God. And there is solace in us all sharing this common thread. Do not go the road alone. Fellowship constantly with other true believers, confess your sins one to another, seek a multitude of council and do not forsake the gathering of the Saints.

2. Individualism: We are each fearfully and wonderfully made. And there is love in the fact that God felt us worthy enough to make us unique. Individual does not mean independent. We are designed specifically to be dependent on God and accountable to the church of all true believers. Be cautious of anything that tells you to increase your self love. You are not your own "nearest neighbor". Depression is not the absence of self love, it's the over abundance of it. Deny yourself. Take up your cross and follow Christ. Don't think less of yourself, but do think of yourself less.

3. Communion: Go ahead, take a swing at God. You can't. Where would you even start if you wanted to try? How could something so insignificant as a human being inflict damage on the Creator of the universe? And yet, we can and we do. There is no greater example of vulnerability, intimacy and love than this, that... GOD... as in the God of all creation (really let that sink in), loves you enough to be broken hearted about His separation

from you. What greater validation of worth, love and value would anyone ever need other than that? God cares so much about us that our sin grieves Him. And when you suffer, God grieves with you. The fact that a completely invulnerable God, would become so vulnerable as to allow us to inflict emotional wounds upon Him, shows the extent of His great love for us. And the fact that He finds you worthy of that love, means that you are in fact worthy to be loved by the only One whose love really matters. This is why self love is such an insidious fallacy. God is the source of love. There is no such thing as self love. A cup can't fill itself. The water that fills the cup came from the well. And the love of God is so perfect, that when it fills you, there is absolutely no room left for anything else. Your cup is already overflowing.

That is your identity. And nothing can change that. No power of hell, no scheme of man. You are His and He is yours. That is the rock on which we need to build our lives. I am not a "doctor" or an "MBA" or a "soldier". Those are all false identities. They can be taken away. They can pull my license, discredit my credentials and cut off my legs so I can't fight anymore. All of these things are vapor. They can be ripped away in an instant, causing an identity crisis as a result.

But if my identity is that I am "a son of God"... good luck trying to take that away. You can literally kill me and it just means I'm going to see Him sooner. It's the rock on which we stand. And that is your rock solid identity. A house built on any other foundation will sink into the sand.

Even if it was all a lie, we are just evolved apes and God isn't real... being a Christian still results in more hope, meaning, purpose, love, stability, identity and joy than being an Atheist. Christianity is, hilariously, a more "Evolutionarily Stable Strategy" than being an Atheist. Perhaps another one of God's cosmic Dad jokes. Being a Christian is still the best use of an Atheist's life.

The doorway to realizing your identity is repentance. Let's take a controversial, relevant and highly offensive topic as an example: Homosexuality.

Here's what the church should explain to homosexuals but doesn't know how to articulate.

Homosexuality is an identity crisis that replaces your true identity as a son or daughter of God with the sin in question. This is why homosexuals often struggle with identity above and beyond all other issues. But there is actually nothing inherently unique about this brand of sin from any other.

There are some strong Biblical arguments that homosexuality is in fact a unique sin. For example, it's the only sin that God reigned fire down on people for doing in Sodom and Gomorrah. I do believe it is somehow uniquely heinous to God. But I do also believe pretty much all sexual sin falls into that category. Either way, any sin that becomes your identity is going to cause an identity crisis.

The reason you're depressed is because depression itself is just the inevitable result of the endless pursuit of unobtainable happiness.

You are pursuing happiness rather than seeking righteousness and the seeking of righteousness (which is justification, sanctification and glorification) is a prerequisite to living the Christian life. This is why church is incompatible with accepting a lifestyle of sin, whatever that sin may be. Because the definition of being a Christian is literally refusing to accept a life of sin.

You are not a homosexual. That is a false identity. You are a son or daughter of God that struggles with lust (no different than my own struggle with porn and lust). And the refusal to lay down that sin blocks you from realizing your true identity, because repentance is the door that leads to the path of inevitable identity stability.

If you never open the door of repentance, you haven't even started the journey yet. Your conscience (which means "with knowledge [of sin]") is the law of God written on your heart and mind. To accept homosexuality, or any other sin, as your identity is to effectively attempt to mute the conscience (aka, reject the law of God).

That's why you feel constantly persecuted even in a world where no one cares anymore. The world is actually celebrating your sin alongside you now. So why do you still feel persecuted? It's because the voice of persecution was never coming from the world. It's been coming from inside you this whole time (your conscience). It's literally your loving Father telling you to stop and come back home to Him.

I know this is hard to hear, but who are your friends really? The ones fueling your identity crisis to protect their own sin life, while celebrating a lifestyle that is ripping you apart on the inside... or the ones who love you enough to tell you the hard truth?

You must have noticed the intent behind these people who claim to support you, right? Can't you see that you are the tank they are standing behind in a fruitless war to bulldoze their way through their conscience? You're just leading the charge for them. You are their useful idiot.

We have used our knowledge of good and evil (that we gained in the Garden of Eden), to change the meaning of words, in order to make sin appear to be less heinous than it actually is. But when we realign the terms with their vulgar definitions, it's clear to see why God is so angry about it. He never changed His definition when we changed ours.

Have you noticed my occasional use of unnecessary vulgarity in this book? Have you enjoyed it, because it makes me more relatable by justifying the fact that you like to swear too? Or do you despise it because you don't see why a Christian man would see fit to be needlessly profane?

But is it actually needless in the first place? What utility does vulgarity serve in a Christian book? Allow me to explain, but know that this is going to upset everyone even further, and for very different reasons.

When we describe sin in fluffy terms, it becomes hard to see why it's so bad. But vulgar words offer us a means through which we can describe vulgar actions. For example, and this is the example that got me fired from the Nashville Rescue Mission, by the way:

If we define "homosexuality" as "two people loving each other", it's hard to see why that's a problem. But if we define it rightly as "a man fucking another man up the ass and cumming into his feces", it doesn't quite have the same ring to it.

The truth is, no matter who you are, even just hearing a glimpse of the reality of sin, is disgusting. I've even had gay friends tell me that's disgusting, and they are the ones doing it. If you can't even hear it, imagine what God is thinking watching His own children do it, then downplay it.

Despite offending those with a religiously dogmatic background, or those who wish to weaken the description of sin in order to preserve it, it is appropriate to describe vulgar actions in vulgar terms. To fail to do so restricts you to a subset of the language, in which you are rendered unable to describe atrocious acts with accuracy. It's a meme manipulation attack and it works because sin grows in darkness. To redefine sin in lesser terms, is to reeducate the populous which uses those terms.

When Christians accept and embrace secular reeducation, sin is effectively camouflaged in our society. Since God will only be mocked for so long, we are not doing anyone any favors by going along with it. We will all answer to God, here and on Judgement Day, for even every idle word, let alone a lifetime of celebrating sin alongside a perverse, wicked and Godless generation.

If you are only permitted to use words that your captors have allowed, you become a slave confined to their brand of Creole. It's like: "You may retaliate against us in any way you like, as long as your actions and words are from the list of approved actions and words we have given you".

In Ezekiel 23:20, God Himself describes sin as the Old English equivalent of "horse cum" and "donkey dick". But when I say "shit", all hell breaks loose. This is not a well thought out outrage on the Christian's part and it's definitely not spiritually discerned.

If it was, you would be equally as outraged at the use of "God damn" in a secular movie, or "holy crap" by a kid at church. "Holy crap" is the lesser version of "Holy shit", which is just "Holy Spirit", with "Spirit" changed to "shit". I think we can all agree that this is a more intimate insult to God than even simply saying "God damn". So why are we ok with one, but not the other? If your outrage was spiritually discerned, you would be triggered more so by that, than by this.

"Fuck" isn't even in the Bible. Why are we so offended by it? Its etymology is only 400 years old. What if I made a new word called "Wubba-Lubba-Dub-Dub" and in a hundred years it becomes offensive in society? Will Christians now have to repent for saying it, simply because society has now dubbed it offensive? Christians need to think deeper about these things and stop simply accepting society's altered definitions of good and evil as fact.

Now don't get me wrong. I myself have been convicted of vulgarity since writing this book and look forward to a more wholesome life hereafter. I get it. But we should be outraged by the taking of God's name in vain in more than just words. If God is our very breath, then taking His Name in vain could be as simple as taking a single breath for granted. I don't think we should have a free pass to swear, I think we should expand our understanding of this life and live each moment in ways that better align with the reason God put us here in the first place.

The reason I get in trouble in the Christian community for this is because of a misunderstanding of motives. I'm not technically a "Christian" like you are. Rather, I am a truth seeker, and it just so happens that Jesus is telling the truth. We believe the same things, but through an entirely different path and mechanism. My goal is not to blindly further the Gospel. I only wish I had such simple faith, and may God grant it to me going forward. But my goal thus far has been to seek truth wherever it goes, and then spread it along the way... which means to spread the Gospel, but only because it's actual truth.

If the world is pushing hard to soften the definitions of these words into something less offensive and more palatable, then shouldn't Christians be clarifying in the opposite direction? When the lost call themselves "good" people, they are doing so by utilizing a weakened standard of goodness, based on their own set of moral law, that is propped up by the altered definitions of words they have twisted the meaning of.

If we clarify the correct definitions of these terms, it weakens the foundation of the false standards they are using to justify their own false self righteousness. It's uncomfortable sure, but some might be saved.

We see this same type of scenario in medicine as well. Often times a patient is in denial about the severity of their condition. As doctors, it's part of our job to communicate a harsh reality to them, despite it being uncomfortable. The uncomfortable truth is that they might need to get cut up in a bloody surgery, in order to save their very lives.

Likewise, if we can lovingly destabilize their delusion, we might be able to spend eternity with them. Just beneath the mask of "I'm a good person" rests the reality of "God can never forgive me for what I've done". I've seen it a thousand times. I've watched hardened atheists, who profess their own goodness, crumble into a puddle of tears in a matter of minutes.

The shift did not come from anything I said. It is merely the fruition of the Holy Spirit moving in their hearts all the years of their life. It's not a new realization they gain in their intellect, it's that they have lost their ability to continually fight the work God is already doing in them.

It's the point of surrender. It's the moment at which God strips them of their final justification, which they have been using to fight Him all this time. They are not saved because they start doing something new. They merely stop resisting Him and accept what they already knew to be true all along.

And so you collect "I'm a good person" points to pay your conscience to leave you alone so you can sin in relative peace. It's like you're slicing off slivers of your spirit as a currency with which to rent sin time from the Devil. Fighting God constantly is exhausting, which is why you feel constantly exhausted.

You have to stop using your conscience as a sin vending machine, that you pay in "I'm a good person" points to vend pre-paid sin cards from. That was never the purpose of it. And you are really pissing God off by using it that way.

Again I tell you, your identity is not about "who you are", it's about "whose you are". It always has been. To find your identity, you need to go down the Path of the Prodigal (which is Death, Burial, Resurrection) by sincerely asking 3 questions and realizing the inevitable answers:

1. Death of Self: You reach the point of, "God can never forgive me for what I've done." And then you'll get the answer: "He already has". This is represented by the Prodigal son dropping his pride and eating with the pigs in desperation.

2. Burial: Then ask, "Why would God forgive me"? And you accept the answer: "Because He loves you". This is represented by the Prodigal son realizing that even his Fathers servants have it better than eating with pigs, and developing a willingness to give up the old life and serve.

3. Resurrection: And then finally you ask, "Why does God love me so much?" And you come to that final answer: "Because He is your Father and you are His child". This is represented by the Prodigal son returning humbly home, being embraced by his loving Father and receiving his unearned inheritance.

And then you realize your identity. As a son or daughter of God... who struggles with sin (lust in this case) like the rest of us... and the Devil loses another one. You have now exited the matrix. Welcome to the real world.

If you never repent of homosexuality (as nothing more than a sin addiction to lust, rather than your faux-identity), how can you even get to the first step? And that is why you feel judged at church.

You are trying to eat your sin and have it too. You are screaming "I just want to follow Jesus! Why won't they just love me and let me live?! I was born like this!" And the answer is because we were all born like "this". "This" meaning predisposed to sin. It's just that your particular sin happens to be public. Being born a sinner is no excuse.

Although, I am highly empathetic to the particular struggle of my gay friends and family. As someone who struggles with lust myself, I have not yet managed to beat it even in my own life. This is not about me judging you. I do not judge you. I love you. It is for you to judge yourself based on your conscience, as we all must. The Bible calls this "working out your own salvation in fear and trembling".

You want so badly to be on the path of pushing sin from your life (which is part of what it means to be a Christian), as long as you can take your little sin backpack with you for the journey.

But here's the hard truth my friend. Your sin baggage just won't fit through the church door. It's not about the sin. Everyone in the church is a sinner too. It's your acceptance of sin that is the problem. It's your insistence on bringing sin with you on the journey to purge sin from your life. There is nothing wrong with gay people. We are all sinners.

But the way salvation seems to work, it will be better to face Judgement Day as an active gay person who is trying unsuccessfully to resist, than it will be for the straight professing Christian, who supported the gay cause and justified sin in their heart.

It would be better for you on Judgement Day if you literally died getting fucked up the ass... to death, while repenting of it, than it would be if you were a church Christian saying there's nothing wrong with it, or a Christian rightly condemning homosexuality, while ignoring your own rampant and unrepentant pride.

You are no better than the worst of them. All have fallen short of the glory of God and if you say you're without sin, you're self deceived and there is no truth in you. If not, what is the need for Christ in the first place? There is no condemnation for those who are in Christ Jesus and the love of God covers a multitude of sin.

I'm not telling you anything you don't already know. No one is judging you for being a sinner (except your own conscience). The church is just trying to tell you that you have to be willing to lay everything down at the foot of the cross. And that means everything.

That is what you must do to find your true identity: Repent and follow Christ.

CHAPTER 16

Men Worth Marrying

If you take two sheep and lead them to an altar with a priest, before God... what's about to happen? Everyone knows they are about to be slaughtered as a sacrifice. Now toss a dress and a tuxedo on them and invite some friends with a cake and music... now what's about to happen? That's right. The same thing. Marriage is murder and a wedding is just a spiced up funeral.

The reason you become "one flesh" is because you're both cut up into pieces, thrown into a single pile of mingled meat and lit on fire as a pleasing aroma to God. And as the smoke rises, there is no longer any distinction between what used to be two separate individuals. The only difference is that the man is required to spontaneously combust right then and there, as an example to his wife of how she should gradually smolder for the rest of their lives.

Congratulations! I now pronounce you husband and wife. May you live righteously ever after.

Marriage is death to self and if you're excited about it... you don't understand what is about to happen.

You're the over excited puppy who thinks he's going to the park, but you're really going to the vet to get snipped and put to sleep. This is a real problem because it cheapens the sacrifice if it's not a willing death. The Bible says Christ went to the cross with foreknowledge and that distinction matters.

If you're unaware of what's about to happen, you're motive in marriage is actually lust (which is "happily ever after"), rather than love (which is "til death do us part").

You can think of lust as: "For better, for richer and in health." And you can think of Love as: "For worse, for poorer and in sickness."

The Bible says "Greater love hath no man than this, that he would lay down his life for his friends." It says that a man should love his wife the way that Christ loves the church (unto death).

The Bible says a woman should pick a man who is a mature Christian (which the Bible describes as a "Daniel man"). And a man should pick a submissive woman (which the Bible calls a "daughter of Sarah"). Instead men are picking the hottest chick they can find and women are picking the richest man they can find. And we wonder why things are falling apart and so absolutely miserable.

Marriage has 3 purposes:

1. Procreation,
2. Illustration, and
3. Sanctification.

Men, you shouldn't be looking at your wife thinking: "Mmmm... girl, I'ma tear dat ass UP!" If you understood the real meaning of marriage, you should be looking at her like: "Mmmm... girl, I'ma sharpen you so hard into the image of Christ!" That's what marriage is, two people sharpening each other into the image of Christ, until death do us part. The love you have for each other is what keeps you together, and from killing each other in the process. It doesn't have a whole lot to do with "happiness". The reason you are disappointed by hearing this is because you had false expectations going into it in the first place.

Jesus' walk to the cross was the groom walking to the altar. That's why we call it our "walk" with Christ, despite Paul later referring to the Christians journey as a 'race'. Jesus wasn't just crucified on a cross, He had to carry His own death mechanism to the place He would be hung upon it. If you are complaining about carrying the burdens of this life, you're really not going to like what happens when you finally get to the destination (which, of course, is Judgement Day).

His path to the cross was the wedding march to marry His bride (the church). If you remember, He wasn't particularly excited about it. I believe His exact words were "please take this cup from me". Jesus loves you as the Father first loved Him, but no one is excited about an arranged marriage to a cheating whore, not even God. He surely got the short end of the stick in His marriage to us.

Think about the trade off. Jesus is God. The perfect Prince and heir to everything. And yet we walk into the wedding, covered in the filth of fornication with other spirits. We have nothing to offer Him except a feeble, yet sincere: "I'm so sorry I didn't take better care of myself and my life before this moment. I wish I had something more I could offer you."

By the church marrying Christ, we become shared heirs to everything. We have everything to gain and nothing to lose. Truly that is "Good News". Truly that is the best deal ever offered. And what's crazy about it is that the majority of the world won't even accept the offer, because they are too proud to say they're sorry to God in the first place.

Salvation follows the "death, burial, resurrection", or the "justification, sanctification, glorification", theme:

1. Death: You get married at an altar, because animals are slain there. That's why you give your vows (which are your last words) before the final act. The breaking of bread is actually your last supper. That's why a man leaves his mother and father and becomes one flesh with his wife. They lose their son because he dies that day, once and for all. Your wife is legitimized by your marriage, as a mirror of the church being justified by the death of Christ.

2. Burial: During His burial in the tomb, the Bible says Christ descended to hell. And so will you in marriage. Ask... literally anyone. It sucks. But if you're going through hell, keep going, because through this suffering the old you is truly put away, dead and buried. This is the process of glorification.

3. Resurrection: Ask any successful couple who endured until the end. They will say: "After the honeymoon phase wore off, it was really hard for a time. But we both learned to compromise and things got better". What they are really saying is: "We died that day, were buried in hell for a time... and learned to submit (which they call "compromise") and the suffering ended up leading to perseverance, character building and hope... and inevitably joy." It didn't get easier, they got stronger by persevering through the suffering, after being crushed under the weight of it. This is

the part of marriage that is a mirror of resurrection and new life.

This is why feminism is so toxic. The goal of feminism is literally to "take down the 'Patriarchy'". If you didn't know this already... Patriarch means "Father". Their stated goal is literally to overthrow God, hidden right in plain sight. Men are just collateral damage in their war against Him. Feminist hate men, because in marriage, men represent a mirror of Christ and they actually hate the "sky bully" telling them to turn from their sin. They are trying to smash that mirror because they want to see themselves in it, not God.

But marriage is a mirror of God and there is no way around it.

The reason a man leaves his home, goes out into the world to earn a wage, endures that pain, and pays the debt of his family, is because...

Christ left heaven, came to earth, died for our sins and paid our debts for us. This is why the man is the mirror of Christ in a traditional marriage. The stronger vessel.

The reason the woman stays home, cleans, takes care of the kids, cooks and waits for the husband to return, is because...

We are told to endure this life, keep our temple clean, tend the sheep, prepare a wedding feast and wait at the gate for the master to return. This is why a woman is the mirror of the church in the marriage. The weaker vessel.

This is part of what it means to "be about your Father's work". It's just a different role for the stronger verses the weaker vessel.

We all know there is something beautiful about a man returning home and his children running up to lovingly embrace him, but we can't quite pin down why it feels so divine.

It's because we know somewhere deep down inside of us that we are the children of God and our Father is coming home to hold us too.

Men, when you go to work, you are sharing in the sufferings of Christ.

Women, when you make your husband breakfast, it's symbolic of serving Christ His last supper. And when you make him dinner, it's symbolic of preparing the wedding feast for Jesus' return.

This is why you are suppose to do these things as if you are doing them unto the Lord... because you are.

Men, every dollar you earn, every bill you pay... you're doing unto the Lord.

Women, every meal you cook, every room you clean... you're doing it unto the Lord.

Every time a man sacrifices for a woman and every time a woman honors a man, you are serving God. You are polishing the mirror that your marriage is of Christ.

We don't submit, sacrifice and serve because your husband or wife deserves it. You submit, sacrifice and serve because your marriage is a mirror of God, and Christ deserves it.

Wives submit to your husband in all things. Husbands submit to Christ in all things and sacrifice for your wives as He sacrificed for you. Both of you serve each other.

Everyone's receiving love language is sacrifice. And everyone's sending love language is honor. The Bible says if you love the Lord, obey His commands. Obedience is a subset of honor, as the 10 Commandments are a subset of the 2 commandments. If you honor the Lord, you will also obey Him. But you can technically obey Him, while still failing to honor Him, which is called legalism and is what the Israelites in the Biblical stories were infamous for.

There is nothing wrong with traditional marriage. You can always tell what's important to God by what the world is trying to destroy. This is why an attack on traditional marriage is an attack on Christian values. To say there is something wrong with traditional marriage, is to intentionally blur the mirror of Christ.

The nuclear family is the cell of a God fearing society. They are trying to infect God with cancer by attacking Him at the cellular level. Why do you think it's called a "nuclear" family. "Nucleus" is defined as "the central and most important part of an object, movement, or group, forming the basis for its activity and growth."

God doesn't see us as male and female. The Bible says there is no gender in Christ. He sees us as souls and children. So how then are there different roles? Because some children are first born and others are not. Paul's reason for not permitting a woman to teach a man or exercise authority over him is "because Adam was first born". The first born child has a specific role to protect, pour into and die for the younger.

This is why women are the "weaker vessel" because they are second born children poured into by the first born. The same is true of men with Christ. Men are the weaker vessel of Christ, as He is the first fruit that pours into us. There is actually no need to use the word "lead" at all, because male leadership is Biblically defined as "following Christ". And so you could just describe the whole thing as: Children follow your mother, wives, follow your husbands, and husbands follow Christ, as Christ follows the Father. And of course, the Father follows no one. Everyone dies, submits and follows. Everyone must do exactly what they don't want to do.

Christ is the stronger vessel of man, in the same way that men are the stronger vessel of women. Likewise, men are the weaker vessel of Christ, as women are the weaker vessel of man. It's a mirror. Men don't get to escape following, submitting or being the weaker vessel. As a matter of fact, our job is to be a daily living example of what following, submission and being the weaker vessel looks like.

The Bible saying: "Wives submit to your husbands in all things" isn't because men are better than women or that they deserve it. We don't deserve it. But Christ does. You're supposed to submit to your husbands because they are the image of Christ in the mirror of marriage. The only way to die to self is to live for Christ.

Feminism was the original sin. In The Fall, the gender roles were flipped. The correct order was:

- God with dominion over man.
- Man with dominion over women, and
- Men and women with dominion over the animals.

And then The Fall:

- The snake took dominion over the woman by deceiving her.
- The woman took dominion over the man by coercing him, and
- The man attempted to become God by eating from the tree of knowledge.

The roles were switched in The Fall and so marriage and family are intended to be a mirror of the correct order, so we can all align ourselves with God's will again. That's why the Bible doesn't care if you get married or not. You can, but it's just a moral lesson on your relationship with Christ.

The reason the Bible says "if you burn with sexual passion, get married." Is not just because it will give you an outlet for that passion through unlimited marital sex whenever you want it. If you get married for that reason, you're gonna find out that marriage doesn't work that way at all. Another one of God's cosmic Dad jokes. Sometimes His jokes aren't so funny when we realize that we are the punchline.

The reason marriage is the solution to burning with desire, is because burning with desire is a red flag that you're gonna need a "helper" to get a little extra training in submission. And the suffering of marriage is just another mirror that is going to help you see God more clearly. It's no coincidence that the Bible says: "A man who finds a wife finds a good thing" and then in the same breath it also says: "rejoice in your sufferings". Marriage is just remedial humility boarding school for God's rebellious children who just can't seem to get with the program.

By being the example of Christ in your own home, you will feel the things that you're doing to hurt God, as your wife and children do those same things to hurt you. If you already are totally submitted to God and don't need that extra training in righteousness, the Bible actually says it's better not to get married and just serve God with your life instead.

I know this is a hard teaching, but is it really that bad?

Men, why are you complaining about having to provide for the weaker vessel? The only other option is having to become the weaker vessel yourself, and I know you don't want that. For the literal love of God, have some mercy on her.

Women, why are you complaining about submitting to your husbands? Do you want to be the ones to have to die? Or do you want to be the ones died for? If you were on the Titanic and they said: "Alright! All men and children to the life boats!" You wouldn't have some innate intuition inside of you that says "Wait a second! It's supposed to be women and children! I'm not supposed to die. I'm supposed to be died for." Well where do you think that instinct came from? It's because your actual love language is salvation and sacrifice, while your husbands is submission and obedience.

Women, you do realize this means your husband has to be loyal to you, care for you, listen to you, gently nurture you, protect you, serve you and love you unto death, right? Why is that such a bad deal? Given, he's only going to be as good at actually doing it, as you are at actually submitting to him, which is not good at all. But don't you want to be married to a man who at least tries to conform to the image of Christ everyday of your lives?

Men have to stand before God someday and not just account for their own sin, but also for their wife's sin. They have to answer God when He says: "How did you treat and take care of my daughter, which is a mirror of how I should deal with you today in this very judgement?" You do not have to do that for him. And we need to remember this as we are living our daily lives.

The Bible does not seem to give concession for divorce due to an unbelieving spouse, or even an abusive one. That sounds unconscionable in our modern culture.

But the Bible only allows divorce in the case of sexual immorality, of which, even a single episode of watching porn seems to count, since the Bible says: "If you have lusted, you have already committed adultery in your heart". But it just points again to the mechanism of the mirror.

Considering that marriage is a mirror of our relationship with God, then if there is only one unforgivable sin (which is the blaspheming of the Holy Spirit), and only one reason for marital divorce (which is sexual immorality), then God seems to sees sexual immorality as the physical equivalent to us spiritually blaspheming the Holy Spirit. It's a mirror.

Again we see that sin has a sexual connotation to it, because sharing one flesh with foreign spirits is spiritual sex with the enemy, which defiles the wedding bed of the church's marriage to God. And so dying in sin, which is failure to accept the atoning blood of Christ, is the one sin you will go to hell for. Really, you're going to hell for any one of the millions of sins you committed in your life time, but it's the lack of having them atoned for, that causes them to count against you at Judgement.

The Devil's main mechanism of deceit is simply misrepresenting what God actually said. Many people get outraged that the Bible seems to tell an abused wife to stay with her abusive husband, and that seems to be true. But they over look the fact that you could technically divorce him over watching porn a single time, which... is like... everyone. I'm guessing a guy who beats his wife is probably also lusting after other women, right? And so divorce would actually be pretty easily justified Biblically, in fact. Given, you should try to work it out, of course, as God worked it out with you when you did the same thing to him spiritually.

My point is that God seems to have a particular disgust for sexual sin above all else. And so I would say my own struggle with lust and porn is somehow worse to God than if I was, let's say, addicted to heroin, which, thank God drugs are not something I struggle with. I don't judge people who do, rather I know life is hard and I just pray for them and try to help.

But the Bible says that the wrongs that other people do to you are God's right to seek vengeance for, not your own. If an abused wife, for example, knew what God was going to do to her monstrous husband on Judgement Day, she would pray daily that God have mercy on him instead. Every time he hits you, he is storing up your Father's wrath. It's going to be worse for him on that day than either of you could possibly imagine. As much as you hate him and want to kill him, you would beg God for mercy on his behalf if you knew how God is about to repay him for his violence against you.

Isaiah 3:14-15 says: "The Lord will enter into judgment with the elders of His people and His princes: "For you have eaten up the vineyard; the plunder of the poor is in your houses. What do you mean by crushing My people and grinding the faces of the poor?" Says the Lord God of hosts.

And Mark 9:42 says: "If anyone causes one of these little ones to stumble, it would be better for them if a large millstone were hung around their neck and they were thrown into the sea."

Reading this, you may think I would be the absolute worst husband to ever live with. But actually my understanding of these things makes me more sensitive to the unique needs of a woman, which I can now be more cognizant of, patient with and merciful towards. My love for my wife will be based on Christ's love for me, as Christ's love for me is based on His Father's love for Him. And since it's all rooted in something that stems from God, my love, mercy and patience will not only be unchanging, it will only increase over time as I become less of me and more of Him.

- When I don't want to take out the trash, cook dinner or change the baby's diaper, I will see it as suffering I'm supposed to delight in, and so I will get up and do it anyways with a smile on my face, because I am doing it unto Christ.
- When I don't want to get up and go to the gym, I will remember that my body is a temple of God and I need to be a good steward of it. I need to keep my body clean as it is God's house.
- When I want to sit and watch TV, I will remember that I have a fleshly predisposition to laziness, dereliction of duty, and not wanting to lead. And so I will get up and go do something honorable and productive with my time instead.
- Not to mention I would be as loyal as they come since I understand that I either have the choice of complete loving devotion to one woman or to completely be a eunuch for the Kingdom.

That's why the Bible tells women to only marry mature Christian men. It's your prior ignorance of scripture, and your blatant refusal to submit to it that has cost you everything you actually need and want now. God's punishment is always going to be to give you what you want, and then realize the consequences of not doing it His way. God allows this to teach you the cost of failing to align your life with scripture. He allows it in mercy because if you can understand that here and now, even though it hurts, you may accept that difficult lesson before judgement and be saved through the process of the pain.

God knew all along how to take care of you. He created you. But you have to submit to Him in order for that to happen. When we submit to God's plan for our lives, everything is taken care of. Matthew 6:33 says: "Seek first the Kingdom of God and His righteousness and all of these things will be added unto you."

Accept your sufferings. Delight in the suffering. You were never meant to be happy, prosperous and comfortable in this training simulation. Literally, none of this matters. You're entitled to as much happiness in this life as a steak is in a meat grinder.

Men, I know you think you have more important things to do than listen to her emotionally drone on all day. But there's nothing more important in this life than righteousness training, which listening to her most definitely is. Talk about building patience and becoming slow to anger. Making her feel heard, understood and honored is not about her. It's not about you either. It's about Christ. You're not her salvation anyways. You're job is to point her to Christ, who is her salvation.

Men love the whole concept of: "wives submit to your husbands, not because they deserve it, but because by submitting to him, you are actually submitting to Christ, who does deserve it." But they hate their half of that same humble pie: "Husbands, lovingly listen to her problems as Christ listens to yours."

You know you have reached a fair and equitable exchange when both parties are pissed off about the agreed upon arrangements. It's almost like it's a curse or something. Everything that both of you want, is just on the other side of submission. This is where we get the common cliche: "Women need love and men need respect". What is should say is: "women need salvation and men desire obedience". This is again a mirror of how our love language is salvation and God's is honor (which automatically denotes obedience).

Men who like the idea of their wife submitting to them haven't figured out yet that this means they are going to actually have to lead. Women who think they want to lead, haven't figured out yet that this means they have to be the ones to die as well. More importantly, neither of them have come to terms with the fact that their rebellion and refusal to live in accordance with God's design is not about their comfort in this life, but their soul surviving to the next.

And yet "submission" is such a dirty word in our culture today. I once put the word "submissive" in my description of what I was looking for in a woman, in a (supposedly) Christian dating app... and they literally blocked my account.

Wives, if you refuse to submit to your husbands in all things, it's a red flag that you will fail the test on judgment day when God searches your heart and mind to see if you have truly submitted to Him. You don't submit to your husband because he's competent, deserves it and leads you Biblically. You submit to him despite his inability to do any of that, otherwise it wouldn't be called "submission". If it's easy, there would be no sacrifice in it. And if there is no death in it, there can be no resurrection from it.

A truly "good" man knows this and slowly, patiently, lovingly encourages you to submit to him over your shared lifetime. This is not for his sake, but for yours, as this is the meaning of marriage in the first place. If the first born fails to prepare the second born for Judgement Day, he therefore fails to assist you in submitting, and he will have a lot to answer for on Judgement Day as to why he let his inaction and predisposition to laziness lead you to hell. And women, if your man is doing this, and you are fighting him and telling him to stop, you're the one who will have a lot to answer for on Judgement Day, as he is not doing anything wrong in God's eyes.

Christ saved us not because of ourselves... but rather despite ourselves. That's the same way you need to submit to your husband. I know he's a screw up and a jerk. He's a sinner just like you. You submit to him despite the fact that he sucks at all of those things because it's not about him, it's about the mirror of Christ and the state of your own heart on judgement day.

This is why God cursed us so specifically in Genesis 3. He basically said "Since Adam failed to lead and Eve failed to follow, I'm going to bake this issue into the foundation of every single relationship hereafter. Women will desire to lead, but will be forced to follow. And men will desire to follow but will be forced to lead. Both will have to submit to do exactly what they don't want to do."

That's because this life is a submission simulation training. It's literally God's powerpoint presentation and the topic is "How to Submit". Because if you can learn to submit in life, you might just survive the judgement when God searches your heart and mind to see if you've truly submitted to Him. This life is a slow cooker crockpot softening the meat of your heart... so that it's tender for God on Judgement Day.

That's why the Bible tells Christians to submit to authorities and the government. Do you think God is under the delusion that your government leaders don't suck? Do you think God ever looked over at Jesus and said "Jesus! How did You let that one get through!? I told you to only put in people that we want in office!" It's never happened.

God allowed every poor leader throughout history to rule because it's hard to live under difficult leadership. But if you can learn to submit under a horrible leader, you'll have no problem living in submission under the perfect One. We refused to submit to God, and so He is teaching us a lesson by giving us what we said we wanted. It's training. This whole life is training in righteousness through submission.

This is why the Bible says that if you obey Him, you will get good leaders and have good times. And if you disobey, you will be ruled by women and children, your cities will be destroyed and you will suffer. Because that's God's whip and He loves us enough to discipline us. It breaks His heart to see us suffer, but He knows, as a Good Father does, that He must do it to save us.

For us to have free will, and still somehow end up Holy, this life is the process. If we didn't have free will, it would be easy but pointless because God would end up with a family forced to love Him. If we didn't end up holy in the end, there would be no guarantee that Heaven would be without tears. And so this is the way it must be for all things to be true in the end. Anyone who is going to be a trouble maker in heaven, as evidenced by their lack of submission in their life on earth, never makes it there in the first place. This is so God can keep His promise that there will be no more tears in Heaven.

If you are a peace keeper, you may make it into Heaven by the skin of your teeth. Maybe not. But blessed are the peace makers, for they will be called Children of God. It's not about works. It's about the heart that those works flow from. If you love the Lord, obey His commands. If you obey His commands, you will not need to be disciplined, but also will desire to be disciplined, because you now understand what discipline is and the full effect it has in us.

This is why it seems like karma, but it's not quite karma. Karma is a heretical rearranging of this actual mechanism. Karma mirrors this truth, and so it appears to be anecdotally true, yet it slants towards being a good person, which we see is true of all heresies. Karma says "If you are a good person, you will get your reward according to your own goodness." The real mechanism is "If you have already submitted to God through repentance for not being a good person, there's no need for God to continue to discipline you as a mirror of how you're making Him feel."

There's a chilling quote by G. Michael Hopf, that "Hard times create strong men, strong men create good times, good times create weak men, and weak men create hard times."

But it should more accurately say that "Discipline creates submissive children. Submissive children don't require discipline. Good times create spoiled children, and rebellious children need to be disciplined."

And so if it's not "karma" is there a word for this situation? Yes, it's called "love". This life is your childhood and your Father in heaven is raising you.

Submission is defined as: "The action or fact of accepting or yielding to a superior force or to the will or authority of another person." Sound familiar? That's what God wants from us and since we refused to submit to Him, rather than kill us, in His great mercy He bankrupted heaven to give us a remedial course on humility, so we can take the test again at a later date. This life is that finishing school, so we will know which forks and spoons to use at the wedding feast when we get there. When you get your new body in Heaven, you'll need to know how to breathe in it. God is teaching you how to spiritually breathe now, so you'll be ready for it then.

When Paul told us to submit to the government, Nero was throwing Christians into the lion's den to be eaten alive with honey smeared on their genitalia so the lions would eat that part first. He was burning Christians alive in steel cages to light the streets of Rome. That's where the term "Roman candle" comes from.

And yet Paul told us, while under the rule of Nero, who later had Paul beheaded, to submit. Because it's better to submit even unto death than it is to walk into Judgement Day with an unsubmitted heart. This is why the Bible says "Do not be afraid of those who kill the body but cannot kill the soul. Rather, be afraid of the One who can destroy both soul and body in hell." (Matthew 10:28)

What does that look like in practice? The life of Christ. God sent His Son to come show us what the perfect life looks like so we can emulate it. This whole thing is about preparing us for Judgement Day. This life is the class before the final exam.

This is also why there will be no excuse on Judgement Day, because God will say "Didn't I already give you enough chances? How can you say you didn't know?"

But why doesn't God just tell us all of this instead of leave us here to figure it out? He already tried that. Adam knew. Solomon knew. And it didn't change anything. Knowledge is not really what matters. God's standard is strict. This is why Solomon said God has placed a heavy burden on man. We all think we can handle more, but what God expects of us is hard enough already. He only wants the ones whose hearts are truly submitted.

As King Solomon says in Ecclesiastes 3:9-13: "What gain has the worker from his toil? I have seen the burden that God has given to the children of man... I perceived that there is nothing better for them than to be joyful and to do good as long as they live; also that everyone should eat and drink and take pleasure in all his toil—this is God's gift to man."

The wisest man to ever live (who knew all of this) is literally telling you that to find joy (and in some translations "happiness"), you need to take pleasure in accepted suffering because it's a gift from God.

Men pay their love to their wife in a one time lump sum, as they die once and for all at the altar of marriage. Women repay their respect to their husband in a life long subscription based model of installments. This is why the woman takes the man's last name. It signals the death of her old identity. Likewise, Christians take Christ's name to signal the death of their old self. We must ask God to erase and replace us. To become the absence of ourselves and the presence of Christ in that absence. The disciples formerly known as ourselves.

Women are multipliers. Give them food and they will multiply it and give you a meal. Give them a house and they will turn it into a home. Give them sperm and they will multiply it into a child. It has also been said that if you give them grief, they will multiply that as well and give it back to you.

Women take what man has supplied and make it better, beautiful and usable. This is a mirror of God offering us salvation and us going and multiplying the seed in evangelism. It's worth mentioning that perhaps the greatest evangelist in the Bible was the woman at the well. In less than a day, she brought an entire town to the feet of Jesus. You could be like her. You could do the same, if you will believe the way she believed.

Marriage is a mirror of the next coming of Christ, just as the unblemished animal sacrifices in the Old Testaments were foreshadowing. A man leaves his home in the morning and goes into the world to pay the price of his wife's life. The wife prepares the home, tends the children and waits at the gate for him to return. How much more obvious does God have to make these Easter eggs for us? Any deviation from the Biblically described marriage is analogous to sacrificing a blemished lamb as an imperfect foreshadowing of a perfect Christ.

You should treat God the way you wish your children would treat you. That's actually why God is allowing you to suffer in the way that you are, even though it grieves Him to see you in pain. He is showing you a mirror of how you're making Him feel. And He's doing it in love, that you might be saved. Because if the issue is not fixed by Judgement Day, his wrath will consume you completely. He is making you acceptable to Himself now, because if you are not acceptable to Him at Judgement, you won't survive the experience. The pain you're feeling now is God actually protecting you from Himself then. He has cursed us to salvation. Even His curses are blessings.

Fix your vertical relationship with God, and your horizontals will take care of themselves. Seek first the Kingdom of God and His righteousness, and all of these things will be added unto you. The way you do that is by accepting suffering, repenting and dying to self.

You don't get to treat your spouse the same way they have treated you. You treat them how you wish they would treat you. That is the Golden Rule. Picture the perfect version of them, that is everything you've ever wanted, flawless and complete. Then treat them as if they were actually that better version of themselves. See the potential in them that God has seen in you. Is that not the very least we can do? Don't do this because they are perfect, but rather love them despite the fact that they are imperfect.

The one thing you need to know about married life, is that marriage doesn't end in death, it starts with it.

CHAPTER 17

Emotional Support Jesus

The answer to "What would Jesus do?" includes the possibility of flipping tables and beating people with whips. If you think "Jesus is always gentle", allow me to introduce you to the Lion of Judah.

What if I told you Jesus doesn't love you. At least not in the way you think. The Bible never says "Jesus loves me, this I know. For the Bible tells me so." It says Jesus loves the Father and the Father loves you. The only time Jesus talks about loving us directly, is in relation to His love for the Father, the Father's love for Him or our obedience to the Father (which is God's love language).

Jesus' motivation for saving us, doesn't actually appear to be about us at all. The Father loved us so much that He gave His only begotten Son, but the son's motivations may have not been about us in the first place. Revelation 5:12 says "In a loud voice they sang: 'Worthy is the Lamb, who was slain, to receive power and wealth and wisdom and strength and honor and glory and praise!'"

Romans 5:8 says: "But God shows his love for us in that while we were still sinners, Christ died for us." Notice the transaction here. God the Father loved us, and as a result, Christ died for us. It does not say that Jesus died for us because He loved us, but rather that He was obedient unto death, because He loved His Father... who loved us.

Calm down, calm down. I'm just trying to make a point here. Your entire life is a lie, but not because you think Jesus loves you, He does:

John 15:13 says: "Greater love hath no man than this, that a man lay down his life for his friends". This makes it clear that Jesus does love us, with the greatest love, and that this was exemplified in the fact that He died for His friends, which means us.

Galatians 2:20 says: "I have been crucified with Christ. It is no longer I who live, but Christ who lives in me. And the life I now live in the flesh I live by faith in the Son of God, who loved me and gave himself for me." Paul is clearly saying that Jesus loves him. And it can be inferred that this means He loves you too.

John 13:34 says: "A new commandment I give to you, that you love one another: just as I have loved you, you also are to love one another." Which is Jesus Himself saying He loves us.

I'm not trying to get you to accept that Jesus does not love you. I'm trying to break your theology a little bit to take you deeper down the rabbit hole. The Bible is not some fluffy love story fairytale. It is dark. It's not a magic man in the clouds who is just goofing around with a toy He created because He was bored. This is serious stuff. What He is doing is a very important and very great thing. And we must try to understand our role in His plan, so we can serve Him in truth and spirit.

"Hallelujah" is what the angels cry out in Revelation when God is burning the "whore" of the earth. It seems to be their way of saying "It's about time these little bastards finally get whats coming to them". Just because our sin is forgiven, we tend to think of God as ok with it. Like we can just go whore around with foreign flames and then cuddle up to Jesus as if He doesn't mind the stench of our grave clothes. In reality, no one is happy about our sin. Not God, not Jesus and not the angels.

God's love is unconditional, but salvation is heavily stipulated. The Bible says that God loved the world and desires that all be saved. Yet, the fact that He loves us all is not enough to save us all. It is not the love of God alone that saves us, since God loves even the ones who will parish. God gave us grace because He loves us. And we are saved by His grace, through our Faith in Jesus. This faith alone in Christ alone is what saves us. Simply being offered that opportunity is an example of God's love and grace.

If God desires that all be saved, yet many will still parish, does that mean that God does not get what He wants in the end? He does get what He wants in the end, yes, but what He wants is not what you think. God wants a family who loves Him. That means the bar is set at accepting only those people who humbled themselves in faith and repentance. But as for the ones that will be lost, it seems that God does not get what He wants, no. And this is a theme we see throughout the Bible.

God wanted the Israelites to choose life, yet they chose death. He wanted to be Israel's King, yet they chose a man. God wants you to stop sinning. Does he get what He wants when it comes to you? No, of course not. Jesus died to free us from the slavery of sin, yet most Christians (myself included) are using the grace He purchased as an "all you can sin" pass to the amusement park of life. God is a good good Father, long suffering with rebellious children who drive Him to constant wrath.

This is a hard pill to swallow, but Jesus went to the cross willingly, yet reluctantly. He didn't want to die for you and He shouldn't have had to. Jesus' love for us is an overflowing of His love for the Father and the Father's love for Him. This only serves to further elevate the love of Christ, that He would be obedient unto death to save His very own enemies. Greater love hath no man than this, that He would lay down His life for His friends. It would mean nothing if He was happy about His death. Rather, the sign of Jonah seems to indicate that Jesus felt about us the way Jonah felt about Nineveh. His focus was on His Father's glory, not our salvation.

The reason this distinction matters is because herein lies your assurance of salvation. Your salvation is sealed by 3 things that will never change:
- The love of Christ for the Father,
- The love of the Father for His creation, and
- The Glory of God.

The reason you cannot lose your salvation through sin is because you never gained it through works in the first place. Salvation isn't really about you. It's about God's own Great Name sake.

The Devil will never be able to talk God out of saving you, because God was under no delusion of how painful it would be to save you in the first place. He knew the pain He was accepting in the beginning and when He made that decision then, He made it once and for all.

There are 3 types of enemies:
- Enemy of Anger: I hate you and want to kill you!
- Enemy of Apathy: It's nothing personal. I'm just doing my job.
- Enemy of Empathy: I am so sorry. I don't want to do this, but I have to.

The worst one is the Enemy of Empathy, because while you can calm down the

Enemy of Anger and pay off the Enemy of Apathy... good luck convincing someone who never wanted to kill you in the first place, and who already tried to talk themselves out of it, but came to the inevitable conclusion that it must be done all the same.

There is no way to talk God out of trying to save you because He has already considered and accepted the pain of it. The Devil can't tell Him anything He doesn't already know about His decision. And so this is a good thing, right? It's actually a double edged sword. It also means that you will not be able to talk God out of your wages on Judgement Day. He will even agree with everything you're saying, with tears in His eyes. He might even say that He is sorry things worked out this way, that it has broken His heart and that He had hoped for a different outcome... and then He will cast you into the pit of hell and call in the next one to be judged.

General Mad Dog Mattis once said to the leaders of Iraq: "I come in peace. I didn't bring artillery. But I'm pleading with you, with tears in my eyes: If you fuck with me, I'll kill you all." That's a threat you take seriously, because it's not really a threat at all. It's a promise. And it's the same promise God is making to you. There will be no excuse on Judgement Day. I absolutely promise you this, 100%. Anything you have to work out between you and God, do it now, and do it in fear and trembling. That's what this life is for. It's a fleeting moment of time to reconcile with God before judgement.

People think God will have mercy on them because He is a just and righteous Judge. But that is exactly why He won't show you mercy. He will show you justice. He is showing you mercy right now and you're not taking it seriously.

In comparison to how much you love God, the Bible says you should hate your mother (whom you obviously love). Likewise, God loves you so much, that in comparison, the Bible says He took pleasure in crushing Jesus severely (which He obviously did not enjoy doing).

God asked you to love Him so much that it looks like you hate your mother, because He first loved you so much that it looked like He enjoyed killing His Son.

That's how much God loves you. Imagine His heart break at sending you to hell. God did not spare the angels. Think about that. God did not even spare His own sinless Son.

Isaiah 53:10 says: "Yet the LORD was pleased to crush him severely. When you make him a guilt offering, he will see his seed, he will prolong his days, and by his hand, the LORD's pleasure will be accomplished."

By the way, Jewish tradition holds that Isaiah was hung upside-down and sawed in half, starting from between his legs, by the order of Manasseh, the 14th king of Judah. Why wouldn't "gentle Jesus" go and save him? Why would Paul write, in Philippians 1:21: "For to me, to live is Christ and to die is gain"?

If God was pleased to crush His own sinless Son, how much mercy do you think He will show you on Judgement Day?

The Bible is the story of a Good Father making a house for His son (Jesus), then adopting a retarded foreign baby (which is us), and that Down's syndrome baby lighting the house on fire (which is The Fall).

The mercy of the older brother is to say "Forgive them Dad, they don't understand what they've done" and the love of the Father is to ask the older son to clean up their mess for them, which He agrees to do. It doesn't mean He had to have a smile on His face while doing it.

Notice the direction of love in the following verses:

- John 14:21 says: Whoever has my commandments and keeps them loves me. Whoever loves me will be loved by my Father, and I will love them and reveal myself to them.
- Romans 8:38 says: I'm convinced that nothing can separate us from God's love in Christ Jesus our Lord...
- John 15:9 says: As the Father loved me, I too have loved you. Remain in my love.
- Romans 5:8 says: But God shows his love for us, because while we were still sinners Christ died for us.
- John 16:27 says: The Father himself loves you, because you have loved me and believed that I came from God.

Let's break this down:

- Whoever has and keeps Jesus' commands loves Him.
- Whoever loves Jesus will be loved by the Father.
- And as a result of the Father loving you, Jesus then loves you, completing the cycle of love.

This is the transaction of salvation:

- God is the source of love who first loved us,
- God's love for us is a currency which is backed by God's Glory in Heaven,

- That love is made accessible to us through Jesus,
- God first loves Jesus, and
- Then Christ loves us, as His Father first loved Him.

Think of it like this:

- The bank has an unlimited amount of money,
- That money is back by gold at Fort Knox,
- We can access that money through an ATM,
- The bank authorizes the transaction of money at the ATM, and
- Then the ATM dispenses money to you, from the bank.

The love of the Father first fills the cup of Christ and that cup of love overflows to us. "Cup" is another name for a "vessel". That's why Jesus is our stronger vessel and we are His weaker vessel. The vessel is a catchment device for God's love. The reason we can't hold God's love is because we're not supposed to contain it. We are broken vessels so that the love of God (that comes through Christ) will leak out of us to quench the thirst of a lost and dying world. He is strong in our weakness. His love best flows through our weaker, cracked, broken vessels.

This is also why men are the bread winners. It's a mirror. Men earn money and give it to their wives to leak into the home and feed the children. That's why the woman is the weaker vessel of the man. It's not an insult. It's a beautiful mirror of Christ. Please stop trying to shatter it.

Christ is the middle man transferring love back and forth between you and God. He's the ATM machine, linking you to an unlimited account, that pumps out love money endlessly, which you go and spend in the world to feed the hungry, clothe the naked, visit the prisoner, heal the sick and buy water for the thirsty.

It's a distribution network of love. We are supposed to be leaky love vessels. We are not meant to store up God's love, but rather spend it freely, as it was freely given to us. It will never run out because it comes from a source that will never run dry. This is why when you write a check of love, you know your Father is good for the money. And if you run out, go back to the ATM and get some more.

Notice that this entire banking system is already in place, but the actual transaction is triggered from our end (which is us going to the ATM). Your faith goes up the chain to Christ and then perfect love comes cascading back down from God... to Jesus... then to you... and then, hopefully, to the World. Albeit, sadly most Christians never share their cup at all and keep it to themselves. God help you on judgement day for that.

If you never answer the call to go to the ATM in the first place, which we Christians call "come to the well", then this entire transaction never even starts. If you don't even believe the ATM has any money to give, you'll never even trust enough to ask for it, which we Christians call "taste and see that the Lord is good".

Notice the If/Than statement of it all. If we love Jesus... Then God will love us. That is why we are saved by the Grace of God through our Faith in Christ. The Grace of God is activated for us when we have Faith in Christ... because The Father will love us... if and when we love Christ. Then because the Father loves us... Jesus then loves us too. But unless the Father first gives Jesus your name, He doesn't even know who you are.

And this is if we keep His commands. And what are His commands? To love God and love our Neighbor. It doesn't say how well we have to do it, and thank God for that, because we absolutely suck at it. But God is merciful to accept a sincere and sustained life long effort.

We are not saved by faith in Christ or our love for Him. We are saved by the grace of God alone, through faith in Christ alone. It's really faith in God's grace that saves us. It's God's grace to reach out His hand to us. It's our faith to accept it.

Faith in Christ is how we opt into grace, that's true. This whole thing is a class action court case that you have to opt into in order to benefit from the verdict of, but faith is not what saves us, grace is. This is the nuance of why faith is not a work.

Otherwise, you would technically be saving yourself by virtue of having faith, and could therefore boast on Judgement Day. You're saved by the Ark, and must be grateful to the one who built it. You answering the call to the Ark is not you saving yourself, and yet in order to activate the Ark, you have to answer the call because you have faith in the one who is telling you that the rain is coming and faith that the Ark is sufficient to save you from it.

Faith triggers grace, which saves us. Only perfect love can save you. That's why self love (which is imperfect love at best, and more likely just lust) is a fallacy. Perfect love only comes from God, and the only way to get that is to first love Christ. And the way to love Christ is to first love God and your neighbor, which are the 2 commands that Jesus gave us.

We are not saved by works, however if our faith is true, works will be the evidence of true faith. Otherwise, rotten fruit (which means no works) equals a rotten root (which means false faith).

Even when it says "Jesus loved" the rich young ruler in Matthew 19, it was after the rich man claimed to have obeyed the Father's commands since childhood. The Bible says if you love God you will obey His commands. And if you love the Father, Jesus will love you. But when Jesus scanned his heart and found the sin of greed for money there, He grew righteously furious.

The man asked Jesus what He had to do to activate the transaction of God's love. Jesus said he has to obey God. The rich man claimed that he had done so since birth. In other words, he proclaimed his own goodness. Jesus recognized the man's claim of obedience to the Father and this triggered Jesus' love for the man. But when Jesus scanned his heart and found no actual evidence to support his claim, Jesus was pissed.

Everyone's favorite Bible verse, Jeremiah 29:11, which says: "God has plans to prosper me." is not about you at all... it's about Jesus. As a matter of fact, everything you think is about you, is actually about Jesus.

We Christians call these Old Testament physical stories, which are really New Testament spiritual analogies (also called "types of Christ"). For example, you are not Noah in the story of the Ark. We are the animals. Jesus is Noah.

The Old Testament physical is the New Testament spiritual. In the Old Testament, we have the story of:

- One man,
- Who is a carpenter,
- Who builds a refuge,
- For His blood family,
- Who doesn't deserve it,
- With nails in his hands,
- So that they can float above the wrath of God,
- Yet still be tossed around by the waves of it,
- So that they can fear the one who sent it,
- Gain knowledge of who He is through that fear,
- Understand His great love for them in sending the plans for the Ark,

- And sending the One who built it, and
- Henceforward submit to His love, once the Ark lands in a new world.

Sound familiar? That's the physical version of the spiritual salvation Jesus builds for us in the New Testament.

The New Testament is about saving our souls, the most valuable thing in existence, other than God Himself. This is because we are made in the image of God, albeit we are not gods. Simply by virtue of resembling Him, we are valuable above all else. Humans seem to be the vessels in which God horcruxed Himself, and as such, we are part of Him in some deep and mysterious way I am too terrified to attempt to explain further.

Would you sell your eyes for $1 million? What about $20 million? No. No one would because they are clearly priceless. But Jesus says the value of your soul is so great that if your eyes cause you to sin, you should pluck them out. That means that something which we value as priceless becomes instantly worthless when compared to the true value of your eternal soul. And maybe that's why God and the Devil are both fighting over your soul, because they know the real value of it.

Now if someone wanted to purchase your soul, they would have to pay the priceless-priceless price tag of what it costs.

Now multiply that times everyone alive. Now multiply that times every generation that has ever lived (adjusting for population) and who will ever live... and you will start to approach the cost of the cross and the value of Christ who paid it. The only way that's possible... is if He is God.

And that is what Jeremiah 29:11 means. None of this is about you. It is all about Jesus.

The value of your eyes has nothing to do with accuracy. Most people except that what they see can easily be deceived. People who look further into this realize that the eyes play tricks on us all the time. There are blindspot assumptions. The way your eyes work, as well as all the other senses in fact, they are extremely inaccurate. And so why would something so broken to you have any value at all? Why does the accuracy, or lack there of, not change the fact that your eyes are still priceless?

But if your eyes are priceless to you, and your soul is priceless to God. Why is your soul worthless to you? Why do we honestly not care about it at all now?

Your soul is that much more valuable than your eye.

When Jeremiah 29:11 says: "God has great plans to prosper you", this was telling the Israelites to settle down and accept that they had to endure 70 years of slavery. They were waiting on an answer from God as to whether or not He was going to rescue them from the slavery Nebuchadnezzar just oppressed them under. God's answer was not only "no", but it was essentially that He is the one who told Nebuchadnezzar to enslave them in the first place.

God told them that they need to accept their punishment for past deeds, because it is actually training in righteousness to prepare them for future glory, and settle in and take wives. They would not be rescued in their lifetimes. Then He offers them the hope that their children will be rescued, and God has great plans to prosper them, but only after the wicket generation died off.

The reason God sent them into slavery for 70 years is because for the last 490 years, they failed to observe a Sabbath year every 7th year, to let the land rest and for debts to be forgiven. 7o times 7 equals 490. God was taking back what was owed to Him. He was balancing the sheets as an Old Testament physical mirror of New Testament spiritual salvation. Jesus references this when He tells us in Matthew 18:22: "I tell you, not seven times, but forgive seventy times seven times."

He is tipping the hat to the fact that He is the forgiveness that has come, and that forgiveness is not a canceling of debt but a payment of debt in full, with something that is of greater value.

In the Bible, God seems to only call on people who were busy doing work. And the jobs they were doing, seem to be the physical manifestation of the spiritual work Jesus was calling them to. For example, David was anointed King of Isreal, which is the job of shepherding the Israelites, while he was in the field tending literal sheep. The Disciples were called to be fishers of men, while they were catching literal fish. The interesting one to me, is Mathew, who was collecting taxes when he was called. And we then see references to balancing of of books, debts paid in full, sinners redeemed like coupons and reconciled unto God, and all sorts of other financial and accounting terms.

All through the Bible we see the physical and spiritual mirrors.

Again, Old Testament slavery is a physical mirror of a spiritual New Testament mechanism.

Why does the Bible seem to condone slavery in the Old Testament, but condemn it in the New Testament. Many Christians frantically try to explain that it was because God lost control of humanity, they wouldn't listen to Him and so He allowed them to sin, but regulated it. I don't think that's the case. It sounds like a weak cop out to me. It is true that the Bible says "it wasn't supposed to be that way in the beginning", as with the example of divorce, but we must not concede that God has lost control of creation.

It seems to be the case that God's punishment is to give us exactly what we asked for, and so when we attempted to seize control, God allowed it. Therefore, we are in fact in control, not God. And that is exactly why the world is so messed up. However, the Old Testament slavery issue seems to be deeper than the fact that we are in control and simply screwed everything up.

Rather, I would argue that physical Old Testament slavery is a mirror of New Testament spiritual slavery to God and His righteousness.

Look at the way it's described. God said you can beat your slave nearly to death, just don't kill him. Where else in scripture do we see this? God told the Devil he could torture Job, as long as He didn't kill him. And Job was insistent, which God later validated as accurate, that this wasn't about punishing Job for wrong doings, but rather something bigger that God was doing in His superior wisdom. Job didn't know it at the time, but God was allowing him the honor of being the Old Testament physical mirror of New Testament spiritual bond service to God.

Exodus 21:20-21 says: "Anyone who beats their male or female slave with a rod must be punished if the slave dies as a direct result, but they are not to be punished if the slave recovers after a day or two, since the slave is their property.

Job 1:12 says: "The Lord said to Satan, "Very well, then, everything he has is in your power, but on the man himself do not lay a finger."

It's the same thing. You are Job. God created the devil as our drill instructor. In the end, when God kills the Devil, it won't just be a physical death, he will come into the understanding that he served God's purpose all along. The spiritual and emotional pain of knowing that he has been had is going to be worse than any pain of death itself.

For any of it to be real, we had to have free will. And free will without a choice with which to exercise it is also pointless. God had to allow us to sin, in order for us to make the choice to leave it behind. He let us go, told us to return to Him and is allowing for the ones who love Him to do so. It's inception. As sentient beings, we had to realize for ourselves that holiness is better than happiness.

But, with sin entered death, and before we can return to Him, death itself has to die. And the only way to kill death, is for God to bleed. This is the way it had to be. This is the extent to which God loves us. Sin can no more stick to God than paint can stick to the wind. God made Himself into a human form factor so that sin could attach to Him, and in doing so, detach from us.

If you have something that is that valuable, and someone wanted to buy it, what they give in exchange must be of greater or equal value.

God didn't cancel the debt. He paid it. In full. This is an important distinction. Do not miss it. The debt was paid, not canceled.

The reason the blood of Christ was able to buy every soul, who has ever lived, is because it was of that value. The cost was so great because the greater the cost, the more valuable the sacrifice. And the only blood that valuable is the blood of God. All of this points back to the fact that Christ is God.

The only one who could absorb the absolute wrath of God... is God. It blows my mind how some Christians believe in God and Christ and the Bible and still somehow can logic that Jesus is not actually God. Really? What human has blood valuable enough to pay the debt that Jesus' did? Do you think that it could have just been you in His place?

God has never asked anything of you that He didn't first do Himself. Heresies that say Jesus is not God, by default are describing a God who is non-personal and a poor leader. If Jesus is not God, then God never came down and experienced human life first hand, He never beat the game as an example for us to follow, He doesn't understand what you're going through and He is asking you to do something that He never did Himself. That is simply not the God described in the Bible.

Do you think that when Jude 1:5 (ESV) says that Jesus was the one who led the Israelites out of Egypt, that a human could have been that old? How could He have been alive back in Exodus and still only 33 when He dies on the cross in the gospel thousands of years later? There's only one way. Jesus is God.

That is how the death of Christ illustrates the glory of God. It literally assigns an infinite value to His glory and shows you mathematically exactly what that looks like.

Christ didn't die for your sins for your sake. You are saved as a consequence of God flexing His absolute glory. He saved us for His own great Name sake. When the Bible says to fear Him, you might want to fear Him. This is not a joke. God is seriously powerful. We have absolutely no idea who we are dealing with and what He is capable of. Thank God He is on our side.

This idea that the fear of the Lord is just referring to some deep form of respect, doesn't seem to mesh well with "Work out your salvation in fear and trembling". "Work out your salvation with respect and trembling" doesn't quite have the same ring to it.

A better way to say it is that:

- "My people die for lack of knowledge",
- "Fear of the Lord is the beginning of all knowledge", and
- Knowledge of His "perfect love casts out all fear".

And so, yes, the Christian ends up not really fearing Him in the end, but that's only because you now have knowledge of His love for you and His merciful character. You know He could kill you, but also know that He wants to save you. And so fear gets you the knowledge of His love, then knowledge of His love casts out the fear.

We are not supposed to test God. But it seems God has created this place to test Himself. He created a game so hard that He couldn't beat it. And then He beat it anyways. Hallelujah. Glory in the highest.

This is how the Bible describes Jesus in Revelation 19:11-20 (KJV):

"And I saw heaven opened, and behold a white horse; and he that sat upon him was called Faithful and True, and in righteousness he doth judge and make war. His eyes were as a flame of fire, and on his head were many crowns; and he had a name written, that no man knew, but he himself. And he was clothed with a vesture dipped in blood: and his name is called The Word of God. And the armies which were in heaven followed him upon white horses, clothed in fine linen, white and clean. And out of his mouth goeth a sharp sword, that with it he should smite the nations: and he shall rule them with a rod of iron: and he treadeth the winepress of the fierceness and wrath of Almighty God. And he hath on his vesture and on his thigh a name written, King Of Kings, And Lord Of Lords. And I saw an angel standing in the sun; and he cried with a loud voice, saying to all the fowls that fly in the midst of heaven, Come and gather yourselves together unto the supper of the great God; That ye may eat the flesh of kings, and the flesh of captains, and the flesh of mighty men, and the flesh of horses, and of them that sit on them, and the flesh of all men, both free and bond, both small and great. And I saw the beast, and the kings of the earth, and their armies, gathered together to make war against him that sat on the horse, and against his army.

And the beast was taken, and with him the false prophet that wrought miracles before him, with which he deceived them that had received the mark of the beast, and them that worshipped his image. These both were cast alive into a lake of fire burning with brimstone."

How gentle does He sound now? And why would you want such a weak savior in the first place? How could He fight your battles for you if He wasn't first a warrior?

Jesus is not a homeless hipster. He is not a socialist beta male. And He most certainly is not your emotional support teddy bear. He is an all powerful God. He is the light of the world through which all things were created. It's time you start seeing Him as such. As the bride is made ready for the feast, she needs to learn to respect Her husband for the warrior He truly is.

The lack of respect you have for Christ, as a result of treating Him like your boyfriend, is nothing short of blasphemy. Your ignorance of the Bible is unacceptable. On Judgement Day, as mentioned in Revelation 20:12, there seem to be two books, one of which the dead will be judged by. I'm pretty sure that's the Bible. You might want to start reading it. The Bible tells you to fear the Lord over 300 different times. Jesus is not your emotional support peacock. He is God. Treat Him accordingly.

This is an arranged marriage and Jesus doesn't want to marry a whore wrapped in smelly grave clothes. You are saved by His blood, the least you can do is go and get cleaned up a bit for the wedding. Stop sinning. Stop adding nails to His hands and thorns to His head. Go and remove the grave clothes, wash yourself clean of sin, repent, turn from it, take up your cross and follow Him.

As a matter of fact, Jesus offended people so much and so often that His own villagers tried to throw Him off a cliff for offending them.

Christ is a Shepard and we are His flock. When we are saved and we run away with sin anyways, Christ leaves the 99 and comes after the 1. But what happens next is where most Christians are going to have their theology messed with.

Shepards would not just go through all the effort to track down the one sheep, and just assume it wasn't going to run away again. They weren't stupid.

The reason Christ is carrying the sheep on His shoulders is because when He found it, He broke its leg in half so it would have to stay close to Him as it heals. God breaks our lives for our own good. We are rebellious little shits and He loves us enough to discipline us.

The Bible says to "fear God". It says to "work out your salvation in fear and trembling". But does this mean you're supposed to be afraid of Him? Yes! That's literally what it says. The Bible says "Do not be afraid of those who kill the body but cannot kill the soul. Rather, be afraid of the One who can destroy both soul and body in hell."

This concept of telling people what they want to hear because it makes them feel good is about as healthy as letting a diabetic kid eat endless candy because he likes the taste. Or letting a retarded kid play in the street because he thinks it's a game. It's spiritual negligence and it's reckless. And all for the selfish result of you feeling like a virtuous person.

Sin is slavery. If you are patting a slave on the head telling them to celebrate their slavery, then at least don't turn around and pretend you love them as well. If you love them, you will desire for them to be set free. You will grab them by the shoulders and scream "Wake up! Be Free!"

A lot of people think they understand what love is. But love is not a verb. Love is a cycle or process. It's living. Dynamic. Flowing.

The world is in rebellion against God, but this rebellion is fueled by only half the story.

The meme "A Jack of all trades, is a master of none" makes it sound like the quote is saying it's not a good idea to be a jack of all trades. But the full meme originally was "A Jack of all trades is a master of none, but still always better than a master of one". And knowing the second half clarifies the meaning, and may change the way you live your life as a result.

The same is true with love. The Bible paints a picture of a God who only cares about Himself. This life is not about you, it's about His glory, His story, His will, His crown, His righteousness and His interests.

And that's totally true. But if that's all you ever hear, it makes God sound like an evil narcissistic, tyrannical father who just created us out of boredom and arrogance. Like He is just sitting up there jerking off to our misery or has abandoned us completely.

If that were the truth, it would be what it is. We would have no choice. It would just be reality. But that's not the God the Bible is describing. And thank God for that.

You're rebelling against only half of the story. And here's the other half.

Yes, this life is about God's glory. But the Bible also says that you are the glory of God.

Yes, this life is about God's righteousness, But you are the righteousness of God.

Yes, this life is about God's crown. But you are the crown of God.

Yes, this life is all about elevating His great Name. But you are also marked with that Name when you enter His family.

When you lay crowns at the feet of Jesus in heaven, you are laying yourself at His feet, because you are the crown of God.

Do you see the cycle of love in this? It's about Him, but He wants you. And so it's about you, but it's not about you. It's a cycle. Love originates from God and flows to us, and then flows through us, back to Him. We are recharged with love.

The Bible says we love because He first loved us. We are charged with the love of God, and then go and carry that love to others, which depletes us, and causes us to need to be charged back up from the source.

This is the definition of love that is greater than Agape. I call it cyclic Love.

It's not about you, it's about God, but all God cares about is His children, which means you.

He loves you enough to save you despite yourself. If you were allowed to screw it up, you would. He takes control for your own benefit.

The reason the Bible only gives half of the answer is because, unlike the other so called "holy" books, that need to fully round out their points to a reader who is intellectualizing the literature, the Bible is a living Word in which the Holy Spirit gives you the other half in real time. God is not intimidated by your lack of ability to understand, because He is a living God that will meet you where you are, when you read the Word in all humility.

I have read the holy books of the earth. The Bible is the only one that read me.

CHAPTER 18

The 7th Sola

You are in fact saved by works. Just not your own. It is the work of Christ that saves you. To access those works, you only need to have faith in Him. Any of your own works are filthy rags to God and will not save you. But the work of Christ on the cross, which is the only work that saves you, is sufficient.

The 7th Sola of Salvation is knowledge, and it is a requirement for salvation.

This is offensive to Christians because, "What about the retards!?" Calm down, calm down. First of all, as I already explained, we are all retarded. It's just a sliding scale. But we are all, most definitely, on the spectrum.

Secondly, I'm not talking about gnosticism (which is secret hidden knowledge that you have to go and find). I'm talking about public knowledge. Knowledge so public in fact, it's written on everyone's heart and mind. It's your conscience.

It's really identity (which is knowledge of who you are, in relation to God) that is birthed from conscience (which is knowledge of what you've done to hurt Him).

Around 500 years ago, the Catholic Church had a group of protesters split off, thus creating the "Protestant" branch of Christianity. The main issue was whether we are saved by works, or saved by grace, through faith, not works. Catholics were teaching that we are saved by works, not grace alone, through faith alone.

In response, the Reformers created the "5 Solas of Salvation" to clarify the mandatory belief of all future denominations of Protestantism. Sola means "alone" in latin. This is also why I am technically neither a Catholic or a pure Protestant.

All Protestants technically agree that we are saved by the 5 Solas of Salvation, which means we are saved:

1. By the Grace of God alone,
2. Through Faith in Christ alone,
3. As defined by Scripture alone,
4. By the blood of Christ alone, and
5. For the Glory of God alone.

Each of these points is heavily expounded upon and entire discourses can be read about the details of each one. But, personally, I think the Reformers perhaps overcorrected a bit and skipped a couple important nuances. I think there are actually 7 solas, they are not all solas and I believe they correspond with the 7 questions of creation (who, what, where, when, why, how and by whom).

I believe the salvation message would be: "Your soul is saved, by the Grace of God alone, through true Faith (as evidenced by works, but not at all by works), by the blood of Christ alone, for the Glory of God alone, when you humble yourself before God (repent, profess & have faith), as defined by Scripture (as the final authority, not the only authority).

To repeat that, in the format of the 7 questions of creation, it would be:

1. Who: Your soul is saved,
2. What: By the Grace of God alone,
3. How: Through true Faith (as evidenced by works, but not at all by those works),
4. By Whom: By the blood of Christ alone,
5. Why: For the Glory of God alone,
6. When: When you humble yourself before God (repent, profess & have faith),
7. Where: As defined by Scripture (as the final authority, not the only authority).

But what about people who have never heard the Gospel before? What about people who never heard the name of Christ? How can they be saved by a name they never uttered from their lips?

Are we really saved by the "name" of God? And if so, which name? If an uncontacted tribe off the coast of India came into contact with Western culture and through some misunderstanding of the Book of Revelation, and the Transformers movies, accepted the full and correct salvation message... except they referred to Jesus as "MegaDeath 3000!" Would they not still be saved by the name of MegaDeath 3000?" And if not... why should you be saved by the name of "Jesus"? His name was "Yeshua".

For those who never heard the name of Christ, they are expected to realize truth from the evidence in nature around them and through their conscience. This is enough for them to recognize that there is a God, and that they are a sinner. That is enough to seek Him, experience the Holy Ghost and find Christ through that journey because Christ is the only one who tells you that you're a sinner, you cannot save yourself through works and you need a Savior. It also seems Biblical that God will expect less of them on Judgment Day than He will of those who had a Bible but chose to ignore it.

Everyone already knows the Gospel deep down. It's written on our hearts and minds. Your conscience (meaning "with knowledge") is the knowledge of salvation needed to be saved. This is why everyone will hear and no one will have an excuse on Judgement Day. If you say "I didn't know" on judgement day, God will say "didn't you hear your conscience screaming at you to stop?"

Your conscience is your own personal call to the Ark. It would be like if the drowning people were banging on the wall of the Ark, trying to get in as the water's rise and Noah says, "Didn't you hear me screaming at you this whole time to come to the Ark? You only took it seriously once it began to rain. It's too late. Do not say you were without knowledge. You were in fact 'with knowledge', you just didn't believe it. You heard the call, you just chose to ignore it."

We are in fact saved by the name of Christ, as Romans 10:13 says: "for everyone who calls on the name of the Lord will be saved."

And Acts 4:11-12 says: "Jesus is 'the stone you builders rejected, which has become the cornerstone.' Salvation is found in no one else, for there is no other name under heaven given to mankind by which we must be saved."

But our very breath itself is His name, and Romans 8:26 says: "We do not know what we ought to pray for, but the Spirit himself intercedes for us through wordless groans."

Therefore, 7 Fold Salvation looks something like this:

1. Stop fighting your conscience.

2. Designate the 10 Commandments as your standard of goodness.

3. Realize that you immediately fail the standard.

4. Accept that this means you are not "good" and cannot save yourself.

5. Express your need for a Savior to God.

6. Repent of your sins.

7. Trust in Christ as your Lord & Savior.

That is what it means to "Get Saved". Notice there is no mention of earning your salvation through works.

Romans 4 makes it extremely clear that works are not required for salvation. But James 2 also makes the opposite seemingly clear as well. And so this is a point of contention in the Christian world.

Romans 4:3-5 says: "What does the Scripture say? 'Abraham believed God, and it was credited to him as righteousness.' Now when a man works, his wages are not credited to him as a gift, but as an obligation. However, to the man who does not work but trusts God who justifies the wicked, his faith is credited as righteousness."

Paul is quoting Genesis 15:6, which says: "[Abraham] believed the LORD, and He credited it to him as righteousness."

And so we see that in both the old and new testaments, grace through faith is what saves, not works. For example, what saved Adam and Eve? The same thing you are saved by. Faith in Christ. If they were saved by works, then they failed by getting kicked out of the Garden, but God promised them salvation and redemption thereafter. God told them that they would be saved through their children. This was again, foreshadowing for Christ, who would be born from their bloodline.

Adam and Eve, like you, were saved by faith in Christ. They were just saved by the promise that He would someday come (future faith), while you are saved by the fact that He already has. Notice that their sin had devastating consequences, but that did not affect their salvation. That is also the case with you, but if you take advantage of this "loop hole", you aren't actually saved, because someone who is saved, wouldn't want to do that.

This is so blatantly clear in scripture that Paul actually addresses the implication of it. He says in Romans 6:1: "What shall we say, then? Shall we go on sinning so that grace may increase? By no means! We are those who have died to sin; how can we live in it any longer?"

Paul is making the point that works based salvation moots the fact that salvation is a gift from God, because if we earned it through works, it would be owed to us. Notice how the Devil again switched the definitions. The Bibles says "the wages of sin is death". And the Devil says "the wages of goodness is life". It's the difference between "Be good and God will owe you salvation" vs "You have sinned and God owes you death".

Telling you that you can earn your salvation through works is the exact opposite of God telling us that we already have earned death through sin. Romans chapter 4 and Ephesians chapter 4 make it clear that we are not saved by works, but by grace, through faith, as a free gift from God, not works, lest any man boast.

Then... we have the Book of James, Jesus' own brother, throwing a huge monkey wrench into what otherwise seemed pretty cut and dry. James 2:14 says: "What good is it, my brothers, if someone says he has faith but does not have works? Can that faith save him?" And to really drive the point home, James 2:17 says: "In the same way, faith by itself, if it is not accompanied by action, is dead." And James 2:26 says: "As the body without the spirit is dead, so faith without deeds is dead."

James is saying that if someone claims to have faith, but no works as evidence of that faith, their claim is untested, and therefore unreliable. He is not saying that faith alone does not save. He is saying that faith alone does save, but true faith will always be accompanied by works, as evidence that the faith is legitimate saving faith. Otherwise, it's just self deceived virtue signaling.

Let's break that verse down a bit. The flesh is your soul's interface with the physical world. And the spirit is your soul's interface with the spiritual world. It works the same way with artificial intelligence, which lives in the form factor of hardware, firmware and software, which is just another physical mirror of body, soul and spirit that God left us as an Easter egg with which to seek salvation.

If works represents the flesh, and faith represents the spirit, according to James, then works is therefore the manifestation of your soul's salvation in the physical world, as faith is the mechanism of your soul's salvation in the spiritual world. If the spiritual mechanism is in place, then the physical manifestation will be evident.

And so "faith without works is dead", as the body without the soul is dead. As a crime with no evidence is unprovable. As a tree with no fruit is useless. As a well without water is dry. As a coal without heat produces no flame. Faith without works is like a sail with no wind, a marriage with no love and a cross with no King. Or put more simply: "rotten fruit, rotten root".

James is not commenting on losing your salvation once it is secured, he is saying that many people who claim to have it... don't. Jesus says this as well in Matthew 7:22-23: "Many will say to Me in that day, 'Lord, Lord, have we not prophesied in Your name, cast out demons in Your name, and done many wonders in Your name?' And then I will declare to them, 'I never knew you; depart from Me, you who practice lawlessness!'"

But isn't this interesting? They are claiming to have the works of prophesying, casting out demons and performing miracles as evidence of their true faith. But Jesus responds that they may have known Him, but He never knew them. He called them "lawless", despite their claims that their works were evidence of their true faith. Jesus is saying that their works did not satisfy the law.

These men were literally saying "But we did all of these works! Doesn't that mean we are saved?!"

And Jesus is saying (and I of course am paraphrasing here, not putting words in the mouth of God): "You're not saved by works. You are saved by the fulfillment of the law, which I am here to fullfil for you, since you cannot do it yourself. You only needed to have faith that I will do it for you. You had the law given to you, and those to come will have the law written on their hearts and minds. But you deceived yourself into thinking you had satisfied the standard of God and fulfilled the law yourself through mindless rituals and legalistic works. I tell you that these works you claim have saved you are but filthy rags to God. He who attempts to mute his conscience, which is the law, will not inherit the Kingdom of God. And this is despite the outward appearance of their works, which is why only God can judge the innermost parts."

So, let's recap: You are not saved by works alone without faith. You are not saved by works at all. You are saved by faith alone, even without works as evidence. But you will have works as evidence if your faith is real. The distinction Jesus is making is that you can also have the appearance of faith, as evidenced by works, but still be lawless according to God. And so we see that the difference between simply believing, versus having true saving faith, involves the fulfillment of the law.

Jesus fulfilled the law for us and so all that is required for salvation, is to plead His blood over your sins, as the Israelites symbolized when they smeared the blood of the lamb over their doors, and the angel of death passed over them. The angel did not enter the door to see if righteous or unrighteous people were inside, it counted the blood of the lamb as righteousness alone, without even looking at the ones inside. And literally thank God for that, because they would have all died. And yet, "worthy is the Lamb who takes away the sins of the world" (John 1:29).

The law Jesus is referring to is the 10 commandments, which Jesus said boiled down to only 2. He is saying that they are not saved by the works they are claiming, but rather they are damned by their failure to love God with all their heart, soul and mind, and to love their neighbor as themself. He is saying that they failed to follow their conscience, realize they are sinners and repent. Rather, they thought they were good people by virtue of their works, and as a result they go to hell.

James is not saying you are saved by works. James is saying that the currency of Faith needs to be backed with something of substance (works), otherwise it's just fiat faith that you can't take to the bank. That's not too hard to get past, but then James really throws us a curve ball in James 2:24, which says: "You see that a person is considered righteous by what they do and not by faith alone."

That's shocking. And most Protestants aren't even aware of this verse. Martin Luther himself, who held a doctorate of theology and started the Protestant movement, called the Book of James an "Epistle of straw" for this very reason. When the Bible seems to contradict itself, we have to see the verses as two pieces of iron sharpening one another, to give us an even deeper meaning of Scripture.

The Bible is not vague, it's so surgically accurate that sometimes it seems like it clashes. But those verses are not smashing together and dulling each other out. They are actually passing closely by and sharpening one another. The truth can be found in the uncomfortable friction coefficient between them.

For example, Deuteronomy 5:9 says: "You shall not bow down to them or serve them; for I the Lord your God am a jealous God, visiting the iniquity of the fathers on the children to the third and fourth generation of those who hate me."

And Numbers 14:18 says: "The LORD is slow to anger, abounding in love and forgiving sin and rebellion. Yet he does not leave the guilty unpunished; he punishes the children for the sin of the parents to the third and fourth generation."

But then Jeremiah 31:29 says: "In those days people will no longer say, 'The parents have eaten sour grapes, and the children's teeth are set on edge.'"

So which is true? And the answer is... both are true. As a matter of fact, it's giving you a hint as to how it all works. One argument is that sin, at one time, did in fact revisit the children, but not anymore. Meaning the conflicting verses are regarding different times or covenants. But if those verses are talking about physical death through gene dilution, death is still going strong till this day. The curse of Genesis 3 is clearly still in full effect, despite a misreading of Galatians 3:13, which says "...Christ redeemed us from the curse of the law by becoming a curse for us, for it is written: 'Cursed is everyone who is hung on a tree.'"

The curse of the law here may be referring to the Moral, Judicial or Ceremonial laws mentioned in the Bible. By harmonizing Scripture we see that it's likely the Ceremonial Law that is no longer necessary, as all of the Old Testament laws about sacrificing an unblemished animal were just foreshadowing of the sinless Christ yet to come. Since Christ already came, there is no longer a need for the Ceremonial Law. Jesus also fulfilled the Moral Law (which is referring to the 10 Commandments). This doesn't mean the Moral Law no longer applies like Ceremonial Law. But the curse of Genesis 3 is still in full effect, as evidenced by the fact that:

1. We still die,
2. Women still have labor pains,
3. We still have to work the earth for food, and
4. Snakes still crawl on their bellies.

But think of it like this. If you make a cake using a mold, and the original mold has a dent in it, all the cakes made from that mold, will have the same dent. But if one cake is ruined, because it has sour batter, that doesn't mean the next cake made after it will be sour. The batter changes generation to generation, but all of us have the dent of the original mold. Both are true. We still are dented from Adam's original sin, yet we also each have our own sin account with God, for which we will be judged on Judgment Day.

The same is true of the dispute between James and Paul. It becomes clear that we are saved by grace, through faith, not works, when you weigh the book of James out with all of Romans 4 (which clearly says faith alone is credited as righteousness) and Ephesians 2:8-9: "For it is by grace you have been saved, through faith, and this is not from yourselves, it is the gift of God not by works, so that no one can boast."

Basically, Paul is yelling, "You're not saved by works! That's the whole point! You couldn't earn it even if you tried! Just walk through that door! You'll be fine!"

And then you enter the door of Christ and become a Christian and there is James standing on the other side saying "Hi! Welcome to salvation. Can I see your works please?"

And you explain to him how Paul told you that salvation has nothing to do with works. To which James replies, "That's true. You can't earn it, but you do have to prove it."

James is actually supporting the "saved by grace alone, through faith in Christ alone, not works at all" narrative, he is just making the point that talk is cheap. He is explaining that people will proclaim their own goodness, they will even call themselves Christians, but the way you can tell them apart is if their life is laid down for Christ, and works are the evidence that they are living the life.

James is giving us an algorithm with which to oust false converts. He is surgically separating the wheat from the tares. He is drawing a distinction between the nuance of "belief" vs actual "saving faith". He is saying it's not enough to simply profess your belief in God, as even the devil and demons believe in God's existence. You must be transformed by your faith, or your faith isn't actually faith at all.

For example, James 2:19 says: "You believe that there is one God. Good! Even the demons believe that and shudder".

James is also not alone in his assertion. King Solomon writes in Proverbs 20:6: "Most men will proclaim each his own goodness, But who can find a faithful man?" Notice that Solomon is saying the same thing. People will use works to try to justify their own goodness, but they have no real faith. James is pointing out the inverse, that you cannot claim to have faith, if there are no works as evidence. But you can also have only works, and still no true faith as well.

So again, and I'm really just trying to drive this home because this is the single issue that separates the teachings of Christ from all other man made, Satan authored, Nephilim inspired, religions, including the ones who claim to believe in Christ (such as Catholicism, Mormonism, Jehovah's Witnesses, Seventh Day Adventist's, and all other supposedly Christ cults):

- Solomon is saying: you can have works, but that doesn't mean your faith is real.
- James is saying: you can believe, but that doesn't mean you're faith is real.
- Paul is saying: Even for those without works, your faith alone is credited

as righteousness.

They are boxing salvation in for us so we can see the mechanism clearly. And the only way for all 3 of them to be true at once is if: we are saved "by the grace of God, through faith in Christ, and this is not from yourselves, it is the gift of God, not by works, so that no one can boast (which is literally just a quote of Ephesians 2:8-9)".

That's it. Cut and dry. You are not saved, at all, by works. If you were, it wouldn't be a gift. And yet if your saving faith in Christ is true, there will be works as evidence of that true faith. That is what the Bible seems to be saying. That's what the famous verse John 3:16 is all about: "For God so loved the world that He gave His one and only Son, that whoever believes in Him shall not perish but have eternal life."

Great! That is all fine and dandy. I get it. God loves us and Jesus died for us. But didn't God just decree all of this in the first place? The Bible says God knew all of this before the foundation of the world, came up with the plan of events, rubber stamped it and pressed play. Considering that, why does it matter that Jesus died for us when it is God who just made up this horrific story line to begin with? Doesn't it ruin the love of Christ once we realize that God just decreed all of this stuff to happen from the beginning?

No, as a matter of fact, it shows a deeper level of the Father's love for us. And here's why. Do you remember in the movie "Avengers End Game", when Dr. Strange saw all the possible outcomes, and there was only one way they could beat Thanos. Things had to go a very specific way, and Dr. Strange couldn't tell them certain things because they wouldn't do them if they knew.

Dr. Strange gave up the time stone to Thanos, in much the same way that God handed the earth over to Satan. It wasn't ideal. It didn't make sense in the moment. A lot of suffering and death came as a direct result of it. But it had to be that way for the right things to happen in the end.

Before the beginning, God looked at all the possibilities of how 3 things could become true.

1. He wanted a family who loved Him to glorify Him for all eternity,
2. They had to be free will, sentient beings who chose to love Him, against all odds.
3. Once the family was together, there had to be no more tears, no more sin and no more death. In Heaven we will never again suffer Death, Divorce

or Displacement. And neither will God.

God looked out and saw the one way this impossible paradox could ever come to be. And the only path by which all of these things could possibly happen, is the life we are living now. The Bible says that God has foreknowledge of everything because He already saw it before the foundation of the earth. It also says that our actions are predestined according to His will, but if we knew everything that would happen, it wouldn't. If we knew everyone who would be saved, we would stop evangelizing, which would mean they wouldn't be saved. For it to all work, it must be a mystery, which is why the Bible says we "see through a glass darkly."

Dr. Strange coming up with a list of events that must happen in a specific order and at a specific time in order to win, is the whole idea behind Biblical prophecy. God laid out key events that must take place, at a certain time and in a certain way, in order to achieve the desired end goal.

Jesus then went and fulfilled those prophecies, in the right time and order, saving us in the process. Prophecy was also fulfilled in lesser parts by the prophets, disciples, apostles, and modern day saints. Even evil men like King Nebuchadnezzar were used by God to fulfill prophecy. As a matter of fact, every time you obey God, you yourself are fulfilling Biblical prophecy. But none to the extent that Jesus did.

This is how all of this is for the glory of God, yet Jesus (who is only a single part of the Trinity) is the hero of the whole story. God The Father came up with the game plan of prophecy, but Jesus is the one who went and fulfilled it. That's why it's His-story.

Everything is the way it is, the death, the sorrow, the suffering, because that is how it must be for God's will to be complete in the end. It's the only way to get to where we need to and for all of these paradoxical things to become true. Having a bunch of free will souls, who are all reformed sinners, whores and drug addicts, who now all of the sudden can get along for the rest of eternity, without breaking their free will... is a tall order. There are not many ways something like that could come about.

But couldn't God just find another way? He is God after all. Did Eve really have to be tempted by the snake? Did I really have to read this manuscript to my comatose mother on her death bed? Did Jesus really have to die on the cross? Jesus asked God the same question at the Garden of Gethsemane. And God's answer to Him, is also His answer to you.

It seems that there was either only one way, which is perhaps why Jesus is called "The One", or the way it is now is in fact the cleanest cut way to get it done. We know this Biblically because Jesus asked the Father "If there is any other way, please take this cup from Me". God responded loud and clear when He didn't respond at all. The silence was God's way of saying: "There is no other way."

Jesus didn't die because God is a monster who decreed it. Rather, God wanted eternity with you, and Jesus' life was the cost He had to pay to get it. This is what John 3:16 means. Read it again and see if you pick up on it: "For God so loved the world that He gave His one and only Son, that whoever believes in Him shall not perish but have eternal life." God loves you so much that it says He was "pleased to crush [Jesus] severely" if that was the only way you might be saved.

God wanted something that He couldn't have, but found a way to do it anyways. And in doing so, magnified His own glory. There was no other way, other than for a hero to die. In Avengers, it was Tony Stark. In reality, it was Jesus. Did you not realize that Avengers was just another repetition of His-story repeating itself? Avengers copied their story from the Bible, because every story ever written does, and must.

The reason you were so moved by Ironman's death is because our human love language is sacrifice, while God's is obedience. That scene hit us right in the feels because it reminded us of what Christ did for us. And so we got to have an emotional buzz, but without any conviction that we need to turn away from our sin.

God put 3 pins in all of history and everything else shifted into place around them. That is the meaning for this life, the reason God created everything and the reason things are the way they are. To say that God killed Jesus, God wanted Jesus to die, or even that He allowed Jesus to die, would be equivalent to saying Dr. Strange killed Ironman, wanted him to die and allowed him to.

The truth is, it broke his heart, but he loved the world so much that he was willing to suffer the loss and Tony was a willing sacrifice. So in the end, it was a mutual decision. Dr. Strange was pleased to crush Tony because his focus was on the world being saved, not the one being sacrificed.

The same is true of Christ and God. Tony's motivation was his daughter, that's who he thought about as he died. He died knowing it meant that she could live. Jesus' motivation was you. You are who Christ thought about as He breathed His last. Because of His death, you can have eternal life. Please do not let His sacrifice have been for nothing.

In the end, it was Tony's sacrifice that everyone remembered, not Dr. Strange's plan. Tony Stark's name was elevated above all names, and that's the way Dr. Strange wanted it, because even though Dr. Strange is the one who made it all possible, Tony is the one that made it all happen. The reason Jesus is the one, is because it's His name on the grave, His body on the cross, and His blood on the doorway.

In Avengers, the world was saved by the wisdom of Dr. Strange, through the sacrifice of Ironman. And so you are saved by the grace of God, through faith in Christ, not your own works, lest you cheapen the sacrifice by claiming any credit for your own rescue. The humans who didn't disappear in the snap of Thanos represent the Israelites in the Biblical narrative. They were alive for the battle, but played no part in it other than to be rescued.

The ones who did disappear in the snap represent the Gentiles in the Bible. They weren't even alive when the battle for their lives was taking place. The Bible says we were spiritually dead in our trespasses. And so to claim that you are a good person, who can be saved by your own virtue, would be analogous to a disappeared person, who wasn't even awake during the battle, now claiming he is the one who defeated Thanos in the first place. Not by physically defeating him in battle, but by virtue of being such a good person, and raising the collective consciousness simply by existing, that Thanos realized humanity is worth saving after all.

Imagine how upset Dr. Strange would be if the ones who got snapped back into existence through Tony's sacrifice refused to believe that Tony Stark died for them at all, because they weren't around to see it. Maybe the whole thing was made up. How do we even know it was Tony in the suit at all? There was no evidence that such a thing was even scientifically possible to begin with. And all of the supposed "eye witness" testimonies of the battle, have slight variations and therefore cannot be trusted.

Maybe this Thanos guy isn't even real. It's all just superstition and religious mythology from weak minded people too stupid to figure out the science of what actually happened. The so called "battle against Thanos" was probably just an asteroid hitting the earth, which caused a huge explosion, which some uneducated population assigned religious significance too.

Imagine if the ones snapped back denied ever being gone in the first place. And that if they were gone, surely they brought themselves back to life by their own virtue.

The universe decided that they were good people and allowed them to live again. Dr. Strange might just be pissed off enough to send you back to the abyss, don't you think? He might give you some kind of ultimatum to admit that Tony saved you and honor him properly, or his sacrifice will not cover you. And so, if you deny the blood of Christ, and instead profess your own virtue as your mechanism of salvation, you will burn in hell at the behest of God's wrath.

You don't have a choice in the matter to be honest. The people who made Avengers openly hate God. In interviews they call Him the "sky bully". And yet they needed to use His book to make their movie. This is called sitting in God's lap to slap Him in the face. It is the bane of their existence that creation is locked and they cannot beat Him, but sadly, they will burn for trying. It's not a fun or happy thought. It's just reality. Do not make their mistake.

By the way, if any of you at Marvel are reading this, thanks for the great analogy about salvation and the sacrifice of Christ. I'm sure many will be saved by your movie, which obviously was your motivation for making it in the first place. But all seriousness aside, it's not too late to repent. Nothing you do in this life will ever beat the Sky Bully. You're just rebellious children throwing a temper tantrum at your Father. But He is merciful to forgive you, if you will say your sorry, come home and return to Him.

Remember the feeling of love and warmth and awe and gratitude that you felt when Tony died for you? Well that's what it feels like all the time when you are a Christian. It's like the rest of your life is stuck in that scene and it only amplifies the more you learn about the plot and side stories. You realize from every angle that Christ's sacrifice and love is even deeper than you originally thought.

This is why mature Christians don't tend to do drugs. We don't need them. Drugs blur the line between the physical and spiritual worlds. And since you are dead in spirit, you can only access a peep hole into the spiritual world through psychedelic drugs. You're reaching out for a feeling, but that world you're peeping into, outside of your daily matrix, is where we Christians live permanently. It is the real world, the spirit world.

I say this, as a former New Ager myself, who has experienced the being of consciousness through acid, mushrooms, sex and meditation. I know these things because I've done them.

There are some religions and experiences that can also access the spirit world without Christ. This is what John 10:1 is talking about when Jesus says: "Very truly I tell you Pharisees, anyone who does not enter the sheep pen by the gate, but climbs in by some other way, is a thief and a robber." Jesus is saying that if you enter the spirit world through manmade religion, you are stealing a mechanism of God, while cutting Him out of it. You can imagine how this will play out for you on judgment day.

This glorious elation that we feel in movies when a hero dies for us is also how heaven will feel. It will be like the eternal version of the adrenaline rush you get from being in a crowd, and everyone is cheering for one man, as he carries the ball and scores a goal. Imagine a crowd of all the saints who have ever lived. Imagine standing next to King David, Ester, Mary and Moses, hearing all the stories and cheering on Christ on His throne for all eternity. That love, that high, the beautiful emotion, forever, without even getting old, and only increasing more and more as you understand the infinite wonder of what it is that God and Christ really did for us all.

That is heaven, and I pray that I see you there some glorious day.

If God was pleased to crush Jesus for you, He will be pleased to burn you if you spit on the grave of Christ by not accepting His sacrifice. If you refuse to submit to God, repent of your sins and follow Christ, you will burn. This is not because God is singling you out, it is because He is formatting the old hard drive of earth, to prepare it for the installation of the new heaven.

In the end everything will burn. God won't just throw you into the lake of fire. God is the lake of fire. And when He returns, the only thing that will survive is that which has already become fire. It's not that He will kill you, it's that everything will stay in His presence forever. If you are also fire, you will survive. If you are still flammable at that point, you will burn.

I think the reason you can't just die, is because at that point, death itself will already have died.

1 Corinthians 15:25-26 says: "For [Jesus] must reign until He has put all his enemies under his feet. The last enemy to be destroyed is death."

The Bible seems to be saying that you will burn forever, not because God is a monster, but because eternity is the default life span of a soul in the absence of death. And if there is no more sin in Heaven, there is no more death, since death is the wages of sin.

John the Baptist said in Matthew 3:11: "I baptize you with water for repentance.

But after me comes one who is more powerful than I, whose sandals I am not worthy to carry. He will baptize you with the Holy Spirit and fire."

Fire burns off iniquities, which is the process of sanctification. The way a silversmith knows that molten silver is pure, free of contaminants and ready to be poured into the mold, is that he can see his reflection in it. A clay pot is also finalized in fire, before which it is useless as a vessel. We are here in this life to become baptized in spirit and fire, so that we can finally dwell in God's presence, who is fire, with Him in us, and us in Him, as one flame.

This is not to say that this life is purgatory. The Catholic concept of purgatory is us burning in equal measure to our sins. As we have already discussed, our sins are paid in full by Christ. There's no sin left for us to pay for. Purgatory is us earning our salvation through suffering. This life is us suffering to drive us to repentance to Christ who already paid for our sins. Again, we see the deceit is in the "saved by works" nuance.

And so that's it, right!? Just follow your conscience. Let your conscience be your guide, right? Well. No. Jiminy Cricket said that, not Jesus. "Let your conscience be your guide" is not actually in the Bible.

The Bible does not say to let your conscience be your guide, but rather to let your conscience be guided by the Holy Spirit. It's not the call itself that guides you, it's the one calling out into the wilderness, through the call. This nuance matters because the Holy Spirit is the author of the Bible, and so Scripture is to completely govern your conscience, rather than your conscience govern you completely.

The Bible says your conscience can be burned, and therefore inaccurate at times. This would be like not hearing the caller because you have a poor connection to them. And so you hold what you think was said, accountable to the one who said it. You hold your conscience accountable to the Holy Spirit, through Scripture.

Your conscience is the call to the Ark, and the one calling is the Holy Spirit.

Ignoring a person's call seems to be equivalent to rebuking the one calling.

Ignoring your conscience, which is the call, is equivalent to blaspheming the Holy Spirit, who is the one calling out to you through the conscience.

You don't lose your job for the act of hanging up a phone, you lose it because you offended the person who you hung up on, who in this case is your boss. You don't get in trouble for sending a call to voicemail, you get in trouble for slighting the person you sent to voicemail. It's a sign of disrespect.

If the Holy Spirit is calling out to you through the conscience, and you ignore the call, you are cursing the caller. There is only one unforgivable sin, and this is it, to blaspheme the Holy Spirit.

CHAPTER 19

Citizens Under Siege

The enemy likes to convince people who are damned that they are ok. And people who are saved that they probably aren't actually saved. This leads to a sort of spiritual Dunning-Kruger affect where the lost are always confident that they are going to be ok and true Christians are always second guessing their own assurance of salvation.

Spiritual Warfare is simply the enemies attempt to discourage evangelism through confusion, distraction or apathy. That's it. Anything fancier than that is an example of falling into the trap of Spiritual Warfare itself. The term "demon" was coined by Moses and means "lesser spirit". It's actually an insult to call them demons and most Christians today are terrified to even say the word.

There are 5 stages of Spiritual Warfare (possibly more) that I've come across so far:

1. Denial: Demons don't exist and I don't have to be afraid of something I don't believe in.
2. Fear: They exist but I'm terrified of them.
3. Revenge: I'm fearless but want to make them pay for wasting years of my life.
4. False Warrior: I'm finally in control but constantly exhausted.
5. Freedom: I've stopped fighting a defeated enemy in the dark and simply stepped into the light.

The European countryside is littered with the corpses of castles. These castles were built when an army would push the enemy line back and then erect castles to hold the line. The opposing army would then try to take the castle back and occupy it, rather than build their own. The game became castle warfare and the side that won was the side best at fortifying their castles and defending them by keeping the enemy out. You didn't have to win. You just had to resist.

In the Old Testament, God commanded His people to tear down enemy strongholds, destroy false idols and cut down hill top Asherah poles. He was telling them to remove enemy castles from among them. This whole thing is about castle warfare.

You are a temple of God. Which means you are a castle of God. The enemy cannot tare down your castle (which means kill you) and so they opt to occupy you instead (which is demonic possession), or lay siege to you (which is demonic oppression), or get you to destroy it yourself (which is suicide). This is why spirits desire to "cohabitate" in your temple. They are trying to occupy your castle.

On the face of it, they are looking to drive your soul's vehicle (which is your body) for a good time. But this is just the equivalent of war-torn soldiers (meaning demons) raping the village women because they are depraved. They may have pillaged their way through taking the town, but the goal of taking the town itself was a larger strategic play of the ruler in charge of the army, who, in this case, is the Devil.

The bigger game that the generals commanding the soldiers are playing, is a war for territory. We are the castles of God being fought over. Possession vs oppression is the difference between the enemy occupying the castle or laying siege to it. The effect is basically the same. What differs is how you fight it: one you resist, the other you evict (which is essentially what an exorcism is, a spiritual eviction notice).

To attack the Christian, since the enemy cannot kill you, he lays siege to your castle and tries to get you to kill yourself through fear, misery or boredom. We hunger for sin because we are being intentionally starved and the only thing left to eat is the poison apple the enemy has thrown over the wall. We are citizens under siege.

Whenever you are attacked, the first thing you should do is pray. And in that prayer, ask God to orient you to the enemy attacking you, the weapon being formed against you and the battlefield you're dealing with:

1. The Enemy: figure out if the attack is coming from the World, the Flesh

or the Devil,

2. The Weapon: figure out which weapon is being formed against you. Usually, the weapon being used in the attack will be under the broad categories of Confusion, Distraction or Apathy, and

3. The Battle Field: figure out if the battlefield for this attack is the Path Field, the Rocky Field or the Thorny Field (from the Parable of the Sower).

You can also see if the attack is targeting one or more of the 3 traumas mentioned earlier in this book. The enemy loves to play off your emotions, effectively creating an autoimmune attack where he just triggers you, and you fight yourself. These type of attacks play off of your traumatic longing for:

- Eternity,
- Love, and/or
- Security.

Once you've figured out where the attack is coming from, what its weapon is and where it's taking place, inventory your own weapons and armor to attack it. This is pretty easy because our weapons are always the same. Our spiritual weapons are:

- The Fruit of the Spirit,
- The Armor of God,
- Prayer,
- Fasting
- Fellowship,
- Evangelism,
- Boredom (Dopamine Detoxing),
- Resistance,
- Deep Biblical study,
- Worship, and
- Reading the Word.

Pavlov's Dog is a famous experiment where Ivan Pavlov rang a bell while feeding his dog. Then he rang the bell again but gave the dog no food. The dog still salivated hearing the bell because he already learned to associate the bell with receiving food.

The same is true of humans and sin. We salivate for sin because we have been programmed to hear Beelzebub's Bell (which is temptation) and expect some sort of temporal pleasure (which is sin). This is part of how we are slaves to sin, are born into sin and experience freedom from sin in Christ.

The second have of the study, which is never mentioned, but obviously important, is that as Pavlov rang the bell enough times but denied the dog food, eventually the dog dissociated the two and stopped salivating when the bell was rung. This is why the Bible tells us to resist. Because eventually the temptations will become easier.

This is due to dopamine detoxing and neuroplasticity (the literal, anatomical renewing of your mind in the form of neuron rewiring due to repeated experience). How the Bible knew this 2000 years before any of these things were discovered is... you guessed it... another coincidence.

Your job is not to win, you just have to resist. Like Pavlov's dog, you can't unring Beelzebub's Bell once temptation hits, but you can resist the sin salivation until it rings out and the temptation passes. Don't even try to fight. It's an ambush. You can't win anyways. They will just kamikaze you until you're exhausted. Just occupy yourself with resistance until the urge passes.

The way you fight temptation, is the same way Jesus did in the desert, with Scripture. Jesus resisted the Devil but had to do so 3 times. So read 3 chapters a day, and pull a verse from each one. "3 a day, keeps the Devil away". Those will be your 3 verses to fight temptation that day and if you read 3 chapters a day, you'll finish the entire Bible, cover to cover, each year.

It's also good to pray when you get tempted. And when you pray, address your prayer to the part of the Trinity that fights the enemy you are dealing with. Never pray to angels, saints or Mary. The Bible says that there is an audience watching us and that the angels and saints deliver our prayers to God as burnt incense. But that doesn't mean you address your letter to the mailman. They may deliver it, but the recipient is always God.

The Structure of the Lord's Prayer, which is how Jesus taught us to pray, is a letter.
- Recipient: Our Father.
- Address: Who art in heaven.
- Salutation: Hallowed be Thy Name.
- What they want: Thy will be done...
- What you want: Forgive us our sin...
- Signature: In Jesus Name, Amen.

God's love letter back to us is the Bible. God wrote His letter back to you before you wrote yours to Him, which shows is command of time itself. Prayer is sending mail to God. Reading the Word is reading His letters back to you. And this makes up the communication in your relationship with God because salvation is not something you do, it's someone you know (Jesus).

Catholics are having their mail intercepted by demons, who help them find their car keys, or whatever, and they think because their request was granted, God must have heard it and answered it. This is why Catholics predominantly struggle with understanding what it means to have an intimate relationship with God. As such, their sterile, repetitive, monotone church services make sense to them, because it mirrors their sterile, repetitive, monotone relationship with God.

One of the best examples of spiritual warfare is how the Devil convinced Catholics to replace the Holy Spirit with mother Mary as their comforter, replace Jesus with dead saints and angels as their advocate, and replace the Father with priestly fathers as their source of grace, despite the fact that Christ clearly said "Do not call anyone on earth 'father,' for you have one Father, and he is in heaven." (Matthew 23:9).

Catholics get around this by calling it "proof texting" the Bible. They claim to "take the Bible seriously, not literally". Whatever that means. The reason they claim authority to do this... is hilariously based on a proof texting of 1 Timothy 3:15, which says: "...This is the church of the living God, which is the pillar and foundation of truth." Catholics claim to be "the church" mentioned in this verse and then use their self proclaimed status as the "pillar of truth" to throw other, less convenient, scripture under the bus.

For example, Catholics say that in Titus 1:4, Paul calls Titus his "son" in the faith. And therefore it is logically fitting that Titus would reciprocate in calling Paul his "lower cased f" father in the faith. And since we know this is true, it's ok for all of us to do it, despite the fact that Jesus Himself literally says In Matthew 23:9: "...do not call anyone on earth 'father,' for you have one Father, and He is in heaven." Then, using this assumption as a foundational rule, they stretch it to the point of calling the Pope their "Holy Father", with an uppercased F.

Ask a Catholic if they are a Christian, and they will correct you with "I am Catholic". This would be like asking them "Are you of Christ" and them replying "I am a universalist", since Christian means "From, related to, or like Christ" and Catholic means "universal". For Christians, scripture interprets scripture. For Catholics, scripture subverts scripture, getting it out of the way so they can get back to church tradition as their source of truth, rather than scripture.

I like to ask Catholics when was the last time they were comforted by the Holy Spirit, rather than by mother Mary? Sometimes you can get them to admit that they think of them kind of as one and the same. Like the Holy Spirit is the mother figure of the trinity, and Mary is the mother of Jesus. And so you can ask them "When Jesus said He would leave us a "helper", was He referring to Mary or the Holy Spirit.

Some of the honest ones will admit they think "both". And so they admit, that they see Mary as a god or in a demi-god like status. This can cause an existential crisis when you remind Catholics that in order to answer everyones' prayers, Mary, the Saints and the angels would all need to be omnipresent, which is effectively worshiping them as a pantheon of gods. Albeit Catholics claim this is veneration, not worship.

You can however address your prayer to any member of the Trinity of God:

- If you're being attacked by the World, you can pray to God The Father, as the Bible says that He opposes the World. 1 John 2:15-17 says: "Do not love the world or anything in the world. If anyone loves the world, love for the Father is not in them. For everything in the world, the lust of the flesh, the lust of the eyes, and the pride of life comes not from the Father but from the world.

The world and its desires pass away, but whoever does the will of God lives forever."

- If you're being attacked by the Flesh, you can pray to the Holy Spirit who opposes the flesh. Galatians 5:16-18 says: "So I say, walk by the Spirit, and you will not gratify the desires of the flesh. For the flesh desires what is contrary to the Spirit, and the Spirit what is contrary to the flesh. They are in conflict with each other, so that you are not to do whatever you want. But if you are led by the Spirit, you are not under the law."
- And if you're being attacked by the Devil, pray to Jesus, who is the Son, as Scripture says Jesus opposes the Devil. Luke 4 and 1 John 3:8, say: "The one who does what is sinful is of the Devil, because the Devil has been sinning from the beginning. The reason the Son of God appeared was to destroy the Devil's work."

The overall battle is already won by our Father and therefore, all we do to fight is resist and all we do to resist is flea to the Father's arms. We are essentially just managing His property until the King returns.

A lot of Christians take solace in the idea that they are owned by God and therefore cannot be possessed by demons. This may be a misplaced hope and here's why. It's true that Christ has bought and paid for you and so you are in His castle network, owned by Him. But this just means that the enemy can never own you (which is demonic possession). You can still leave a door open (through sin) and invite the enemy to squat in one of your vacant rooms. And in that room, he's going to do the same thing he would do if he owned the house... try to burn it down.

Because demons are a defeated enemy, being afraid of them is analogous to calling God a liar. If you fear God, you don't have to fear anything else. As a matter of fact, you're not allowed to fear anything else. Fear is a form of worship. When you fear the Lord, you are worshipping Him, and when you fear demons, you are worshipping them, which is a sin they will use to attach to you.

You're essentially validating them as legitimate enemies, and slapping your Father in the face by saying He never really conquered them in the first place. That, of course, is a sin. And while sin does not separate us from salvation, it does allow demons a foothold to stick around and stir up chaos in our lives... which of course causes more fear, which causes us to be afraid, which is calling God a liar, which is a sin, which allows demons to stay... and so goes this merry-go-round. I call it the "Sin Cycle".

Fear leads to Sin, which leads to Torment, which leads to Fear, which leads to Sin... and so on.

The best place to break the cycle is at fear. It's hard to just magically not be afraid of something that is terrifying you. But the way you do it is to pray that God increase your love and let that perfect love cast out all fear. Don't pray for decreased fear, but rather increased love that drives out all fear.

If you're not willing to do that, you haven't suffered enough and I pray that God increase your demonic problems until you simply cannot take anymore. You cannot unread that last sentence. This prayer is now upon you and so you're only option is to start taking this stuff seriously.

Then and only then will you be desperate enough to get help. I know how messed up that sounds. You'll thank me later when you understand what actual freedom feels like. I hope it's the kick in the ass you need to finally make the decision to repent, turn from sin and actually try to start sanctifying.

If you have truly repented and can't figure out how to break out of the sin cycle, an exorcism might be an option. But I would still recommend against it. Here's the problem with exorcisms. If you are not sincere and willing to turn away from sin, it won't work. And if you're only sincere in the moment, but not determined long term, the demon will leave, you will relax and then it will hire 7 more stronger than itself and come back. Now you've really got an issue. I've actually seen this happen to a person I exercised a demon from and almost had it happen to me.

Exorcism is like a weight loss surgery. After the surgery you have to stay on a 1500 calorie a day diet for the rest of your life, or you can just gain the weight back anyways. But if you have the fortitude to maintain a 1500 calorie a day diet... you don't need the surgery in the first place. The weight will eventually drop off over time by itself. And so the surgery is a bit of a catch 22.

The last exorcism I performed (for free), the Catholic Church tried to charge upwards of $3,000 for. A real exorcism looks more like a psychiatric interview with the demon inside the person and can easily take upwards of 4 hours or require multiple sessions if the person hosting the demon is refusing to be honest about their sin life, or sincere in their repentance of it.

The reason Catholics are so good at casting out demons, is because their pagan rituals and demonic worship invites them in, and so they have a lot of experience kicking them back out. It would be like bragging about your bucket dumping skills, while ignoring the holes in your boat letting the water in in the first place. This is also the problem with protestant deliverance ministries. They are big into casting out demons, but not big into telling people to stop sinning thereafter.

They require zero qualifications before handing someone a church branded puke bucket, sticking a DSLR camera in their face, slapping them on the forehead and screaming "COME OUT IN JESUS NAME!" as theatrically as possible. Brownie points if you have some sort of annoying dog bark or high pitched shrill as you repeatedly slap the person's forehead. As if the louder you shout, the more authority and sufficiency Christ gains.

Charismatics claim to hear from the Holy Spirit, yet they never test that familiar spirit against 1 John 4. They are also notoriously light on sin, despite the fact that Jesus said: "Go and sin no more, lest worse things happen to you" after He exorcised a demon. Instead, they get emotionally pissed when you suggest they test the spirits. I had one lady scream at me, saying: "I HAVEN'T BEEN TALKING TO A DEMON FOR 20 YEARS!!" But how would she know? She never tested it. And this begs the question, should the people with the most sin, the least discipline, the lowest adherence to Scripture and the worst discernment of spirits really be the ones casting out the demons?

What happens when a demon is cast out in a room full of hundreds or thousands of other unrepentant sinners? You guessed it. It's the spiritual equivalent of going to the hospital with a cough, and coming back with full blown antibacterial resistant pneumonia. If you are successful at casting that demon out, and that's a big if... chances are it will just go into someone else in the same room a few seconds later.

But don't worry! The church is there to kick it back out next Wednesday night! And there will be cookies and bingo after service! And so the game of demonic musical chairs continues so the church and ministry never runs low on relevance, funding, social media content or people to exorcise. It's basically the spiritual equivalent of the medical industry which treats symptoms with medications but has no interest in actually curing the underlying disease.

Be weary of any ministry that claims to be experts in demonic exorcism. It means they have experience in it. Which likely means they are doing something to welcome those demons in in the first place. Reckless, feminist, hyper grace ministries who are light on sin and call everything "legalism" tend to be the best examples of this.

With that said, physical proximity does not seem to matter. Demons are rulers of territories, but this doesn't seem to refer to geographical locations. Rather they seem to be rulers of sin real estate. Meaning if they are a spirit of lust and they leave one person who repented of their lust, they will either wander and try to re-enter the original person if they return to their sin, or they will look for another person struggling with lust, and attached to them.

Think of a demon as a specialist in a particular type of sin, which is its preferred type of territory that it rules over. This is also why there appear to be generational curses, even though the sins of the father will not revisit the son. It's because that demon attaches to a specific type of sin, and children tend to mimic their parents in every way, including their particular brand of sin.

Most of the exorcism knowledge out there is not Biblical. It "works" but for relatively unknown reasons. It came into the Christian world from ex-Wiccan converts who brought over their knowledge of the spiritual world and occult with them. It's not to say they are wrong, but the information they possess was largely given to them by interviewing demons. And so... you can kind of expect a fair amount of baked in deceit and twisted truth.

I will say that I was in a desperate place at the time of learning all of this. I was at a point of torment so deep that I don't know how I would have skipped the exorcism and went straight to sanctifying. I feel I needed the exorcism (which provided a moment of peace) to bridge the gap and break the chains. And so I don't necessarily throw all of the exorcism stuff under the bus, just like for some people a bariatric surgery makes sense as a way to kick the process off. But only for those who will actually stay on their diet long term afterwards.

I felt for a long time that God was denying me relief. But looking back, I realize now that He knew I wasn't really ready to change. And so He withheld deliverance from me until He knew I wouldn't just turn back to sin right after it. It wasn't sadism, which I actually accused Him of at the time. It was mercy based on His foreknowledge that I would just be tormented by even more demons if He delivered me before I was sincere in my desire to continue to sanctify once I had received peace.

It was a rock and a hard place and the exorcism bought me some time and peace of mind. It brought me to the next level of tricks, and then I fell for all of that too, but at least it was progress. At least the constant torment stopped for a minute and I could breathe. But mark my words. If you take the moment of peace for granted, and don't actually change your ways, or at least try like your life depends on it, the hell you're about to experience is going to be at least 7 times worse than you originally went through.

If you are experiencing heavy demonic problems, like lights flickering on and off, voices heckling in the darkness, dropped phone calls, shadows on the wall, torment, nightmares, cold temperatures at night, feelings of worthlessness, suicidal thoughts, fear of the dark, etc... then you might want to consider an exorcism to get to the next level, not to get completely out of the woods.

An exorcism is an eviction notice for the demon squatting in your vacant room.

That's it. If you kick it out but don't shut the door, it will just return with its new friends. You are a house, and God's name is on the deed. Only someone stronger than God can take it from Him, and since there is no one stronger, no one can touch you... unless you give them permission... which you do through sin.

To get rid of him, you have to go to the court (which is the secret place), and use the law (which is Scripture), to get a formal eviction notice (which is repentance), then notify him of the order to leave (which means you ask God to cancel any ground or territory your sin gave to the demon(s)) and kick his ass out (which means rebuking him back to the pit, until the day).

After the exorcism, you will have to shut that door to sin, rededicate that room (meaning that area of your life) back to God, invite the Holy Spirit in and start cleaning that room regularly. But... what if you just did this part now, without the exorcism? The demon will leave on his own and not come back. And so again, you don't actually need the exorcism at all. It's like nuking the battle field. It hurts the enemy, but it's dangerous for you as well.

An exorcism is just a simple 3 step process:

1. Repent all sin: "I confess (the specific sin). And repent of it (repentance being a willingness to turn from it)".

2. Cancel all ground: "I cancel all ground and revoke all permissions that my sin has given to demons".

3. Rebuke the demon, or demons, back to the pit: "May the Lord rebuke you back to the pit, until the day".

If that doesn't work, repent deeper. Repent of ancestral sins that happened before you were even born, break soul ties, lay down even unknown sins... the whole 9 yards. If that doesn't work, find footholds in your life and delete them too. If there are old videos of you having sex with your hot ex girlfriend saved on your computer, as was true in my case, delete them. If there is an old t-shirt a gothic friend gave you, burn it. If there is an old picture of you partying with your Devil worshipping friends, rip it up. Think about the thing you don't want to give up or the problem you don't want to address... and that is what you must get rid of. To get what you want, you have to give up exactly what you want to hold on to. To start doing what you should, you have to do exactly what you don't want to do.

Purge sin from your life any way you can and repeat the 3 step process until something starts to move. It's not really about the objects themselves, or the demonic power attached to them. Demons actually only have as much power as you give them through sin. It's about making a clear declaration that you belong to Christ and are willing to burn anything you have to to make that point clear. It is Christ they are running from, not you. It's your burning of the objects, not the objects being burned that lets the demons know they have to go. A squatter won't leave because you tell him to. He will leave when he can see it in your eyes that you're not going to let it go until he's gone. You have to make yourself a harder target and no longer worth their time.

The first thing you will notice is the voices stop laughing and mocking you. They will get serious, short with their answers and more respectful. This means that they know ground is being canceled and they are afraid to get cast back to the pit. You will also hear less and less suicidal thoughts about how worthless you are and how no one loves or respects you. They will stop telling you "God can never forgive you for what you've done" because you will have begun to realize that He already has.

Rather than try to destroy you, they will instead try to negotiate a cease fire agreement, where they will stop tormenting you as long as you stop trying to get rid of them. Do not take this deal. Fight on. Resist more. Repent deeper. Pray harder. Fast longer. Do not give up. The cease fire is just another trap anyways.

Do not engage in deep conversation with them. Just do the work, give God the glory for any progress and move on. They will try to trick you into thinking you are powerful in the spiritual world now and will try to coax you into going on a revenge rampage. Avoid this. They aren't scared of you, it's an exhaustion trap. They are afraid of the Lion of Judah standing behind you. Crush them and move on. Let it go and live in the light.

Realize that their little parlor tricks of flicking lights on and off and freaking you out at night are not evidence of their power, but rather the extent of your sin. You have allowed them to have that level of power over you by refusing to be totally owned by God.

You are a rebellious and run away slave who is complaining about getting thorns in your feet because you ran away from the Master. Go home. Go back into the light.

It's like if Mario stopped listening to the commands of the player, went to the desert level, saw the hole in a cactus and decided to have sex with it. And then he gets cactus needles in his ass and shakes his fist at the player screaming, "Why did you do this to me!?!?! What did I do to deserve this?! I am a good person! Answer me!!"

If you think this is entertaining and crazy, because you have never had any of these demonic issues happen to you, that's not evidence that demons aren't real. It just means you are right where the enemy wants you. You haven't even begun this journey yet and their first level of deceit is to convince you that they don't exist. You are not exempt from it, you're the biggest sucker of it. Try to obey your conscience for a year and see what happens.

Once you're through this, you will laugh at demons, like: "All you can do is flicker some lights on and off? That's your A-game!? How sad and pathetic. What a bunch of losers. This big bad wolf and all he can do is a cheap parlor trick of flicking lights on and off".

I know that this can seem like an impossibility, but I promise, once these chains start to break, their whole little game falls apart pretty fast. If you're pinned down under the weight of a demonic attack right now, and you can barely whisper a single word into the darkness, whisper "Jesus".

Depression is not a lack of self love, it's an overabundance of it. Suicide is the ultimate act of selfishness. Like we've seen over and over again, what the world tells you is backwards. What you've been taught to believe is love, is actually lust. Learn to embrace the upside down Kingdom of Christ where the first is last, the greatest is the least of these and the one who loves his life will lose it.

Be careful with binding and rebuking spirits. Do not rebuke them yourself, but say "May the Lord rebuke you". It's true that Jesus' only remedy for demons was to cast them out, but be sure you're ready for them to leave and not find the door still open when they return.

Remember that demons are the birds in the Parable of the Sower. They want to steal the seed (which is the Word) lest you hear it, believe it and be saved. If you walk up to a bird and bind it with duct tape, does that stop it from eating the seed? Or does it just stop it from flying away? By binding and rebuking evil spirits, all you're doing is chasing the birds around the path field with a stick.

The reason I rarely do exorcisms is because most people who say "Please help me get rid of this demon!" Are really saying "Please help me alleviate the consequences of sin... so I can go back and sin some more." You have to actually be willing to stop sinning in order to get out of this. If not, you have not yet suffered enough. Once you just cannot take it anymore, it will be a no brainer.

But as long as you want to hold onto your sin, you will deal with the consequences of it. It's not even really about the act of sinning. You cannot out sin the grace of God. I still sin all the time, but have no demonic issues at all anymore. And that is because I have committed to turn from sin and try and fail constantly. It's the heart that is set on sanctification that will get you out of this mess. But it must be sincere. You must learn to hate sin as God does. Not love it and pretend.

If you been through all of this, you feel you have already deeply repented, you have turned away from sin and you are living the life, but you're still suffering from demonic torment, here are 5 things you can try:

1. Read the Bible every day without fail.
2. Pray continuously for increased love that casts out all fear.
3. Fast. The Daniel fast is a great place to start. I've never once fasted where it didn't have amazing results. It's a spiritual cheat code if ever there was one. If that doesn't help, ask your friends and family to commit to fasting with you and praying for you.
4. Learn to rejoice in your sufferings. That'll finish them off for sure. When something bad happens to you, instead of getting mad, find a way to thank God for the pain instead. For example, next time you stub your toe, as you're about to yell "SON OF A..." Calm down, take a deep breath and say, "Thank you Lord for this test. I have prayed for increased emotional intelligence and spiritual discernment and I see You are being faithful to answer that prayer. Thank You Father for Your love and Your grace and Your mercy..." Boy will the demons run from a heart that begs God for trials and thanks Him for suffering.
5. Evangelize. Remember that Spiritual Warfare is just an attempt to get you not to spread the Word of God. So... go spread the Word of God.

If any of these things are too hard, you're not ready to get out of the hell you're in. When you are ready, you know where to find the information you need to escape.

If you're already doing all of this and you're still not sure what's going on, demons are likely not your problem. Look to the world and flesh to see if the issues are coming from there. If it is for sure still demons, it may just be a test or an indication you're on the right track.

God seems to outsource the training of His children to Satan. Satan is actually an accidental servant of God. God is going to strengthen you through these trials. It's kind of like a dad letting his son get in a fight at school because he knows it will do him good in the end, even if he gets a little banged up in the process.

Increased demonic torment may be a test from God, an unorthodox answer to prayer, or a blessing in disguise. Although if it's really bad and you find yourself growing desperate, I would say it's sin you're missing in your prayer for repentance, especially if the demons are disrespectful and taunting you.

The mature Christian that is tested in this way is usually being further trained in spiritual warfare so they can help others and they usually already understand this and are patiently wrestling their way through the annoyance of it.

Remember that this life is a suffering simulator. That's the whole point. It doesn't get easier. We are supposed to get stronger.

If you are wrestling a demon, remember that it is probably a dead Nephilim spirit. He had a body once and he desires to reattach to the flesh, through your body to have a good time. The last thing he wants you to do is dopamine detox. If all else fails, bore his ass to death.

The Bible says "resist the devil and he will flee". It also says "this kind only come out through prayer and fasting".

If you are terrified of demons, because they seem mysterious, let me remind you what they all have in common. There is only one spiritual world, and all demons live there. There may be different types and classes of demons, but all demons are lesser spirits. That's what demon literally means.

- All demons are beings who were created by God as angels (or the half breed children of those angels),
- They once lived in heaven,
- They all bought into lucifers lies,
- They have all been defeated by God,
- They are all terrified of Jesus, and
- They are all under your feet.

Keep these things in mind, but above all, test the spirits to see if they are of God. Ask the spirits directly "Do you confirm that Christ has come in the flesh" (1 John 4:1-3).

If the spirit says anything other than "Yes", it's not of God. And they will say all sorts of things, ranging from "Maybe"... to "He came in the flesh but He did not die for our sins"... to "Thou shall not test the Lord your God!"

Stay the course brothers and sisters. Freedom is within sight. We are almost home.

CHAPTER 20

All Things to All Men

You just watched me get ripped in half by a bus. There's blood everywhere and a child across the street is screaming in horror. I look up at you with terrified eyes and say "I only have 60 seconds to live. I don't want to go to hell. Please tell me how I can go to Heaven!"

What would you say to me?

When I ask this question to people on the street, the conversation always goes something like this:

They always say some variation of "I would tell you not to worry. If you lived a good life, you will go to Heaven".

"But I haven't lived a good life!" I respond. "I stole a candy bar once as a child and I lied a few times!"

They laugh and say "That's not that bad. You'll be fine. A candy bar and a few lies are not going to send you to hell. Everyone does that! You're still a good person."

I respond "But I'm not a good person! I raped and murdered 8 children! I don't want to go to hell! Please. I have 10 seconds left! How do I go to Heaven!?"

They get a sober look on their face as they think "Well, maybe you deserve to go to hell."

But as I count down the final seconds.... "9... 8... 7... Hurry up! I'm going to die!"

They shout out "Just... um. Apologize! Apologize and believe and you'll be ok!"

"Times up! I'm dead." I say. "Looking back, do you feel confident that what you told me sent me to Heaven?

They think about it and say "Yeah, I think so."

"Alright. I agree. Sort of. Let's recap what just happened." And I go over it with them.

And so I'll tell you, the reader, what I tell them.

This question got your attention for a few reasons:

1. It's about everyone's favorite topic (themselves),

2. You already subconsciously know the answer (but can't access it), and

3. You recognize that it's a soul survival question (and you too will die someday).

You saw a man dying and recognized that he was scared of going to hell. You told him he was a good person because if you admitted that his sins made him a bad person, then you too would have to shatter your own image of yourself as a good person.

And so you drew a line in the sand just past what you yourself had done. You created your own subjective standard of goodness based on what was necessary to save yourself. If you had raped 8 children, the cut off would be 9. Our standard of goodness is always just past what we have done, and then we let the door of damnation slam on the guy behind us. You used your own life as the standard and judged him according to that standard.

When we ate from the tree of knowledge of good and evil, we then used that knowledge to redefine the definitions of good and evil for ourselves. Based on these new definitions of good and evil, we created easier standards and then held ourselves up to those lesser standards to find ourselves righteous in our own eyes. But the Bible is a dictionary, preserving God's definitions of these terms. God's standard of good and evil is the 10 commandments, but we all automatically fail that standard and so we come up with our own to avoid having to repent to God for our sins.

But once you found out he was a child rapist, you judged him and realized that his sin was far beyond your own. So you threw him under the bus and immediately recognized the victims' right to justice being served, so much so that death itself seemed like a fitting punishment.

But as I counted down the final moments of life, it induced a Freudian slip and you yelled out "apologize".

But apologize to who? And for what? The victims are dead. They can't forgive him. You can't forgive him either. And he doesn't have the authority to forgive himself.

And how is this apology going to instantaneously change the destination of this man's soul from hell to heaven? Because that was the question, wasn't it?

Another way to say "apologize" is "repent".

More specifically said: "You are guilty of sin. You are not a good person. You cannot save yourself. You are bound for hell and you deserve it. To be saved, you need to repent of your sins (which means apologize to God)."

What if he would have said "But I occasionally donate to the Red Cross!" Would anything good he has done matter at all? Or would his good works be filthy rags compared to the evil he had committed? Even if he had done more good than bad in his life, we are judged based on our crimes, not our good deeds.

Sometimes people say "forgive yourself" or "say you're sorry". But it's always a variation of "Repent". Everyone is already a Christian, they just haven't submitted to God yet.

How did I know they would say repent? The same way I knew you could finish "Mary had a little..."

Because I knew to look for that meme deep down inside of you. I knew it would be there, because the Bible says God wrote His law on your heart and mind.

And Conscience means "With Knowledge". More specifically, "Con-Science" means "With-knowledge [of Sin]". Everyone already knows. That's how I knew to look for the salvation meme in their heart and mind.

See, you don't have to find God. God finds you. You just have to stop fighting Him. There is a little muscle in your eye called the Levator Papillae that lifts your eye lid to open your eyes. When you die, your muscles will all contract into rigor mortis. And when that happens, that little muscle will contract, lifting your eye lids and you will die with your eyes open. God wins in the end. Literally, it takes more energy (ATP) to remain willfully blind than it does to just relax and let your eyes open to see the truth. Again, God's cosmic sense of humor.

This question cuts right through their worldview armor, defense mechanisms and general minutia, right to the mechanism of salvation. And so they start with the salvation message of the second religion: Be a good person and live a good life based on your own subjective standard of goodness.

I also knew to look for that meme there because it has been programed into them by the enemy.

But the second reality hits them, that argument falls apart and the Freudian slip reveals what was written on their heart and mind all along: We are sinners, justice must be served, the wages of sin is death, I cannot save myself, I need to repent of my sins and have faith in a Savior.

You really knew it all along. What you might not know is this. While you judged that man based on the standard of your own life, Jesus will judge you based on the standard of His. And Jesus never stole a candy bar. Jesus will see you, the way you saw the child rapist. Sin must be atoned for by blood. It's either going to be your blood or the blood of Christ. Choose wisely.

This question of "What is the mechanism of salvation" is what broke the Catholic church in half. Catholics believe that we are saved by faith and works, not faith alone (with works as evidence of true faith). They call it "Faith in love" but that's just fancy Catholic talk for faith + works.

Protestants believe: Grace through Faith = Salvation + Works.

Catholics believe: Grace through Faith + Works = Salvation.

Catholics are odd. They have one foot in each religion. I believe this is what the Bible is referring to when it talks about "lukewarm" Christians. Catholics don't believe they are good people like the second religion, at least not all the time. Instead they believe they are sinners by default, except when in a "repentant state of grace" (which is the time period between their last confession and their next sin). During this state of grace, they would technically consider themselves "good" or at least "without sin" (momentarily). Which is what saves them, dying in a repentant state of grace, or aka "dying as a good person".

At least they don't seem to be in any danger of proof texting the verse that says: "If you say you're without sin, you are self deceived and no truth is in you".

This "state of grace" idea creates a sort of subscription based salvation model where every 5 minutes you fluctuate between being saved and not saved. As a matter of fact, Catholics don't believe in getting "saved" (as a singularity) at all. This means you have to run back to the confession booth constantly, which means you are dependent upon the Catholic Church, which is just another example of mass population control by religion.

When the Bible says, "Don't even eat with wicked people", who is it referring to, since Jesus Himself often broke bread with whores, sinners and tax collectors? Clearly it's not talking about sinners. It's talking about the Sadducees and Pharisees. The Bible is calling out religious, ritualistic people as wicked. I believe the Sadducees and Pharisees saw the Jesus movement catching on and highjacked it, thus recreating themselves as what would later become the Catholic Church.

I like to ask Catholics this question: "If you leave confession in a repentant state of grace, and then you walk outside, trip over the curb, take God's name in vain and then get hit by a bus... are you going to heaven or hell?"

Most Catholics will respond that in this case they would have to rely on God's grace to have mercy on them. And by admitting this, they are tipping their hand to show that they believe "Grace alone" is the exception to salvation, not the rule.

What Catholics actually believe is closer to "We are saved by the Grace of God + our own works (unless we die in a state of sin, in which case we will have to rely on the Grace of God alone)". God's grace is their backup contingency plan, not the main mechanism of salvation.

To which I respond: "Great. Take that 'I would have to rely on the Grace of God to have mercy on me' thing and just streeeeeeetch... that out over your entire post-salvation life. That's how salvation actually works." The fact is, we are never without sin, and somehow simultaneously always in a permanent state of grace. The Christian has assurance of salvation and is always ready to die. Not because of anything we did, but because of the sufficiency of Christ's sacrifice.

Catholics have replaced the need for the Father's grace, the Son's intercession and the Holy Spirit's comfort with works based salvation, intercession of the saints and the comfort of mother Mary, respectively. Be careful with these bait and switch, misdirection meme attacks.

Also be cautious of watered down protestant salvation messages as well, like "Believe it and receive it". These salvation messages say nothing of repentance, humility, sanctification, or brokenness before God. Do not take my word for it either. The Word you should take is the Word itself. Pray for a humble heart to understand and then go read it yourself. You may gain a little insight from my book, but you will only gain true understanding from the Good Book itself.

The best way to expose an Atheist who claims to have read the Bible is to ask them to describe the Parable of the Sower to you.

All of life is summed up in the Parable of the Sower, which is probably why Christ said it is the pre-requisite parable for all the rest. The Parable of the Sower (which is also called the Parable of the 4 Fields) is found in Matthew 13:1-23, Mark 4:1-20 and Luke 8:4-15.

The sower who is throwing the seed refers to an evangelist preaching the Word. The seed lands on the soil of the 4 fields (which is the heart of the person hearing the message). The state of the soil determines what happens when the seed hits the field (which is a representation of the Word of God hitting their heart). The fourth field is the good soil, while the 3 bad soils are the battle fields on which the battle for your soul is fought (which is The War Within).

The 3 battle fields are:

1. The Path Field: The path has been hardened from being trampled on. When the seed hits the hardened path, it sits on top and birds come and eat it so it cannot take root. This means your heart is hardened with arrogance and pride. When you hear the Word of God, it sounds like foolishness to you and you reject it. This is also why humility is the decryption key that converts knowledge of what the Bible says into wisdom of what the Bible means. The bird is the devil who comes and steals the Word so that you will not hear it, believe it and be saved. Essentially, you have made an idol of your own perceived intelligence.

2. The Rocky Field: The rocks stop the seed from rooting deep into the soil. As a result, the plant shoots up quickly, but with shallow roots. Without deep roots the plant can't draw water from the soil and the sun burns the plant out. This means you have misconceptions about the Word, and you've created an idol of God that is not aligned with actual Scripture. You're worshiping a more convenient version of god that you want to be true, rather than the Biblically defined God of Israel. And so your faith shoots up quickly, but people being skeptical of your beliefs causes your faith to fall apart and die (which is represented by the sun burning up the seed). The solution is to rip up the rocks (which are false memes), align your understanding of God with the Bible and grow deep roots so that the persecution of the sun only makes you stronger, by driving your roots deeper to find living water in the soil.

3. The Thorny Field: When the seed lands amongst thorns, the thorns block the sunlight, steal all the soil resources, nutrients and water and choke the plant out as it tries to grow. This means that you have allowed the world, pornography, money and other worldly things to choke out your faith in God. Essentially, you have allowed any number of material idols into your life and your faith suffers as a result.

But what about the good soil? What grows in the good field is the tree of life we lost access to in the Garden of Eden. That tree bears fruit that we feed to the lost. That's evangelism. Fruit is defined as seeds wrapped in a sweet flesh. The seed (which is truth) is wrapped in a sweet appetizing fruit (which is love). Fruit is literally truth wrapped inside of love.

A piece of fruit with no seed inside is useless. There is no seed to grow new life in their hearts. You have given them a fish for the day, but denied them the opportunity to learn to fish for a lifetime. It's not enough to just be nice to people, bubbly and pleasant. How are you going to give them the Word... without actually using your words? The old adage: "Everywhere you go, preach the Gospel... and if necessary, use words" is a meme lie from the pit of hell.

Conversely, what good is it to throw a handful of cherry pits at their face? Rather, hand them a handful of cherries and they won't even see the pits. All they will see is fruit (which represents love). And once they are done consuming it, they will be stuck with the pits (which represent truth) to wrestle with. This is how you evangelize in truth and love. This is how you become a fisher of men. The fruit is the bait. The truth is the hook hidden beneath that God will use to reel their rebellious ass onto the Ark. if there's no hook, there's no point.

If I told you that you could eat from the tree of life in the Garden of Eden, would you not do it? Would you not also tell everyone you know to come with you? But that is in fact exactly what I am telling you. The fruit from the tree of life is the Gospel shared through truth in love. It literally results in eternal life, just like eating from the tree of life would have. It's the same exact thing. So why have you all the sudden lost interest now?

This is why the Kingdom of God is already among us, and inside of us. Mary Magdalene first saw the resurrected Jesus as a Gardener. But this was no mistake. He is the Great Gardener. He is gardening the fields of our hearts back to the Garden of

Eden. This is the new heart He gives us. This is the work He is doing inside of us.

This is also how we co-labor alongside Him, not that He needs our help. It's more that He enjoys our company. When the Bible says put your hand to the plow, tear your hearts and work the fields, it is talking about tearing out the thorns, plowing up the path and plowing up the rocks from the soil (which are mutated memes buried in your worldview). It is talking about sanctification.

If works are evidence of true faith, then evangelism is evidence of true love. If you don't love the lost enough to cast out the fear of talking to them about not burning in hell, you don't love them at all.

When you evangelize, stick to what Christ did for them, not what you did for Christ. It's really not about you. A long diatribe about yourself and your own story (under the guise of a testimony) is never going to compare to God wrapping Himself in flesh, coming down here and dying for our sins. Stick to love, but do not skip the conviction of the law. Understand that the law is love. And love fulfills the law. It's not a harsh message. It's truth.

If you truly desire that your love ones be saved, go save others. If you catch 1000 fish for God, it's been my experience that He will throw a familiar fish in your net. To save one of your own, go save others.

I am writing this chapter while sitting on the couch of my old Army buddy Vince, to whom we witnessed to for 15 years. Today, it's with tears of joy that I can report that Vince is now a steadfast follower of Christ. And that only happened after I had talked to about 1000 strangers about Jesus. And now I get to spend eternity with my brother in Heaven.

I am telling you friends, the one thing you think you can't buy, the salvation of your loved ones, is actually on the menu. You just have to pay for it in a currency you weren't expecting. You're going to have to work for it. Otherwise, I think it's pretty clear that you don't actually love them, or you don't actually believe the Bible. Because if both of those things are true, there's no way in hell you would be wasting time walking on eggshells.

Stop asking me to save your friends for you. Do not call me and offer me money to evangelize your loved ones. God made you for a time such as this. You do it. Pray that God increase your love for the lost to the extent that it drives out the fear of talking to them. Pray for daily bread and God will overflow you with opportunities.

Go fishing for strangers, and eventually, I'm telling you, God will weigh heavy on the hearts of the ones you love.

You say you would do anything to save your parents, children, friends or loved ones. If that's really true, you now know what to do. If you don't do it, may their blood be on your head and their sin on your account.

Ezekiel 3:18 says: "If I say to the wicked, 'You shall surely die,' and you give him no warning, nor speak to warn the wicked from his wicked way, in order to save his life, that wicked person shall die for his iniquity, but his blood I will require at your hand."

All of us are commanded to fulfill the great commission. If you don't believe me, tell God on Judgment Day about how you thought you were an elbow or a knee cap in the body of Christ and see what He says. I'm telling you you're the finger tips of God reaching into the darkness of a lost and dying world. Love them enough to tell them the truth. You have found life! Why are you not sharing your cup with the lost?! The only answer I can figure is that you're either a coward or a monster.

Stop waiting for your calling. Go do what the Bible already commanded you to do. Pray for increased love that casts out all fear. God will equip you. Stop over thinking it. Go save the lost. Go serve your King.

CHAPTER 21

Closing Prayer

Our Father in Heaven, our Lord, our Savior, our Judge and our Friend,

Holy is Your Name, oh Ancient of Days.

We repent of our sins. We submit and surrender to You.

We accept the suffering of sanctification to come, and we thank You for Your loving discipline.

Poison us with righteousness. Crush us like olives and pour us out onto the hair and feet of Jesus, that we would be made useful to the Kingdom.

I am so very sorry for the pain we have caused You.

Forgive us. Save us. Show us the Way.

Enter into our hearts. Renew our minds. Dwell in Your temple.

Change the desires of our hearts and make us acceptable to You.

We choose the seeking of Your Righteousness over the fruitless pursuit of our own happiness.

We love You. We adore You.

Holy is our God. Worthy is the Lamb.

You alone are God, faithful to find and mighty to save.

Increase our love for the lost, that it will cast out the fear of telling them about You.

I too, like You, desire that all be saved. Speak through us as empty, yet willing vessels of Your Glory. Holy Spirit go before us and convict their hearts. Prepare the fields of their hearts to receive the Word.

We do not ask more of You. You are sufficient, our portion, more than enough. But we ask You to teach us how to give You more of ourselves. Erase us and replace us.

You do not dwell in part. Wherever You are, You are completely. And You are everywhere. We are the limiting factor. Our faith is weak. But grant us faith. Help our unbelief.

This thing You've done... This thing You are doing... It is good.

You are a good, good Father.

Thank You for Your Great Love for us. Your Mercy. And Your Faithfulness. We do not deserve You.

In the Name of Jesus Christ of Nazareth, and by the blood He shed for us on the cross at Calvary.

Until we meet face to face.

Amen.

END NOTE

Thank you for reading THE WAR WITHIN, by Dr. Michael Cocchini.

This book mainly focuses on the first two questions of:

1. Is there a God? And,
2. Which one is it?

The final question of what God wants from you is simple... He wants you. In a word, what God wants from you is love. Salvation is not something you do, it's someone you know (Jesus). It's not a formula, it's a relationship.

While this is simple, there is infinite depth to its simplicity. I have already begun writing THE WAR WITHIN Volume 2 (WWII), which focuses exclusively on salvation by grace, the Bible and our relationship with God, along with deeper explanations of the matrix (which is mentioned in the Bible 5 times, and means "womb"), the simulation we live in and the Parables of Jesus.

To pre-order THE WAR WITHIN Volume 2 and enroll in the online course which reteaches the lessons of this book in a stunning black board lecture style format, go to www.TheWarWithin.me.

* 9 7 9 8 9 8 9 4 1 6 6 1 5 *

www.ingramcontent.com/pod-product-compliance
Lightning Source LLC
Chambersburg PA
CBHW052109020426
42335CB00021B/2693